No refuge: the crisis of refugee militarization in Africa

ROBERT MUGGAH | editor

No refuge: the crisis of refugee militarization in Africa

Zed Books

LONDON | NEW YORK

in association with

BONN INTERNATIONAL CENTER FOR CONVERSION

B·I·C·C

small
arms
survey

No refuge: the crisis of refugee militarization in Africa was first published in 2006 by:

Zed Books Ltd, 7 Cynthia Street, London N1 9JF, UK and Room 400, 175 Fifth Avenue, New York, NY 10010, USA

<www.zedbooks.co.uk>

Bonn International Center for Conversion, An der Elisabethkirche 25, 53113 Bonn, Germany

<www.bicc.de>

Small Arms Survey, Graduate Institute of International Studies, Avenue Blanc 47, 1202 Geneva, Switzerland

<www.smallarmssurvey.org>

Editorial copyright © Bonn International Center for Conversion and Small Arms Survey, 2006
Individual chapters © individual contributors, 2006

Cover designed by Andrew Corbett
Set in Arnhem and Futura Bold by Ewan Smith, London
Index: <ed.emery@britishlibrary.net>
Printed and bound in Malta by Gutenberg Press Ltd

Distributed in the USA exclusively by Palgrave Macmillan, a division of St Martin's Press, LLC, 175 Fifth Avenue, New York, NY 10010.

A catalogue record for this book is available from the British Library.
US CIP data are available from the Library of Congress.

ISBN 1 84277 788 2 | 978 1 84277 788 6 hb
ISBN 1 84277 789 0 | 978 1 84277 789 3 pb

Contents

Tables and boxes

Tables

Boxes

Acknowledgements

This volume was a collective enterprise. A wide-ranging array of actors – from public policy-makers, practitioners and forced migration specialists to refugee and populations of internally displaced persons (IDP) and community organizations – were involved from beginning to end. It is to both those consulted and those sadly compelled to remain anonymous that this volume is dedicated.

The editor would like first and foremost to extend gratitude to the management and editorial teams of the Small Arms Survey and the Bonn International Center for Conversion (BICC) for their unwavering support to the two-year refugee militarization project on which *No refuge* is based. The commitment and patience demonstrated by, among others, Peter Croll, Michael Brzoska, Eric Berman and Peter Batchelor was vital to its successful production. Special credit is due to Tania Inowlocki for her enthusiastic engagement with both the substance and style of the volume. Appreciation must also be extended to Robert Molteno and Anna Hardman at Zed for taking this volume aboard and seeing it through to completion.

Equally, the tireless inputs of protection and programme officers at the United Nations High Commission for Refugees (UNHCR) in Geneva, particularly Iain Hall, Bruno Geddo, Larry Botnick, Hari Gupta and Sharon Cooper, must also be commended. They, and others associated with UNHCR and the agency's implementing partners, made important contributions to early drafts prepared by the chapter authors. Professor Gil Loescher at Oxford University, who served as an external adviser to the refugee militarization project, also played a crucial role in grounding the project in relevant literature. Finally, the editor is indebted to a great number of others who generously contributed from Kampala and Kinshasa and who, unfortunately, cannot all be named here. This volume is a tribute to their perseverance in climates of what can only be described as extreme adversity.

Guinea James Milner gratefully acknowledges members of the Guinean government for their engagement with this project. In particular, research would not have been possible without the kind assistance of M. Alhousseine Thiam, director of the BNCR, and Moustapha Condé, assistance coordinator of the BCR in N'Zérékoré. M. Condé's support for the research project, in particular, went above and beyond the call of duty. Special thanks are also due to M. René Kamano in Conakry, Lieutenant Colonel Lamine Bangoura, the governor of N'Zérékoré, Commandant Algassimou Barry, the Prefect of N'Zérékoré, and other colleagues for their valuable insight.

Sincere thanks are also due to representatives of the UN system in Guinea, who gave generously of their time and experience and also provided essential logistical support for the research. Particular thanks are due to Louise Aubin (UNHCR) for her unfailing support and willingness to help. Without her, we would still be stuck in N'Zérékoré. Special thanks are due to Stefano Porretti (World Food Programme – WFP) and especially to Milan Sannerkvist (UN Office of the Coordination of Humanitarian Affairs – OCHA). Thanks also to Stefano Severe (UNHCR), Mohamed Azzedine Salah (UNICEF) and Colonel Jean Michel Ntcha (Office of the UN Security Coordinator – UNSECOORD). Sincere thanks are also due to Sani Chaibou (UNHCR, N'Zérékoré) and Etienne Ladandé (WFP, N'Zérékoré).

In Conakry and N'Zérékoré, many non-governmental organizations (NGOs) set aside precious time for interviews. Profound thanks are due to friends and colleagues from Action Contre la Faim (ACF), Mathilde Groh in N'Zérékoré (American Refugee Committee, ARC, and Action by Churches Together–Lutheran World Federation, ACT–LWF), Jeremy Konyndyk in Conakry (Catholic Relief Services, CRS; the International Committee of the Red Cross, ICRC; the International Federation of Red Cross and Red Crescent Societies, IFRC; the International Organization for Migration, IOM; and the International Rescue Committee, IRC), and Binty Kamara in N'Zérékoré (Médecins Sans Frontières, MSF). Particular thanks and appreciation are due to the members of the Mano River Women's Peace Network and the Organisation Guinéenne de Défense des Droits de l'Homme et du Citoyen, and especially to their presidents, Dr Daraba Saran Kaba and Dr Thierno Sow. Their dedication is tireless, and their commitment humbling.

Thank you to Elissa Golberg (Foreign Affairs Canada) for providing valuable insight and for arranging a round-table discussion of the initial findings in Ottawa. Special thanks are also due to Professor Tolo Beavogui for his patience and wisdom, and to Mike McGovern for reviewing an earlier version of this chapter. Thank you also to M. Barry in Conakry and M. Donzo in N'Zérékoré, whose support was as unfailing as their humour. Final thanks and appreciation go to the dozens of refugees James met in Conakry, N'Zérékoré, Lainé and Kounkan. Their courage in facing every day the challenges we study occasionally is inspiring.

Uganda Robert Muggah would like to extend his appreciation to representatives of the Ugandan government, particularly fellow Oxford graduate Felix Kazahura (Office of the Prime Minister) and the national police, including Mvule Richard, Ouma Vincent, Kilama Johnson, Ovuru Jasinio, Lutiva James and Okot Biteck. Representatives of the Uganda People's Defence Force (UPDF), including Lieutenant Colonel Achoka, James Mogira and Obina Alexander, also provided useful insight during his field visits to Gulu, Lira, Adjumani and Moyo.

Representatives from the UN were especially supportive of the field research in various districts of Uganda, Rwanda and the Democratic Republic of the Congo (DRC). In particular, officers of the UN Mission in the DRC (MONUC) – such as Captain Stan Slogrove (Kampala), Guy Houdégbé (Kampala), Danilo Paiva (Goma), Major C. Vera (Goma), and Lieutenant Colonel Gustavo Vila (Goma) – were extremely generous with their time. Auke Lootsma and Enid Nambuya, both of the UN Development Programme (UNDP) in Kampala, provided vital background information at short notice. Dr Olive Kobusingye, currently with the World Health Organization in the Republic of the Congo (RoC) though longing one day to return to her native Uganda, provided important health-related data.

Crucially, the UN Office of the Coordination of Humanitarian Affairs (OCHA) and UNHCR provided ongoing support for the fieldwork. Robert Muggah is particularly indebted to Andrew Timson (Gulu), whose wit and experience facilitated his work enormously. Moreover, useful exchanges with OCHA's Jan Egeland (Geneva), Eliane Duthoit (Kampala), Stephen Lukudo (Kampala), Marc Vincent (Geneva), Dennis Mawake (Gulu), Lars Erik Skansaar (Gulu), Stella Adjwang (Gulu), Dusman Doka (Gulu), Paul Ndaitour (Goma) and Patrick Lavand-Homme (Goma) proved instrumental in rendering a more sophisticated treatment of a tremendously complex environment. For UNHCR, Juan Castro-Magluff (Kampala), Stephen Ghona (Kampala), Nicolaj Sonderbye (Kampala), as well as Veronica (Adjumani), Paul (Adjumani), Lucy (Adjumani), Maurice Moussouravi (Goma), Otim Fred (Moyo) and Salim (Moyo), all gave generously of their time.

Offices of other NGOs in Uganda – including Action Against Hunger (Action Contre la Faim, ACF), the International Organization for Migration (IOM), Save the Children–UK, the inspiring Gulu Support the Children Organization (GUSCO) and Africa Inland Church–Sudan – also provided important insights into the specific historical context and political economy of refugee and IDP militarization in the region. Local NGO and public health representatives, including James Otto of Human Rights Focus, Leander Komakec (University of Gulu) and Martin Ogwang of Lacor hospital, were instrumental in generating hard data on the effects of the phenomenon – and their extraordinary compassion and empathy will be long remembered.

Finally, Robert would like to extend his special thanks to Kennedy Mkutu (Bradford University, UK), Zachary Lomo and David Santino Okwera (Refugee Law Project, Kampala), Matthew Foley and Francis Stevenson (Overseas Development Institute), Andrew Pinto (University of Toronto), Helga Rainer (London School of Economics), Jesse Bernstein (Internal Displacement Monitoring Centre), Tania Kaiser (School of Oriental and African Studies), Karen Jacobsen (Tufts University) Alex Potter (independent editor) and Tim Shaw (Commonwealth Institute) for reviewing the draft report, and providing useful comments. Their commitment to supporting the refugees and IDPs in Uganda and elsewhere is unrelenting and much admired.

Tanzania Edward Mogire would like to make special mention of the support provided by the Centre for the Study of Forced Migration (University of Dar es Salaam) for the logistical support they rendered in obtaining a research permit. The Tanzanian Red Cross not only provided the author with accommodation and transportation in Kasulu but also agreed to undertake interviews. He thanks the Tanzanian Christian Refugee Services (TCRS) camp manager in Kasulu and the doctors at Muyovosi and Mtabila refugee camps and is grateful to UNHCR staff, especially the head of the sub-office in Kigoma region, the protection officer in Kasulu and the ICRC field office doctors at Kigoma. Special thanks must also be extended to the staff of the Ministry of Home Affairs, and to the refugees who agreed to devote their time to interviews and discussions. Last but not least, the author is grateful to BICC and the Small Arms Survey for providing the funding for this research and Kingston University for granting him time and other resources to conduct it.

Rwanda Gregory Mthembu-Salter extends his thanks to the many people who gave valuably of their time to assist him in this study. Needless to say, all errors and omissions are his alone. Sincere thanks are due first to the refugees of the Nyagatare transit camp and Cyangugu town, who generously shared their experiences and perceptions of their situation. He is also indebted to UNHCR's staff in Rwanda and DRC, including Rwanda office representative Kalunga Lutato, Volker Schimmel, Carolyn Ennis and Jaya Murthy, for their kind assistance, and to MONUC staff in Bukavu. The Rwandan government and armed forces fully cooperated with this study, and the author's thanks are due particularly to Richard Sezibera and Joseph Mutaboba in Kigali, Vincent Muragwa, the executive secretary of Cyangugu province, and Lieutenant Colonel George Rurigamba, Cyangugu's RDF commander.

Preface

Armed conflict and violence generate vast numbers of refugees and internally displaced persons (IDPs). In 2004, the United Nations High Commissioner for Refugees (UNHCR) estimated that there were 9.2 million refugees worldwide, while the Global IDP Project calculated that there were close to 25 million IDPs. The great majority of refugees, estimated at 3.5 and 13 million respectively, are in Africa. Refugees and IDPs are often unable to return to their home country or original place of residence in the immediate or near-term post-conflict period. Many thousands of people may languish in camps and settlements, and remain uncertain about their future. UNHCR reports that at least 6.2 million refugees in thirty-eight camps were considered as being within 'protracted situations' in 2004. In such unwanted circumstances, camps can become 'militarized', and, in turn, constitute a threat to internal and regional stability.

No refuge provides the forced migration community with new insights into the many dimensions of refugee and IDP camp/settlement militarization. It draws from new empirical research of refugee camps and settlements in Guinea, Rwanda, Tanzania and Uganda, where UNHCR works to protect refugees and to provide them with critical humanitarian assistance. By exploring the interface between refugee camp militarization and small arms proliferation, it opens a new chapter in our understanding of the many risks refugees and IDPs face, and how better to assist them.

Overall, the volume tells us that the scale and intensity of militarization are influenced by the region or host nation's political economy. Thus, militarization does not take place in a vacuum; it is deeply embedded in historical developments. Second, we can be reassured that cross-border militarization appears to be declining in comparison with previous years, partly because of reduced refugee flows in general, and also because of the successful interventions and situation-specific refugee security strategies applied by hosting states, UNHCR and the international community, including the increase in the number of UN authorized peace operations.

But UNHCR, implementing partners and donors cannot afford to be complacent. It seems that 'internal militarization' is on the rise, as refugees and IDPs are increasingly caught up or directly implicated in internal conflicts – from Guinea to northern Uganda. They may be armed, are often recruited into a militia, and will seek to defend their livelihoods. In some countries, it seems that humanitarian agency efforts to address refugee

insecurity and refugee and IDP militarization – as well as the donor support for these efforts – are only compensating for the failure of asylum
and country-of-origin states to meet their responsibilities. Ensuring the
civilian and humanitarian character of asylum and protecting civilian populations are, and must remain, primary responsibilities of the state. The
1951 Convention Relating to the Status of Refugees, the 1967 Protocol and
the 1969 Organization of African Unity Convention Governing the Specific
Aspects of Refugee Problems in Africa uphold international protection.
While there are no comparable instruments for protecting IDPs, various
guiding principles have been elaborated.

Clearly, ensuring the civilian and humanitarian character of asylum is a
major concern of the international community, especially of UNHCR. In the
late 1990s, UNHCR published a conceptual framework document known as
the 'ladder of options', outlining levels of refugee insecurity and proposing
a range of possible responses to address a given situation effectively. The
ladder included a combination of 'soft' and 'medium' (practical) options,
such as screening borders, community policing and the deployment of
international observers, and 'hard' options, including military intervention
when authorized by the UN Security Council.

Because the latter can be slow to act on the issue, UNHCR has worked
with a number of other actors, such as the UN Department of Peacekeeping
Operations (DPKO), to tackle a problem that is ostensibly beyond their
remit. UNHCR's Executive Committee signalled its concern about refugee
militarization in its Executive Committee Conclusion on the Civilian and
Humanitarian Character of Asylum, no. 92 (October 2002), and set out
important understandings to ensure the physical security of refugees, particularly in refugee camps and settlements. This important Conclusion
called upon UNHCR and DPKO to enhance collaboration on all aspects
of this complex matter.

More recently, UNHCR and DPKO entered into a formal agreement that
placed refugee security at the top of the agenda, and which recognizes the
need for partnerships and a comprehensive approach to attaining UNHCR
Agenda for Protection Goal no. 4: Addressing Security-related Concerns
More Effectively. Together with host governments (and with the assistance
of the international community), UNHCR has also advised on issues such
as the repatriation of foreign ex-combatants or 'armed elements' through
disarmament, demobilization and reintegration (DDR) processes. This is a
fairly new area of activity for the agency, however, and the challenges and
achievements need to be evaluated.

No refuge provides important new insights into how states, UNHCR,
the international community and their many partners can learn from past

scenarios and improve protection interventions. The efforts of the Small Arms Survey and the Bonn International Center for Conversion in working with UNHCR to make this publication possible are to be commended.

Kamel Morjane
Assistant High Commissioner, UNHCR
September 2005

Abbreviations

AAH	Action Against Hunger
ADF	Allied Democratic Front
AFRC	Armed Forces Revolutionary Council
AHA	Africa Humanitarian Agency
APM	anti-personnel mine
ARLPI	Acholi Religious Leaders Peace Initiative
ARN	Anti-Robbery Unit
BAC	Anti-Criminal Brigade
BCPR	Bureau for Conflict Prevention and Recovery
BCR	Bureau pour la Coordination des Réfugiés
BICC	Bonn International Center for Conversion
BMS	Mixed Brigade (police and gendarmerie)
BNCR	Bureau National pour la Coordination des Réfugiés
CARA	Control of Alien Refugees Act
CPU	Child Protection Unit
DDR	disarmament, demobilization and reintegration
DDRRR	disarmament, demobilization, reinsertion, reintegration, resettlement
DPKO	United Nations Department of Peacekeeping Operations
DRC	Democratic Republic of Congo
EAC	East African Community
ECOMOG	ECOWAS Monitoring Group
ECOWAS	Economic Community of West African States
ESS	Emergency Security Services
ExCom	UNHCR Executive Committee
ex-FAR	ex-Forces Armées Rwandaises (ex-Armed Forces of Rwanda) soldiers
FAC	Force Armées Congolaise
FAR	Forces Armées Rwandaises (Armed Forces of Rwanda)
FARDC	Forces Armées de la République Démocratique du Congo (Congolese Armed Forces)
FSA	field security adviser
FSO	field security officer
GDP	Gross Domestic Product
GNF	Guinean franc
GUSCO	Gulu Support for Child Organization

HMG	heavy machine gun
HRW	Human Rights Watch
HSO	humanitarian security officer
ICRC	International Committee of the Red Cross
IDP	internally displaced person
IISS	International Institute for Strategic Studies
IRC	International Rescue Committee
IRIN	United Nations Integrated Regional Information Networks
ISO	Internal Security Organization
JCC	Joint Cooperation Combatants
LCHR	Lawyers' Committee for Human Rights
LDU	Local Defence Units
LRA	Lord's Resistance Army
LURD	Liberians United for Reconciliation and Democracy
MDRP	Multi-regional Demobilization and Reintegration Programme
MONUC	Mission de l'Organisation des Nations Unies en République Démocratique du Congo (United Nations Mission in Congo)
MRUWPN	Mano River Union Women's Peace Network
NIF	National Islamic Front
NLA	National Liberation Army
NPFL	National Patriotic Front of Liberia
NRA	National Resistance Army
NRM	National Resistance Movement
OAU	Organization of African States
OCHA	Office for the Coordination of Humanitarian Affairs
OGDH	Organisation Guinéenne de Défense des Droits de l'Homme et du Citoyen
OPM	Office of the Prime Minister
PDA	People's Defence Army
PoA	Programme of Action to Prevent, Combat and Eradicate the Illicit Trade in Small Arms and Light Weapons in All Its Aspects
RCD	Rassemblement Congolais pour la Démocratie
RCMP	Royal Canadian Mounted Police
RDF	Rwandese Defence Force
RFDG	Movement of the Democratic Forces of Guinea
RPF	Rwandese Patriotic Front
RPG	rocket-propelled grenade
RUF	Revolutionary United Front
SADC	Southern African Development Community
SALW	small arms and light weapons
SAS	Small Arms Survey

SMG	small machine gun
SPHERE	Sphere Humanitarian Charter and Minimum Standards for Disaster Response
SPLA	Sudanese People's Liberation Army
SRS	self-reliance strategy
SSR	Security Sector Reform
ULIMO	United Liberation Movement of Liberia for Democracy
ULIMO–K	United Liberation Movement of Liberia for Democracy–Kromah
UNAMIR	United Nations Assistance Mission for Rwanda
UNAMSIL	United Nations Mission in Sierra Leone
UNDP	United Nations Development Programme
UNDSS	United Nations Department for Safety and Security
UNHCR	United Nations High Commissioner for Refugees
UNICEF	United Nations Children's Fund
UNITA	National Union for the Total Independence of Angola
UNOCHA	United Nations Office for the Coordination of Humanitarian Affairs
UNSC	United Nations Security Council
UPDF	Ugandan People's Defence Force
USCR	United States Committee for Refugees
USD	United States dollar
VCCU	Violence Crime Crackdown Unit
WFP	World Food Programme
WHO	World Health Organization
WNBF	West Nile Bank Front

1 | Arms availability and refugee militarization in Africa – conceptualizing the issues

ROBERT MUGGAH AND EDWARD MOGIRE

There is widespread agreement that unregulated small arms and light weapons – from handguns and assault rifles to man-portable missile defence systems – can kill and maim. But the availability of small arms also demonstrably undermines the protection and physical security of refugees and displaced persons throughout sub-Saharan Africa, the Balkans, the Caucasus, South and South-East Asia and Latin America and the Caribbean. The proliferation of such weapons is a central factor in the 'militarization' of refugee and internally displaced person (IDP) camps, exacerbating already difficult situations, and ultimately contributing to national and even regional instability. The problem of arms availability appears to be especially acute in so-called 'protracted refugee situations'.[1] Moreover, the militarization of refugee and IDP camps and the trans-national contagion effects are the source of persistent and serious concern on the part of the humanitarian community, donors and host states.

This introductory chapter provides a historical and conceptual outline for subsequent chapters of this edited volume. The following case study chapters themselves summarize empirical and field-based assessments of the extent, causes, dimensions and consequences of small-arms availability and misuse in an array of refugee and IDP camps in Africa. The presentation of evidence-based material is particularly important because its insight into the discrete relationships between weapons proliferation and refugees has hitherto been limited. Rather, discussion of the topic has tended to highlight these connections deductively, from an international relations perspective. The introduction also describes the combination of grounded methodologies used to measure these relationships. Finally, the introduction proposes a number of tentative 'entry points' for improving refugee and IDP protection, 'care and maintenance', and the prospects for achieving durable solutions.

The volume is not an esoteric academic exercise. Rather, it is targeted at humanitarian providers and practitioners, international and regional policy-makers, national law-makers and researchers alike. The rationale of the volume was to provide these diverse constituencies with cross-sectional evidence of the scale and magnitude of refugee and IDP camp militarization in Africa, as well as innovative interventions that have been introduced to militate against it. In order for multilateral agencies such as UNHCR and other implementing partners to respond better to refugee and IDP camp militarization, they must ultimately be capable of generating a clear, balanced and unambiguous understanding of the dynamics of small-arms diffusion. As UNHCR personnel and implementing and operational partners know only too well, militarization can rapidly lead to the breakdown of law and order in and around camps, and to serious violations of refugee and IDP rights, thereby endangering the integrity and security of humanitarian operations, the security of host states and the pursuit of durable solutions.[2] But it is only through effective diagnosis that appropriately tailored solutions can be introduced. The volume thus explicitly targets policy-makers – particularly those manifesting a growing concern over the relationship between refugee and refugee camp militarization and national and regional security. Indeed, there is a robust connection between increased criminality and the erosion of public security and refugee and IDP camp militarization – and it is only through an awareness of the regional and domestic security environments that meaningful interventions may be attempted. Finally, the volume should be of interest to scholars and field researchers working in the security and disarmament fields, most of whom – until recently – have had comparatively little engagement with the issue.[3]

The emergence of a research agenda on refugee militarization

Refugee camp militarization is not a new phenomenon. As the subsequent chapters on Guinea, Uganda, Tanzania and Rwanda amply show, refugee and refugee camp militarization have been issues confronting host governments and humanitarian agencies since the inception of the 1951 UN Convention Relating to the Status of Refugees and throughout the independence movements of former colonies during the 1960s (Loescher 1993). Though these post-colonial refugee movements aroused considerable anxiety on the part of newly independent states, early responses to the problem tended to be heavy handed. During the 1970s and 1980s, for example, camps for South African refugees in Mozambique and Tanzania were controlled by members of the military wing of the African National Congress and the Pan-African Congress, and were regularly attacked by the South African armed forces. In Angola during the 1970s and 1980s, Namibian refugee camps administered by the then Namibian liberation movement – the South West Africa People's Organization – were raided by the South African Air Force. In Zambia and Mozambique, refugee camps controlled by Zimbabwean liberation movements were repeatedly assaulted by the armed forces of the former Rhodesian government. In many cases, so-called 'armed elements' were virtually indistinguishable from the civilian population.[4] As such, refugees were thus cast as a 'problem' and their militarization appeared to constitute a threat of the highest order (Loescher and Milner 2005b).

The issue of refugee and IDP camp militarization became a more prominent concern in the post-colonial period. Despite mounting alarm among humanitarian agencies, host states and certain donor governments, the militarization of refugee camps nevertheless continued unabated into the 1980s and 1990s – particularly in western, central and north-eastern Africa. Throughout West Africa, for example, refugee settlements frequently experienced militia recruitment. The movement of heavily armed militia between Sierra Leone, Liberia, Guinea, Côte d'Ivoire and other countries exacerbated already simmering political tensions between states and undermined the physical security and safety of refugees and hosting populations. So too in the Great Lakes, where rebel groups exploited refugee-populated areas of Tanzania and the former Zaire in order to recruit young men, but also as conduits for illegally acquired goods and resources.[5] The pathologies of militarization soon began to leak into other spheres of local and regional economies.

International concern over refugee camp militarization – particularly among those trapped in protracted refugee situations – has grown apace. A growing academic community has evolved to account for the challenges such militarization represents. Many observers began to claim that refugee militarization, while not new, had increased in frequency during the 1990s when compared to previous decades (Loescher and Milner 2005a; Loescher 1993). According to Stedman and Tanner (2003), some 15 per cent of all refugee crises reportedly involved militarized refugees during the 1990s. The former High Commissioner for UNHCR, Sadako Ogata (1998), also lamented the 'world-wide ... problem of separating refugees from fighters, criminals, or even *génocidaires*'. A sanguine observer of the UN, Shawcross (2000), ominously noted that 'in the eighties the militarization of camps had been the exception and in the nineties it had became commonplace'. But dissenters also soon emerged. Other commentators disputed the apparent escalation of refugee militarization in the 1990s. Lischer (1999), for example, contends that refugee militarization was not as widespread as commonly perceived, arguing that 'the dominant view of widespread refugee militarization is reinforced by journalists and scholars who focus on a few notorious instances of violence'. While her conclusions were reached on the basis of a single proxy indicator of refugee militarization – political violence – hers nevertheless remains an important cautionary observation.[6]

Though debates have grown more sophisticated, there is, in fact, comparatively little evidence of the extent and pervasiveness of refugee militarization in Africa or elsewhere. While it is true that many governments are adamantly convinced that uncontrolled small-arms availability potentially fuels refugee and refugee camp militarization, little is actually known about where weapons are sourced or stored, and the extent to which they are present in camps themselves. Indeed, hosting and expelling states often denounce refugee and IDP camps for their being 'awash' with weapons, with 'flows' pouring into and from these encampments, without having any basis for such claims.[7]

There are many examples of governments identifying refugees and IDP camps as the source of insecurity and arms availability. The Chadian authorities, for example, have recently expressed concern to UNHCR over the alleged flood of arms into Sudanese Darfurian refugee camps and complained of their being controlled by militia despite comparatively little evidence to back this up.[8] In northern Kenya, the newspapers have repeatedly pointed to the Kakuma and Dadaab refugee camps as doubling as weapons trans-shipment points: illegal firearms are alleged to have been stockpiled by Somali and Sudanese refugees and ultimately smuggled to urban centres such as Eastleigh, in Nairobi. By way of comparison, refugee camps in Guinea are popularly condemned for harbouring enormous caches of carefully buried Sierra Leonean, Liberian or locally sourced weaponry. In most cases, however, even in the rare instances where weapons caches are discovered in these countries, they are commonly stored outside camps, for fear of detection.[9] In the case of Tanzania, for example, the ICG (1999) has observed that weapons are generally not seen in many camps and that military activities often take place outside the confines of settlements.[10] On the other hand, this suggests that a narrow focus on the prevalence and misuse of weapons in camps alone provides only a partial glimpse of the likely distribution of arms or the severity of their impacts.

It is clear, however, that militarized refugee and IDP camps do exist and can present a legitimate threat to security. But despite the potential political and security risks presented in such contexts and the growing prominence attached to the issue by UNHCR, there is comparatively limited empirical research to explain either the causes or manifestations of the phenomenon on the ground. This is partly because the international relations scholars and politico-legal experts who have explored related issues have tended to underplay the political and military implications of refugee fluxes, preferring instead to treat refugees as an unfortunate consequence (read: collateral damage) of armed conflict as opposed to a potential independent variable in conflict onset (Weiner 1992/93; Ferris 1993). Realist-inclined scholars in particular have tended to emphasize more traditional security threats and tensions between defined nation-states – whether political or resource-related – and to a much lesser extent the particular role of non-state actors. Moreover, as the refugee studies field itself became increasingly shaped by an emergent 'humanitarian paradigm' that privileged rights and needs-based discourses, refugees came increasingly to be cast as 'victims' (and later 'survivors') and not so much potentially active agents involved in possible cross-border political violence (Havinga and Bocker 1999; Chambers 1986).

These two epistemic approaches – the realist international relations and humanitarian perspectives – failed to take into account the many genuine security and military risks presented by refugee and IDP camp militarization. Proponents of the 'realist school' focused primarily on external and well-defined military threats to territorial integrity, while ignoring 'unconventional' military actors (for example, armed elements posing as refugees). On the other hand, ostensibly humanitarian approaches concentrated on the specific 'experience' of displacement – with the displaced person acting as the referent – and paid comparatively little attention to its political and security implications. Fortunately, over the past decade, discursive transformations in both security[11] and so-called forced migration studies[12] have yielded a more progressive inclusion of refugees and IDPs as both a referent object and a dynamic agent of potential social transformation. Many scholars in both fields now consider, to varying degrees, that the presence and movement of refugees across borders constitute a potentially legitimate threat to regional and national security (Loescher and Monahan 1999; Loescher and Milner 2005b).

Refugee and IDP camp militarization has been the focus of growing attention from a combination of researchers, policy-makers and humanitarian practitioners during the last decade (UNHCR 2001c; Lischer 1999). Though a vibrant debate persists over what precisely constitutes 'militarization', whether refugees or IDPs can themselves retain this classification while armed, and the extent to which illegal weapons exacerbate the problem, there is an emerging consensus in key normative declarations and enabling mechanisms that the preservation of the 'civilian' character of refugee camps is essential to safeguarding their non-political and humanitarian character. Unfortunately, however, when measured against the sheer output of rhetoric and policy formulation on the subject, there is actually comparatively little conceptual clarity or empirical evidence from the ground.

Priority areas for research There are no comparative studies of refugee and IDP camp militarization currently available. Rather, instead of over-

5

arching comparative review, researchers have occasionally explored the interface of refugees, refugee camps, host communities and armaments in discrete contexts. Certain reports have described refugee camps themselves as conduits for smuggling and trafficking of small arms, though many of these remain unsubstantiated.[13] It is regularly assumed that refugees – particularly young unemployed men – are themselves the central actors in perpetuating and sustaining a lucrative trade in arms – whether from their country of origin or domestically from a combination of criminal gangs and corrupt police and ex-combatants.[14] Notwithstanding the fact that refugee and IDP camps are themselves primarily home to the elderly, women and children, weapons are often believed to be circulating within camps and between dormant armed actors and their host communities. Governments have been quick to level accusations against the humanitarian community that they are 'sustaining' and 'abetting' this insidious trade, questioning its neutrality and impartiality. They have been even quicker to accuse refugees themselves of trafficking in arms and taking advantage of the host state's hospitality. These same governments seldom admit that they themselves may be implicated in the weapons movements that are in fact taking place.

There can be little doubt that the issue of small-arms availability has potentially profound implications for the work of humanitarian agencies and the fulfilment of their mandates.[15] Worryingly, senior government, representatives of the armed forces and police officials throughout Africa continue to justify restrictions on asylum and forced repatriation by pointing to the 'refugee-related' flow of arms and ordnance, although they can seldom validate the relationship.[16] Coupled with increasing reluctance among developed countries to sanction third-country resettlement, the emergent 'war on terror' and the growing priority attached by donors to in-country protection and care and maintenance for IDPs, there is a real danger that refugee asylum and refugee protection are being threatened by a poor reading of the issue.

Together with the UNHCR, the Small Arms Survey and the Bonn International Center for Conversion (BICC) recognized that comparative research on the issue was urgently needed. Following extensive consultations, it was decided that a systematic empirical investigation in Africa – the continent with the most severe incidence of refugee and IDP camp militarization – should be undertaken. By considering, *inter alia*, the scale and magnitude of arms trafficking into, through and around refugee and IDP camps, the impacts of small-arms misuse on refugee and IDP security and host populations and the response of host states and international agencies to the issue, it was felt that such assessments might provide a constructive contribution to reducing the yawning gap that separates reality from rumour and speculation. What is more, these assessments could usefully raise awareness of the issue among decision-makers working on both arms control and migration policy, and facilitate the design and evaluation of concrete interventions to improve the protection, care and maintenance of refugees by international humanitarian agencies and hosting states.

This volume is guided by five core research questions. These emerged from consultations with a host of international relief and humanitarian agencies, round-table discussions with diplomats and practitioners, focus group sessions with refugee and IDP populations in Africa, South Asia and Latin America, and a thorough review of the literature on disarmament and refugee studies. The selected country case studies include Guinea, Uganda, Tanzania and Rwanda, and field research was undertaken by each of the chapter authors. These objectives seek to respond to the following questions:

- What is and has been the nature and extent of refugee and IDP camp militarization?
- What are the pre-conditions for refugee and IDP camp militarization?
- What are and have been the scale and distribution of arms availability in refugee camps?
- What are and have been the impacts of militarization on refugee and host community security?
- What are UNHCR, host state and regional responses to the phenomena?

Methodological considerations Despite their common usage in humanitarian and development circles, there are no clear or commonly accepted definitions of either 'refugee militarization' or 'refugee camp militarization'. This is particularly disconcerting because such labels confer an array of stigmas and have political and bureaucratic implications for refugee protection, care and maintenance. Following a careful review of the academic and grey literature on the subject, a number of working definitions were adopted for the volume. Thus, 'refugee militarization' refers to 'the involvement of individual (or groups of) refugees and/or exiles (diaspora) in militaristic activities within and outside refugee camps'. These activities can include political violence, military training, explicit or tacit support for combatants, and armed resistance.[17] Second, 'refugee camp militarization' refers to 'the combination of military and armed attacks on refugees within camps; the storage and diffusion of weapons, military training and recruitment; the presence of armed elements, political activism and criminal violence within camps; and the exploitative use of relief/development resources by non-refugee residents and their dependents'. Refugee militarization is in

7

fact a broader concept than 'refugee camp militarization' and includes military-oriented activities undertaken by so-called armed elements within and outside camps.[18] By way of contrast, refugee camp militarization is generally restricted to related activities under way within or at the periphery of the camps themselves. While sharing similar features, the two concepts are in fact not synonymous, and it is incumbent on the refugee studies community to ensure these distinctions. Table 1.1 below lists a range of indicators of refugee and refugee camp militarization explored in the following chapters.

TABLE 1.1 Benchmarking refugee and refugee camp militarization

Refugee militarization	Refugee camp militarization
• Militarized activity in and outside camps • Political activism and violence • Military training and recruitment • Support for combatants and armed resistance	• Armed violence in camps • Political activism and violence • Storage and trafficking of small arms • Inflows and outflows of weapons • Military training and recruitment • Infiltration of armed elements • Use of relief/development resources

The real dividends of this volume are found in its case studies. Drawing on the normative and conceptual review highlighted above, the case studies review the real and perceived experiences of refugees and IDPs *in situ*. A driving concern of the authors of these chapters was to ensure that the voices and concerns of refugees and IDPs were heard, as they are so often neglected in policy debates in Geneva and New York. The chapters were themselves compiled from a variety of sources, including archival and grey literature from the UNHCR and its implementing partners, literally thousands of key informant interviews, dozens of focus groups with refugee and IDP populations and militia and insurgent commanders, small-scale surveys in refugee and IDP camps and host communities, epidemiological studies from the records of public health facilities, and participant observation in camps themselves. A 'research protocol', itself annexed to this chapter, was provided to each of the four case study authors to assist in guiding their fieldwork. For the purposes of comparability, each of the case studies required a consideration of the following factors:

1 The context in which refugee and IDP militarization occurs. All case study authors were required to undertake a general analysis of the vari-

ous political, economic and social dynamics facing the host state with respect to its refugee and IDP case loads. What is more, researchers were expected to review the declared causes of the original and ongoing refugee and IDP movements; the profile and geographic distribution of refugees and IDPs over time; and the number of camps, their sizes and their locations relative to international borders.

2   The existence and extent of refugee and IDP camp militarization. All chapter authors were instructed to describe the scale and incidence of refugee and IDP recruitment inside and outside camps; the extent of military training and deployment; whether camps were being used as staging posts for cross-border excursions; refugee and IDP participation in armed conflict/criminal violence; the presence of financial and non-monetary networks between armed groups and refugees and IDPs; the role of refugees and IDPs in cross-border and internal trafficking of arms; and the presence of armed groups in camps themselves.

3   The pre-conditions of refugee and IDP militarization. A primary focus of chapter authors was on documenting key triggers that contributed to the incidence of refugee and IDP camp militarization. These include the historical antecedents of refugee camp militarization; the presence of external support for militarization; the proximity of camps to borders; the presence, command and control and objectives of armed actors in the vicinity of refugee camps; refugee affiliation with opposition politicians and diasporas; the presence of exploitable resources near camps; and the existence of humanitarian/development aid that could potentially support local war economies.

4   The scale and magnitude of arms distribution and trafficking in and around camps. Wherever possible, the case study authors were required to document and analyse official and unofficial trend data on small-arms distribution and trafficking into and out of the country; reported weapons seizures in relation to camps; reported incidents where refugees and IDPs were accused of taking part in the arms trade; reported incidents of arms use in camps and host communities; the presence and distribution of armed actors; and various police logs and records to this effect.

5   The impacts of small-arms availability on the refugee, IDP and host population. Drawing on the Small Arms Survey's ongoing research on the effects of firearm-related violence,[19] the case studies sought to measure the frequency and dispersion of armed criminality in and outside camps; longitudinal trends in firearm-related mortality and morbidity in and around refugee and IDP camps; victimization rates, including harassment and sexual- and gender-based violence against refugees

9

and internally displaced populations; and, finally, related impacts on humanitarian operations.

6 Host country and UNHCR responses to refugee and IDP militarization. In order to inform practical responses by UNHCR and others to the phenomena, the case studies reviewed national and host state responses to refugee and IDP militarization; UNHCR and policing-based interventions to improve safety and security in camps themselves; and efforts to implement the so-called 'ladder of options' by UNHCR, donors and others.

A major obstacle to longitudinal research on refugee militarization and small arms relates to the availability and reliability of statistical data. Basic aggregate data on national firearm homicide and crime rates, and the distribution and numbers of registered and illegal small arms and the like, are simply unavailable in most countries in the world – and particularly so in the cases analysed in this volume. The gaps in data have, however, been narrowed considerably through a great deal of archival and secondary research.

The primary source of data generated by researchers was interactions with key informants in the field. These included a combination of structured and semi-structured interviews with a wide array of internal and external actors, including UNHCR staff (at headquarters in country capitals and at the sub-office level); refugees and IDPs (including, for example, youths, small adult samples of men and women, and refugee and IDP leaders); and host community leaders/representatives. Chapter authors also drew on secondary data sources such as the incident reporting systems maintained by field security advisers (FSAs), UN Department of Safety and Security (UNDSS) staff and UNHCR country offices. Specific thematic reports and security assessments were also reviewed, as they often included information on reported instances of arms trafficking and smuggling, armed violence in refugee camps and/or involving refugees and IDPs. Such compilations themselves frequently rely on print and radio media reports, police advisories and intelligence gathered by humanitarian agencies – which are known often to underestimate the prevalence of armed violence (Small Arms Survey 2005).[20] As will be made clear in the following chapters, field research also includes small-sample surveys in refugee camps.[21]

Four lenses used to examine refugee camp militarization

Ultimately, there is no single conceptual approach that can adequately capture the complex motivations for and consequences of small-arms possession and misuse in refugee and IDP camps. For the purposes of guiding the overall comparative study, however, four analytical perspectives were generated to inform the case research. Each of these perspectives has been vigorously debated in the literature, but nevertheless, together they form a useful 'optic' through which to consider refugee and IDP camp militarization. A first perspective is that refugees, internally displaced and refugee and IDP camps are often 'manipulated' as instruments of warfare. The second perspective envisions refugees and IDPs as active agents, rather than pawns or passive recipients, in rendering their own decisions about whether or not to become militarized. A third perspective considers the international and institutional humanitarian response to the phenomenon, and the role of international actors in exacerbating or hindering militarization. The fourth perspective examines the issue through the prism of disarmament and arms control. When combined, each of these perspectives helps illuminate the relationship between refugee and IDP militarization and small-arms availability in a comprehensive and holistic manner.

Refugees as instruments of warfare A clear measure of refugee and IDP camp militarization is the tacit participation of refugees or IDPs in and overt support of internal and cross-border armed conflicts. This was an especially common phenomenon during the US–Soviet proxy conflicts in Africa throughout the 1960s, 1970s and 1980s. The concept of 'refugee warriors' emerged, itself a reference to the arming of former mujahidin combatants in Pakistani refugee camps. As Loescher (1993) observed some two decades ago, 'refugees have become instruments of warfare and military strategy'. Indeed, the incidence of refugee and IDP participation in armed conflicts persists today. But a controversial debate has nevertheless emerged over the extent to which refugees or IDPs are either 'manipulated' or 'willing agents' in such activities.

According to Stedman and Tanner (2003), manipulation is commonplace and can occur in a variety of contexts. They point to the opportunistic harnessing of 'refugee suffering' by warring parties to advance specific political and strategic interests. Indications of manipulation range from the siphoning-off of humanitarian assistance and efforts to establish international legitimacy by elites in and outside camps to the prevention of (voluntary) refugee repatriation.[22] In their view, manipulation can itself be exercised through intimidation, the application of coercive and physical pressure, propaganda and the denial of assistance – and often results in the engagement of refugees in military-related activities.

Manipulation has not gone unnoticed. Indeed, refugee and IDP manipulation has been regularly condemned by the UN Security Council (UNSC 2001), which has contended that 'the failure to separate armed elements from civilians allows armed groups to take control of a camp and its population, politicising their situation and gradually establishing a military culture within the camp'. Humanitarian and development practitioners have also observed the repeated manipulation of Rwandan refugees and IDPs in the former Zaire, as well as with Tanzania's Burundian refugee case load, Liberian and Sierra Leonean refugees in Guinea, Liberians in Côte d'Ivoire, and also among the Sudanese residing in northern Uganda and, more recently, Chad.

To many, the widespread manipulation of refugees and IDPs by so-called 'armed elements' comes as little surprise. Refugee and IDP camps are in fact ideal sites for such activities to take place, and provide at least three major advantages for armed insurgents and militia over otherwise purely military sanctuaries: safety, security and resources. For example, the 'protected status' of refugees under international (refugee) law ensures a degree of safety against reprisals and reduces dependence on the political and economic backing of host states. What is more, crowded camps can provide cover for armed groups – whether insurgents or organized criminals – and serve as ideal bases for military or other types of operations. Moreover, their proximity to international borders – if that is the case – facilitates such activities. Ultimately, humanitarian relief assistance in refugee camps often serves as a magnet for and indirectly provides armed elements with (rentable) economic resources independent of external patrons (Terry 2002; Loescher and Milner 2005b).

Refugees are also regularly manipulated by host states and 'third parties' (Byman et al. 2001). Since the logistical demands of triggering small-scale and incipient armed conflicts in Africa are relatively modest, even poor states can readily facilitate the emergence of a resistance movement to trouble their neighbours.[23] In fact, the voluntary and coercive deployment of refugees as 'freedom fighters' and guerrillas has occurred on all continents (Loescher 1992, 1993). In Africa, governments in the Horn, particularly Ethiopia, Somalia and Sudan, have used asylum and assistance to so-called 'refugee warriors' as a surrogate form of support for rebel movements in other states (Sayigh 1990).[24] Many of these activities have antecedents in cold war-inspired conflicts (Loescher 1992). Indeed, the usual strategy of the superpowers was to exploit and exacerbate the fault lines of pre-existing and simmering armed conflicts or to create new ones where they had not previously existed. It is well known that war by proxy entailed an unrestrained and continuous flow of weapons and aid to refugee groups in various theatres of conflict – though verifiable evidence is limited (Barber 1997; Small Arms Survey 2003, 2004).

Refugees as agents and victims of militarization The burgeoning literature on refugee and IDP militarization contains many descriptions of cases where so-called refugees and IDPs applied armed violence to advance their own discrete objectives. In some cases, refugees inhabit politically motivated 'settlements' led by armed leaders engaged in warfare for a variety of reasons, including the recapture of a 'homeland', the destabilization of existing regimes or the securing of a separate state (Loescher 1993; Zolberg et al. 1989). Alternatively, individuals in exile, including refugees, may find that, given their relative destitution, the most socially meaningful and economically rewarding activity is to join militant or criminal organizations (Durieux 2000). Where refugee camps are located close to or form part of the front line of an armed resistance, as is the case of Sudanese refugees in northern Uganda, eastern Chad or north-western Kenya, armed conflict can become a predominant reality for successive generations of refugees. Where they share ethnic affiliations with host populations, they can also militarize previously pacific communities. Zolberg et al. (1989) have shown convincingly that in such scenarios it is conceivable that armed militants appear rather as 'protectors' or safeguards of refugee community values, ambitions and memories, thus forging more closely the links between the refugee and the warrior.

While the expression 'refugee warrior' may itself be a misnomer, the direct and indirect participation of refugees and IDPs in armed conflicts occurs regularly. Brown (1996) has recorded the impact of refugees and gangs of current and ex-combatants that diffuse across borders on the 'internationalization' of conflict. According to Byman et al. (2001), 'refugee flows and insurgencies feed into one another' – and can regularly lead to full-scale war. Stedman and Tanner (2003) agree that 'there are cases in which refugees grant legitimacy to the warriors by supporting their activities'. In addition to war, militarized refugees can also contribute directly and indirectly to the outbreak of political violence.[25] These and other presumed quantitative relationships are briefly treated in the case studies and the final chapter of this volume.

There is also ample anecdotal evidence of militarized refugees and IDPs harnessing humanitarian and development aid to support their own war chests. According to Loescher (1992), 'humanitarian aid is used widely, both by small and big powers and even by refugee warrior groups [*sic*], to serve strategic and military goals'. Others have documented how relief assistance has in the past contributed to the procurement of weapons by refugees to sustain armed conflicts.[26] According to Barber (1997), 'the aid that flows to the camps where the refugees are gathered can be skimmed by militants based in camps'. Even where insurgent groups enjoyed the support of powerful patrons and diaspora communities, humanitarian and development aid have proved indispensable supplements. As the following chapters will show, voluntary and involuntary contributions or 'taxes' on rations are not uncommon, and have been documented in Rwandan camps in the Democratic Republic of Congo (DRC) and western Tanzania, as well as among Sudanese refugees in Uganda and Kenya, and Burundian refugees in Tanzania (Stedman and Tanner 2003; Terry 2002).

Not surprisingly, refugee and IDP camp militarization is particularly acute where refugees and IDPs are known to acquire, possess and traffic arms, as well as where camps and host communities are used for arms storage and trans-shipment. As potential (voluntary or involuntary) agents in armed conflict, refugees can contribute to the proliferation of small arms as both end-users and intermediate suppliers.[27] In other words, refugees can be users of small arms as well as potential traffickers and dealers. Refugee camps are also themselves often part and parcel of a military strategy by belligerents in a conflict. The Rwandan camps based in eastern Zaire in 1994 are a well-known example (UNHCR 2001c). In such situations, the tightly prescribed mandates of the UN peacekeeping operations are regularly exploited, as was the case with arms trafficking undertaken by the then Mobutu regime.

While the ascribed motivations for small-arms possession and misuse are highly pertinent, it is also important to acknowledge that refugee and IDP militarization can be inspired by defensive motivations. The physical protection of camps offered by host governments can range from predatory to inadequate. In the absence of credible policing or privately provided security, refugees and IDPs often have to cope with extremely precarious situations, for instance because of attacks from hostile armed groups or forced recruitment drives by militant groups. Female Somali refugees in the Kenyan refugee camps of Dadaab and Kakuma, for example, have been attacked when collecting firewood and subsistence market goods (Crisp 2001; Muggah and Berman 2001). The provision of perimeter security, substitution of fuel-efficient stoves and privately contracted fuel-collection services are all examples of ways to prevent gun-related violence perpetrated against refugees and IDPs.

Whatever the motivation for refugee and IDP camp militarization, the response by host governments has most often been severe. For example, Posen (1996) has documented how military interventions have been launched against camps themselves to redress the alleged 'root causes' of the problem. Mechanisms have also been introduced to meet the security threats of incoming refugees. Mtango (1989) has described how direct military actions have been initiated in camps involved with or suspected of supporting armed insurgents. Not only do such camps become potential targets for official armed intervention or unofficial attacks, but refugee, IDP and host communities suffer directly from the proliferation and misuse of small arms. First, refugees and IDPs are known to suffer acutely from fatal and non-fatal injuries, as well as increasing exposure to armed criminality and harassment in areas that are heavily militarized.[28] The consequences of the pervasive climate of insecurity for durable solutions are especially dire. This has recently been highlighted by UNHCR, which noted in a statement to the UN Conference on Illicit Small Arms Trade and Trafficking in All Its Aspects in 2001 that 'the proliferation of small arms in camps and cross-border attacks impedes voluntary repatriation and undermines the reintegration of refugees'. As the final chapter of this volume makes clear, the implications of insecurity for durable solutions have also figured prominently in recent UNHCR Executive Committee (ExCom) statements since 2002.

Refugee militarization and the humanitarian community This volume devotes considerable attention to the political and programmatic responses to refugee and IDP militarization elicited by UNHCR, as the foremost international organization charged with the protection of refugees. With its primary statutory mandate to protect refugees, UNHCR has confronted the issue of militarization in a predictable fashion – by focusing on refugees and IDPs themselves (UNHCR 2002). Over the past decade, UNHCR, donor and host states and implementing partners have elaborated a number of normative and practical measures to demilitarize refugees and refugee camps (UNHCR 1982, 1983, 2001a, 2002). As such, UNHCR has established a basic doctrine to reduce refugee and IDP militarization that currently informs its practical responses.

As stipulated in international refugee law, the responsibility for ensuring the physical security and civilian character of refugee camps rests in the first instance with host governments. In some cases, however, UNHCR recognizes that governments are unable or unwilling to prevent militarization from occurring. Though limited screening and disarming of incoming refugees have occasionally been undertaken by host authorities, they have not always been effective in the face of mass influxes that have so often accompanied Africa's wars. Moreover, unless combatants are prepared to abandon their weapons voluntarily or through organized disarmament, demobilization and reintegration (DDR) programmes,[29] it is exceedingly difficult for poorly armed or unarmed customs officials – much less UNHCR protection officers – to disarm them. As soon as armed combatants merge with civilian refugee populations, screening and separation become exceedingly problematic, if not impossible. Indeed, where there is outright resistance to demilitarization, armed military intervention may be required. But as the case of militarized Rwandan refugees in eastern Zaire has shown, even disciplined and heavily armed military forces may refuse or be unable to take up the task.[30]

UNHCR has reluctantly come to recognize the importance of enhancing security – and controlling the spread of small arms – to achieve its basic protection mandate. For example, Goal 4 of UNHCR's Agenda for Protection highlights a variety of arms-control-related concerns. The agenda emphasizes the pivotal importance of preserving law and order, curtailing the flow of arms into refugee camps and settlements, disarming 'armed elements', and identifying, separating and interning combatants as practical approaches to addressing the problem. Recent ExCom conclusions have likewise called for concrete steps to deal with the problem of refugee militarization and the importance of adopting practical measures in camps themselves to improve security. For example, ExCom Conclusion 94 (c) (II) (UNHCR 2002), has referred explicitly to the need for measures to identify, separate, disarm and intern combatants during refugee emergencies. It further calls upon UNHCR and the UN's Department of Peacekeeping Operations (DPKO) to deploy 'multi-disciplinary assessment teams to clarify the situation on the ground, evaluate security threats for refugee populations and consider appropriate practical responses' (ibid.: para. [g]).[31]

Partly in response to failures to prevent or deal appropriately with the aftermath of the Rwandan genocide of 1994, UNHCR introduced a 'ladder of options' five years later to identify, prepare for and respond to particular (militarized) situations as they arise. Recognizing the limits of ostensibly humanitarian interventions – and the need in some cases for more overt political or military interventions – UNHCR advanced a threefold approach to improving the physical security of refugees in camps. 'Soft options' focused on ensuring the permanent presence of international personnel in or close to camps. They also included the locating of camps at a suitable distance from international borders and ensuring that they did not exceed a certain population size (for example, no more than 20,000). Soft options also included the election of refugee leaders to promote the civilian and humanitarian character of the camp. 'Medium options' included working with local law enforcement agencies, providing training and support to establish national law enforcement capacity, and deploying international civilian/police monitors with the consent of the host state. Finally, 'hard options' were to be used in only the rarest of cases, and included the deployment of multinational or regional forces in situations where other interventions had failed.[32]

The ladder of options was institutionalized at headquarters and field levels after the issuance of recommendations by a UNHCR standing committee in June 2000. Early efforts to mainstream the concept yielded some early dividends. For example, UNHCR introduced the concept of field security officers (FSOs) – staff security experts – to be deployed as part of emergency response teams at the beginning of a refugee crisis to work with national and local public security institutions.[33] It also established an arrangement with DPKO collectively to assess threats and consider appropriate responses through 'reconnaissance' and 'assessment' missions. Finally, UNHCR's Emergency Preparedness and Response Section and the Field Safety Section were merged into the Emergency Security Service (ESS) administered by a senior-ranking official.[34] These interventions have been criticized by Stedman and Tanner (2003) and Durieux (2000) for their inability to address uncooperative host states and armed elements. They have observed a distinct absence of 'policy alternatives' should the UN Security Council refuse to intervene with a Chapter VI or VII mandate – a likelihood that most in UNHCR themselves privately concede.

Since the introduction of the ladder of options, UNHCR has advanced an array of practical and country-specific interventions on the ground. For example, in Tanzania a 'security package' was developed to improve security in Burundian camps, and FSAs were deployed to support the process.[35] In Guinea, UNHCR relocated refugee camps away from the border to protect refugees from attacks by Sierra Leonean and Liberian rebels. UNHCR also entered into a formal agreement with the Canadian Ministry of Foreign Affairs and the country's Royal Canadian Mounted Police (RCMP) that led to the deployment of two RCMP officers who worked with the Guinean Brigade Mixte (gendarmerie and police) in capacity-building efforts towards improved camp security. In Kenya's two protracted refugee camps, police reservists and armed security guards were hired by UNHCR to guard refugee populations (Durieux 2000; ICG 1999).[36] Though these interventions have arguably enhanced the physical security of some refugee populations, they have not necessarily prevented the militarization of refugees or refugee camps. More recently, the ESS has developed a number of supplementary operational responses to deal with the problem of militarization, including the development of so-called Humanitarian Security Officers (HSOs) likely seconded from DPKO and international police. Drawing on the experience of Tanzania, Kenya, Guinea (with the RCMP) and elsewhere, these efforts have allowed UNHCR to develop a specialist role to be filled by the Refugee Security Liaison Officer (RSLO).[37]

The debate on small-arms control Despite their ubiquity in areas where refugees and IDPs reside, it is not altogether surprising that small arms have been slow to emerge as a priority for UNHCR. To be sure, the issues of small-arms availability and diffusion have only recently become a priority for the disarmament community itself and are only occasionally identified as a humanitarian issue, much less one related to refugees and IDPs (Muggah with Griffiths 2002; Small Arms Survey 2002). To many humanitarian and development practitioners, small arms are decidedly 'political' and thus 'someone else's problem'.

Though the early 1990s witnessed an explosion of descriptive studies on the issue of small arms, it was not until the release of various reports by the UN Panel of Experts (UNGA 1997, 1999) that the negative effects of such weapons were highlighted in a public multilateral forum (Laurance and Stohl 2002; Small Arms Survey 2001). The politically binding 2001 UN Programme of Action (PoA) laid out a number of basic principles and concerns with regard to controlling the illicit trade in small arms and light weapons (SALW) – including marking and tracing regimes, controls on brokers and harmonized legislation – though many issues have been left off the agenda.[38] Despite the prevailing conventional wisdom that massive refugee flows are a form of 'contagion' and can contribute to arms flows across borders, the phenomena of refugee and IDP militarization are not mentioned in the PoA and seldom discussed by disarmament negotiators. Acknowledgement of the attendant risks associated with militarized refugee camps and contagion are emphasized, however, in the 1969 Refugee Convention of the Organization of African Unity (OAU).[39]

As with the issue of refugee camp militarization, Africa has witnessed considerable activity in terms of small-arms control. In West Africa, for example, members of the Economic Community of West African States (ECOWAS) signed the Bamako Moratorium on the Importation, Exportation and Manufacture of Light Weapons in West Africa, covering both licit and illicit transfers. In southern Africa, the Southern African Development Community (SADC), whose members formally endorsed the Southern Africa Regional Action Programme, has undertaken several initiatives.[40] Also active has been the OAU (now Africa Union, or AU), which announced the Bamako Declaration (2000) to control small arms. The East African Community (EAC) launched the Nairobi Declaration (2000), which seeks to increase cooperation to control arms trafficking and transfers between virtually all the countries of the Great Lakes, Horn and EAC regions. Though these initiatives acknowledge the link between conflict and small-arms proliferation, they have not fully articulated the linkages between refugee and IDP camp militarization and small-arms availability.[41]

The humanitarian community has also gradually begun to take up the challenge of small-arms control as an integral part of its response to refugee camp militarization. UNHCR's activities with respect to ExCom Conclusion no. 48, which *inter alia* states that refugee camps and settlements should have an exclusively civilian and humanitarian character, have been discussed above (UNHCR 1987).[42] A number of key issues have been identified as essential in reducing refugee and refugee camp militarization – including screening and disarmament, the removal of weapons from camps, the separation of armed elements and the internment of combatants, and other practical interventions. At risk of stating the obvious, however, a first and vital step to demilitarizing refugee camps is practical disarmament. This continues to pose an enormous challenge to both host communities and the international community. On the ground, the de facto disarmament of armed elements and combatants mixed within large refugee populations entering host countries or residing in camps has only been attempted sporadically. Successful disarmament has been limited. A major problem continues to be the difficulty in differentiating armed elements from genuine refugees – a problem also encountered by proponents of DDR activities the world over. As Yu (2002) has made clear in the context of the DRC:

> preliminary screening may identify some armed elements, [but] the lack of clear markers on militia members or other irregular forces makes it nearly impossible to differentiate between combatants and bona fide refugees. In cases where combatants can be clearly identified, unless they are willing to give up their arms, unarmed border guards or UNHCR Protection Officers will be ineffective in preventing camp militarization.

Ultimately, effective practical disarmament depends on the enduring commitment of host states and the international community. But perhaps, as the Zaire case shows, political will cannot always be relied upon. The host country can, and often does, nurture a completely different agenda, which it pursues while stringing along the international community through endless meetings and ad hoc commissions. As the chapters on Uganda and Tanzania show, in many cases police forces are themselves affected by systemic corruption, and are poorly staffed and under-resourced. So the choice for the UN and humanitarian agencies is no small challenge: abet or leave.

Even where political will exists, the actual removal and collection of weapons from refugee camps is an intrinsically complex process. Past efforts have been coercive and generally unsuccessful: the experiences of Rwanda were tragic in this regard, as the Rwandan chapter shows. Although the majority of small arms were stored outside the camps, some arms were known to be stored in camps at Kibeno in the south of the country. Responding to the growing concern of the Rwandan government and the international community, the United Nations Assistance Mission for Rwanda (UNAMIR) sought coercively to disarm the camp. Before it was able to undertake the operation, armed elements had escaped and buried their weapons. In response to this failure, the Rwandan government raided the camp and massacred a large number of otherwise innocent refugees.

Other interventions to reduce refugee camp militarization have involved the internment of previous combatants and the relocation of camps themselves. UNHCR (2001b) has recommended that:

> once armed elements among refugees have been separated and disarmed, the fighters (combatants) should be interned at a suitable location far from the border, or otherwise prevented from continuing their armed struggle or endangering the refugee population. Those confined are entitled to the basic necessities of life, and to be protected from forcible return to their own country under international humanitarian law.

Nevertheless, as the chapter on Tanzania reveals, it took UNHCR well over a year to convince government officials to separate armed elements and relocate them to internment facilities. Though a facility was ultimately identified (in Mwisa) and some forty Burundian combatants relocated there in 1999, the majority have since absconded (Durieux 2000).

Greater acknowledgement of the small-arms control issue by the international community has also recently provided impetus for bringing the issue to the fore in refugee and IDP situations. There has, however, been relatively little transmission of information from refugee studies into debates on small-arms control. This volume expects to begin redressing this imbalance, though the road ahead is long and challenging.

Four cases of refugee militarization in Africa

Africa registers by far the highest incidence and severity of refugee and IDP militarization in the world. The case studies presented in the following chapters were themselves selected according to a number of criteria. For example, in order to highlight regional variations, cases were selected from East, Central and western Africa. Countries were also chosen according to their 'security context', whether proceeding, at or emerging from war. Other criteria included the relative expertise and familiarity of the chapter authors, practical considerations associated with data availability and collection, and networks.

The comparative approach adopted by this volume does not presume to be representative of either refugee/IDP militarization in Africa or policy responses introduced by the international community. It does, however, assume that the selection of case studies is sufficiently broad and diversified for a qualitative evaluation of the principal objectives and perspectives discussed above. Importantly, the case studies provide compelling new evidence, at a detailed and disaggregated level of analysis, to allow interested parties to begin asking the right questions relating to the motivations of refugees and IDPs, the dynamics and contours of refugee camp militarization, and the relevance and probable impact of arms control measures. The introduction closes with a brief review of some basic findings emanating from each of the case studies, before turning to the chapters themselves

Guinea Guinea is often overlooked in studies on refugee militarization, with the focus often (deservedly) on the Great Lakes or Horn of Africa. But the case study chapter on Guinea by Milner and Christoffersen-Deb reveals some new insights, with lessons for West Africa and the continent as a whole. The chapter notes that by the end of the 1990s Guinea hosted one of the largest refugee populations in Africa: an estimated 450,000 refugees. Most lived not in camps but in refugee settlements close to the border with Liberia and Sierra Leone, where many are alleged to have achieved a certain level of self-sufficiency. Their livelihoods were shattered in late 2000 as a result of a series of cross-border attacks. These attacks had profound consequences for humanitarian work in Guinea, as the refugee populations dispersed and settlements became militarized, and as humanitarian actors and resources themselves became an explicit target of the raids.

The Guinean case also offers some instructive lessons for proactive responses to refugee militarization. The authors found that UNHCR and its partners responded to militarization by providing refugees with the opportunity voluntarily to relocate to newly established camps, and subsequently facilitating the return of refugees to Sierra Leone. Security arrangements were established to ensure the civilian nature of the new camps. At a later stage, the specific support of the Canadian government through the deployment of RCMP officers was offered. As a result of these initiatives, coupled with the (positive) change of circumstances in Liberia, the camps in Guinea were effectively demilitarized. Nevertheless, at the time of the research in 2004 it appeared that southern Guinea faced significant challenges related to the presence of armed elements and the proliferation of small arms.

Because the boundaries between refugee camps, settlements and the local community in the region are blurred, and given that the security of the region as a whole has direct consequences for the security of refugees and relief workers, attention must be devoted not exclusively to the security

Conceptualizing the issues

of refugee camps, but also to the security of the refugee-populated areas. The authors contend that if the international community is serious about ensuring the protection of civilians and refugees in Guinea and finding solutions to their plight, urgent intervention is needed to address the presence of foreign and domestic armed elements in southern Guinea, the flow of SALW through the region, and the escalating tensions between refugees and the local population.

Uganda Though once described as a 'development darling' by international donors and lauded for its progressive 'self-reliance' strategies for refugees, Uganda continues to be affected by refugee and IDP militarization. In fact, Uganda has hosted refugees from twelve countries since the 1950s. The chapter reviews how the profile of refugees themselves has changed, ranging from Europeans fleeing the Second World War to former combatants from neighbouring countries who regrouped in the post-independence period. Hundreds of thousands of Ugandans have also been violently internally displaced since the mid-1960s. Hence, the contemporary manifestations of refugee militarization and the militarization of IDPs are not new phenomena, but ones that are deeply embedded in the political culture of the country (and the region).

Muggah finds that Uganda's current populations of 216,000 refugees and over 1.6 million IDPs are geographically and ethnically differentiated. Though often lumped together, the majority of the country's Sudanese, Congolese and Rwandese refugees are concentrated in relatively small 'settlements' throughout the north-western, western and south-western districts. Many of these populations share common ethnic affiliations with communities across international borders. Though it is difficult to establish with certainty given the low reliability of census data, between 5 and 20 per cent of the overall population of the western districts are refugees. By way of contrast, IDPs are concentrated in large 'camps' predominantly in the north-western, north-eastern and central districts of the country and are primarily of Acholi origin. Alarmingly, between 60 and 90 per cent of the total aggregate population of the north-east are considered to be internally displaced.

The chapter finds that the militarization of refugee and IDP camps and settlements, as in Guinea, Tanzania and Rwanda, is rooted in long-standing international, political and ethnic animosities. It is not uniquely a product of the notorious Lord's Resistance Army (LRA). Rather, the experience of displacement and subsequent militarization in Uganda is conditioned to a large extent by the instability of its neighbours to the north, west and east, and domestic politics and ethnic tensions. Despite recent bilateral agreements between Sudan and Uganda to reduce their support for competing non-state armed groups, the current insecurity facing Ugandan IDPs and Sudanese refugees is tied to political relations between the Ugandan government and the Sudanese People's Liberation Army (SPLA), and between the Sudanese government and the LRA. In addition, long-standing ethnic tensions between northern and southern tribes, as well as with the pastoralists from the Karamoja region, have contributed to concomitant displacement and militarization.

The chapter reveals that most IDP camps are fortified with Ugandan People's Defence Force (UPDF) barracks, a military presence and increasingly heavy deployments of UPDF forces and militia groups. Though the majority of IDP camps are not 'militarized', a considerable number of young men have been recruited into self-defence units. Such units are trained by the UPDF, with some members actually being redeployed in other parts of the country or even abroad. As a result, in the central and north-eastern districts, Acholi leaders and displaced populations are increasingly reluctant to volunteer for 'militia' service or civil defence without guarantees against redeployment to other districts. The widespread presence of militias, with relatively ambiguous statutory controls, potentially constitutes a long-term threat to the protection of refugees, IDPs and civilians more generally.

While some improvements in the protection of refugees and IDPs have been achieved since the enactment of the government's Operation Iron Fist I (2002) and II (2004), refugee settlements and IDP camps remain 'targets' for increased militarization. Both settlements and camps have been exposed to escalating levels of armed violence by LRA combatants, non-state armed groups based in the DRC and Karamoja pastoral fighters, as well as army and criminally motivated banditry. The motivation for attacks appears to be a combination of forced recruitment; the pursuit of assets, including food and non-perishable goods; and politically motivated violence. Arms caches, usually of assault rifles, grenades and ammunition, are occasionally uncovered outside of the refugee settlements, though most are believed to have been left on the other side of the border in Sudan or the DRC.

The current policy of the army appears to be to 'drain the sea' (of civilians) in order to pursue LRA combatants and to 'protect' refugee settlements and IDP camps. Despite donor constraints on national defence expenditures and a recent retrenchment (demobilization) in 2002, the government has pursued an explicit policy of reinforcing the army in 'high-risk' areas and has formed armed civilian militia groups throughout the north and east. The army is concerned that by relaxing 'protection' for refugees and IDPs, its own legitimacy will be compromised, leading to increased militarization, and more recruits and greater sympathy for the LRA.

Taken as a whole, the physical protection of refugees and IDPs in Uganda has been increasingly compromised. Though cross-border activities of refugees are in decline, the 'inward militarization' of IDPs is increasing. It is estimated that actual rates of fatal and non-fatal injury are likely much higher than publicly reported owing to under-reporting and constraints associated with access to public health facilities. Actual rates, however, are difficult to determine, owing to the total absence of a police presence outside of urban centres, and unreliable monitoring and evaluation capacities of the humanitarian sector.

Tanzania As with those on Guinea and Uganda, the chapter on Tanzania demonstrates that refugee militarization is not a recent phenomenon, nor has it been restricted to refugees from a particular country. In fact, militarization can be traced to the independence movements throughout the 1960s, while today's refugee camps continue to show only a lingering degree of militarization. Nevertheless, there continue to be regular firearms seizures in refugee camps, a persistent demand for small arms in refugee-populated areas, and refugees incarcerated on arms-related offences.

The author, Mogire, argues that refugee camp militarization was in fact underpinned by five contiguous factors: the support of the Tanzanian government for refugees fleeing colonialism and for Ugandan and Burundian refugees; the heterogeneous nature of the influxes (Burundian and Rwandese refugees); a variety of root causes tied to resources and ethnic persecution; the protracted nature of the refugee problem; and persistent regional armed conflicts that have contagion effects.

As a result, the refugee camp militarization issue has remained high on the domestic political agenda. In fact, in contrast to its earlier policy of 'hospitality' towards refugees in the 1960s and 1970s, political and security considerations have conditioned the Tanzanian government's position towards refugees in recent times. Its official position is that it strongly opposes militarization of refugee camps in all independent African states. But as the author notes, this has not always been the case, as it once directly supported the militarization of Ugandan refugees and has allowed, if not actively supported, the militarization of Burundians residing in its territory.

On the basis of comprehensive evidence, however, it appears that the militarization of Burundian refugees in Tanzania is not as widespread as before. The signing of the Arusha Peace Accord by Hutu rebels, who had been widely held responsible for militarizing refugee camps, seems to be the main factor for this sea change. Ultimately, the successful implementation of the Arusha agreement will determine the future of refugee camp militarization. Thus far, the Hutu ex-rebels appear to have endorsed the political process, and military activities in the camps have subsided. There is no doubt that if the peace process breaks down, refugee camp militarization may begin anew. In other words, the problem of refugee militarization will remain as long as the Burundi conflict remains unresolved. Recent progress in the Burundian peace process provides some grounds for optimism. The chapter reports that widely publicized UNHCR and Tanzanian government efforts to address refugee militarization have not been entirely successful in eradicating the problem of firearms availability. Even so, it appears that the measures have succeeded in ensuring that weapons proliferation does not expand out of control.

Rwanda Rwanda is notorious for its mass exodus of refugees to neighbouring states in 1994 following the genocide. As the case study shows, the current security threats posed by the militarized remnants of this exodus still resident in the neighbouring DRC serve as the Rwandan government's justification for its current threats to reinvade that country. Less well known, perhaps, is the fact that Rwanda has hosted Congolese refugees since 1996, and received a new inflow in June 2004 following ethnic cleansing by the Congolese armed forces, directed at Banyamulenge (Congolese Tutsis from South Kivu province) residents of Bukavu and Uvira. There was widespread concern that these refugees would become militarized, particularly since a 300-strong, fully armed Banyamulenge military unit fled to Rwanda at the same time, after clashing with the UN Mission in Congo (MONUC).

The chapter author, Gregory Mthembu-Salter, finds that while the Rwandan government appealed to UNHCR to recognize these soldiers as refugees, UNHCR has thus far refused. As UN guidelines require, the Rwandan government has disarmed the soldiers and kept them separate from civilian refugees, which has retarded the latter's militarization. The government has also implemented many other of the UN's guidelines intended to prevent refugee militarization, including preventing any firearm possession or military training in the camps. Banyamulenge refugees, however, remain far closer to the DRC border than the UN guidelines dictate.

Rwanda's Congolese refugee case load from the 1990s mostly consists of North Kivu Banyarwanda, and there is some evidence of their militarization, including unconfirmed reports of forced abductions from civilian camps and clandestine military training for the abductees. That said, the level of militarization among Congolese refugees in Rwanda remains low and has no significant humanitarian impact. In addition, the military threat to the refugees is low, largely because of the fearsome reputation of the Rwandan Defence Force (RDF). This situation strongly contrasts with neighbouring Burundi, where 150 Banyamulenge refugees were massacred in the Gatumba refugee camp in August 2004, despite the nearby presence of the Burundian armed forces. Indeed, after this massacre, many former Gatumba residents fled for safety to Rwandan refugee camps.

The chapter finds that there is widespread concern that Rwanda might step up the militarization of its Congolese refugee communities to assist with its destabilization of eastern DRC, and that if it did, the international community could do little to stop it. There is considerable and lingering mistrust between the Rwandan government and the Banyamulenge, making their refugee militarization unlikely, but more trust between the government and the North Kivu Banyarwanda, for whom militarization could be an option. Thus far, however, the Rwandan government has pursued a different strategy: encouraging DRC-based Banyarwanda warlords to stoke sufficient conflict in the Kivu provinces to 'prove' the need for MONUC to disarm by force militarized Rwandan refugees living there.

Conclusion

The strength of this volume resides in its empirical treatment of the experiences of four African countries where refugee and IDP militarization has been pervasive. The focus on Africa was not accidental. Given the sheer scale and magnitude of protracted refugee situations on the continent – and the fact that two-thirds of the world's refugees are found in such contexts – this comparatively narrow geographic focus is warranted. Nevertheless, it is equally important to recall the range of subtle and often provocative lessons that can and must be drawn from parallel cases of refugee militarization such as occurred in Central America and Indochina during the 1980s (Loescher 1993). The distillation of insight from the past could usefully inform ongoing policy formulation and programme design. A historical treatment of these latter cases is a critical challenge that the practitioner and research community should take up in the coming years.

Each of the case study chapters demonstrates that refugee and IDP camp militarization can affect the physical safety and security of those involved and the prospects of achieving durable solutions for refugees. Though humanitarian agencies are obstructed and often forced to evacuate, it is refugees and IDPs caught in protracted situations which are most at risk. Each of the chapters also finds that militarization can compromise the security of host states – and undermines the durability and sustainability of humanitarian and development interventions. Of critical importance, the case studies reveal that repeatedly a key factor in increasing the lethality and protracted nature of refugee/IDP and refugee/IDP camp militarization is small-arms availability and misuse. And yet, troublingly, the scale and dynamics of arms proliferation in many areas considered as 'militarized' remain poorly understood.

This introductory chapter has identified a number of features that shape and condition refugee/IDP and refugee/IDP camp militarization. These included, *inter alia*, refugee and IDP participation in armed resistance; support for armed conflicts; the use of camps for military activities, including training and recruitment, and as bases; the presence of 'armed elements' – rebels, militias, police, paramilitary forces, vigilante groups, criminal gangs and brokers – in camps; the active diversion of humanitarian assistance for military ends; and the increased militarization of host communities. Each of these factors is treated in detail in the chapters that follow.

It is worth recalling the primary research objectives of this volume. They relate to identifying the scale and dynamics of refugee camp militarization; the pre-conditions under which such militarization occurs; the volume and distribution of small-arms availability and misuse in and around refugee camps in Guinea, Uganda, Tanzania and Rwanda; the impacts of small-arms possession and misuse on the physical security of refugees and host communities; and the institutional and operational responses to the problem. This chapter has sought to provide a conceptual overview in which to situate the case studies, and a review of a number of the methodological approaches advanced by the individual authors. Delivered as they are in a straightforward and practical style, it is anticipated that these findings will find an audience in both the refugee and arms control communities currently seeking to promote the 'human security' and protection of civilians, displaced and otherwise.

The overall goal of this volume is to raise the profile of small-arms control on the refugee agenda, as well as of refugee issues on the small-arms control agenda. By providing an evidence-based analysis of a select array of cases, it attempts to shift the debate from anecdote to fact. By considering the motivations, profiles and frequency of arms flows into and out of camps, as well as other manifestations of refugee camp militarization, it aims to help demystify a topic that has recently surfaced on the international agenda. It is expected that the chapters that follow raise more questions than they answer, but that this is a debate that is nevertheless urgently required and long overdue.

Appendix: Research protocol

Objective	Indicators	Methods	Risks and assumptions
Assess the extent of refugee and refugee camp militarization	*Refugee recruitment:* Total reported cases of forcibly and voluntarily 'recruited' refugees, incidence by year, ratio of recruited refugees to overall camp population, sources of recruitment, etc.	*Secondary* Review UN and UNSC reports, resolutions, and internally/ independently commissioned studies; academic reports; consultancy reports Review UNHCR protection reports on Uganda, Tanzania, Rwanda and Guinea	Reliability and validity of secondary data/statistics generated by UNHCR and government sources (e.g. army and police) Locating appropriate media, consultancy and evaluation reports Time constraints
	Military training: Presence of training facilities, total reported cases of 'training activities', total number of refugees arrested for 'training', etc.	*Primary* Key informant interviews with representatives of UNHCR (FSA, protection officers), police, army, key media figures, etc.	Sensitivity to the issue of small arms and camp militarization among humanitarian providers
	Use of camp for staging cross-border attacks: Reported cases, source and target, etc.	Commission archival review of publicly available media/newspaper reports from local partner. Review would appraise reported cases of recruitment, and training in the use of, trade and trafficking in small arms	
	Use of camp resources for supporting military action: Relief assistance, reselling of relief inputs, use of health facilities – including medical supplies, use of shelter, use of camps as 'hideouts', etc.		
	Refugee participation in armed conflict: Estimated number of participants,	Assess existing data on reported incidents of recruitment,	

reported deaths and violently injured camp residents (post-arrival), assassinations reported, reported male adult population over duration of the conflict, incidence of ethnic and political violent conflict in camps, etc.

Financial/material assistance from refugees to armed groups: Proportion of refugee population contributing, proportion of total income contributed, amount (USD) contributed over time, in-kind or non-financial/financial contributions, etc.

Cross-border and internal trade in small arms: Reported cases of arms trafficking, total number of refugees arrested for aspects of the arms trade, rates of armed criminality/drug use in camps/host communities, etc.

Presence of armed groups (types and numbers of factions): Army and police actors, militia and paramilitary groups, (ex-)combatants, organized criminal groups/bandits, etc.

training, refugee participation in armed conflicts, and cross-border trade maintained by national police, prison services, customs, army and/or DPKO

Appendix: Research protocol (cont.)

Objective	Indicators	Methods	Risks and assumptions
Explain under what conditions refugee and refugee camp militarization occur	*Geopolitical factors*: Review and examine: (i) incidents where host states and/or third parties use refugees as proxies in a conflict with neighbouring state(s); (ii) cases of external military support – arms supplies, training, logistics and political support – to refugees; (iii) incidents of refugee participation in liberation or guerrilla wars; and (iv) cases of refugee involvement in armed resistance against home state for political goals (e.g. regime change, autonomy, secession, etc.) *Spatial and demographic factors*: Review and document: (i) the distance of the refugee camp from the national border; (ii) the presence of armed elements in original refugee flow/movements in and out of camps; (iii) the presence of ongoing conflict or armed violence in and around camps; (iv) the size and population of the camps; (v) the proximity of camps to military settlements and the presence of armed combatants; (vi) the presence of 'armed elements' (e.g. active soldiers/militia, ex-combatants, armed civilians, etc.) in the camps, etc. *Political and economic factors*: Highlight and identify: (i) reported cases of refugee affiliation with	*Secondary* Analysis of speeches made by refugee leaders and their supporters justifying military actions by refugees Analysis of speeches/declarations and reports by the host states, UNHCR, UN, DPKO on refugee militarization Textual/narrative analysis of documents – newspaper reports, UNHCR, UN, consultancy, academic reports – to identify the political, economic, and demographic factors given to explain refugee and refugee camp militarization *Primary* Key informant interviews with UNHCR, host state representatives, refugee representatives and academics to explain the	Reliability and validity of secondary data/statistics generated by UNHCR and government sources (e.g. army and police)

opposition politicians; (ii) the presence of diaspora and/or remittance flows; (iii) evidence of armed activity by refugees to gain access to economic resources; (iv) the proximity of rentable and exploitable resources such as minerals and timber to refugee camps; (v) reported cases of refugee involvement in illegal activities such as arms, people and drugs trade/smuggling, etc.

Causes of flight: The origin of any refugee crisis directly influences the level of the refugees' political and military activity. Thus, identifying the root causes of flight – collapse of state, unconstitutional change of government, authoritarianism, oppressive political systems, genocide, ethnic cleansing, abuse of human rights – and analysing how they may lead to refugee militarization will be important

Humanitarian factors: Identify how humanitarian factors, such as international protection of refugee camps and settlements and humanitarian assistance (financial and/or material) have been utilized (directly or indirectly) to support refugee militarization

Support from diaspora/exile/s: Identify the remittances (flows and USD value), nature (e.g. arms, finances, campaigning) and extent of refugee involvement in funding particular groups

phenomenon of refugee militarization

Review of UNHCR and other implementing agencies' documents on demographics and composition of refugee camps. Identify the level and extent of militarization of the population at these sites

Analysis of GIS maps of refugee camps to determine location of camps relative to borders, urban centres, (exploitable) resources, areas of high conflict/criminality, etc.

Appendix: Research protocol (cont.)

Objective	Indicators	Methods	Risks and assumptions
Assess the scale and magnitude of small arms distribution and trafficking in and around refugee camps	*Reported weapons seizures:* Review and identify: (i) total numbers of small-arms seized or collected per month; (ii) types of firearms seized; (iii) quality or serviceability of weapons, etc.	*Secondary* Review UN and UNSC reports, resolutions and internally/independently commissioned studies; academic reports; consultancy reports	Mandate issues may influence cooperation or data obtained Lack of cooperation from the police due to 'sensitivities' of the small-arms issue
	Refugee involvement in the arms trade: Document: (i) the number of refugees arrested locally/ nationally/cross-border for arms-related offences such as trafficking and armed robberies (per year); (ii) reports of illegal weapons trade in camps; (iii) reports of using refugees as mules for cross-border movement of arms; (iv) reports of trafficking in other illegal commodities, etc.	Review UNHCR protection reports on Uganda, Tanzania, Rwanda, and Guinea, as well as reports of implementing partners (e.g. Oxfam, Save the Children Fund [SCF], Red Cross, etc.)	Limited access and availability of medical, police, prison data Missing and/or inconsistent data
	Reported arms use in camps and host communities: Document and map out: (i) frequency of reported gunshots (per month); (ii) frequency of weapons seen in public; (iii) number of complaints registered with police/UNHCR associated with small-arms availability or misuse; (iv) proportion of all robberies, assaults and harassment involving firearms (in camps); (v) proportion of all homicides and external injuries involving firearms (in camps); and (vi) use of firearms in	Review humanitarian agency reports/ records and police/prison, military, DPKO data on reported incidents of arms seizures in camps, number of refugees involved in arms trading, and police incidents reports *Primary* Develop a retrospective review of existing police records and reports (minimum of five to ten years)	

violent conflicts involving refugees (in camps), such as between refugees and host population, etc.

Criminals from elsewhere in the host country are said – in Guinea, at least – to travel to refugee camps to purchase weapons. This could be monitored through press reports and also crime stats in the capital city to investigate alleged connections with refugee sources

Size and number of armed groups: Record the estimated type, ethnic composition, size and number of armed elements in refugee camps and host communities, e.g. (i) army forces; (ii) paramilitary forces; (iii) police recruits; (iv) armed private security forces; (v) rebels; (vi) militia factions; (vii) ex-combatants; (viii) foreign ex-combatants; (ix) armed vigilante groups; (x) organized criminal gangs, etc.

Distribution and organization of armed groups: Appraise: (i) the informal command and control structures of armed groups within camps/groups; (ii) storage and concealment practices of armed groups; and (iii) ownership patterns among refugees and IDPs

Key informant and focus group interviews

Small-scale survey ($n = 20$–40) of ex-combatants and/or refugees to determine command and control patterns, as well as storage and concealment patterns for weapons

Appendix: Research protocol (cont.)

Objective	Indicators	Methods	Risks and assumptions
Assess the impact of small arms on refugee protection and security	*Basic baseline data on the camps:* Generate baseline data on: (i) total number of refugees in the camps (since inception, by year); (ii) total number of new arrivals (per year); (iii) total number of departures (per year); and (iv) total crude mortality rate (CMR) per year (per 100,000)	*Secondary* Review UN resolutions and internally/independently commissioned studies; academic reports; consultancy reports; UNHCR protection reports	Reliability/validity of government-generated data/statistics
	Injuries, criminality and victimization: Review the: (i) distribution and scale of overall fatal and non-fatal injuries; (ii) proportion of all external injuries committed with small arms; (iii) rates of armed robbery, rape and intimidation (per month) in host communities and camps; (iv) proportion of these 'criminal' acts committed with small arms (as compared to other instruments) in host communities and camps; (v) proportion of injuries and criminal acts affecting men, women and children in camps; (vi) estimated costs (financial) of referral and trauma support for refugees; (vii) total amount spent on increasing security measures (e.g. fencing, patrolling, radios, body armour, etc.); and (viii) perceptions of armed violence in camps	Consult police and prison records, court records, hospital and morgue records, etc. *Primary* Key informant interviews with representatives of UNHCR (FSA, protection officers), police, army, key media figures, etc. Review of statistical public health/security data of UNHCR and implementing partners (e.g. SCF, IRC, Red Cross, etc.) Commission archival review of publicly available media/newspaper reports from local partner to	

Impact on humanitarian delivery: Identify and document: (i) total amount of resources (financial and human) expended on security (e.g. protocol, intelligence, armed guards and private companies, logistics, etc.) by UNHCR/ implementing partners in camps across time (over previous *x* years); (ii) reported number of cases in which refugee repatriation is prevented due to intimidation by armed elements; (iii) proportion of refugees denied access to food owing to insecurity caused by small arms; (iv) reported incidents of humanitarian agencies being denied access to refugees; (v) number of homicides, injuries and security incidents (including hostage-taking, abductions, harassment, extortion) reported among UN and humanitarian personnel; (vi) incidence of (forced) withdrawals of humanitarian agencies from refugee camps, etc.

appraise reported cases of recruitment and training in the use of and trade and trafficking in small arms

Small-scale survey (*n* = 20–40) of refugee residents to document perceptions of crime and victimization across time. Also, undertake focused semi-structured interviews with refugee representatives

Appendix: Research protocol (cont.)

Objective	Indicators	Methods	Risks and assumptions
Assess responses of host states, UNHCR and refugees to militarization	*Legal responses:* Review and identify gaps in: (i) existing domestic legislation – particularly immigration and refugee acts – with respect to militarization in case study sites; (ii) regional legislation – including 1969 OAU Refugee Convention, Africa (Banjul) Charter on Human Rights, etc. – in relation to refugee militarization and small arms issues; and (iii) UNHCR legislation – including ExCom and other resolutions – regarding militarization and small arms in-country	*Secondary* Review refugee law and immigration acts in countries under study, the 1969 OAU Refugee Convention, 1965 Declaration on Subversion, independent evaluations and ExCom Conclusions	Availability of and access to appropriate policy documents Adequate time and human resources to undertake the review
	Operational: Review, describe and develop a typology for UNHCR/implementing partner operational responses to refugee militarization and small arms, including: (i) internment; (ii) separation of armed elements from civilians; (iii) closure and/or partial relocation of camps; (iv) creation of safer zones in country of origin; (v) forced repatriation/expulsions; (vi) closure and increased security at borders; (vii) use of private/public security agencies, including army, police, vigilante, paramilitary, community policing; (viii) specialized military responses (DPKO); (ix) altered role of FSAs; (x) implementation of the ladder of options, etc.	Review government and in-country UNHCR policy documents Map key interventions, i.e. develop a typology of key interventions executed by UNHCR, host states and refugees *Primary* Key informants interviews with host state, UNHCR representatives and policy-makers, and refugees	
	Political: Review and identify gaps in bilateral and multilateral arrangements designed to improve security and reduce arms trafficking, including: (i) Nairobi Declaration; (ii) ECOWAS Moratorium; (iii) SADC Protocol; and (iv) others		

Notes

1 A protracted refugee situation is characterized by Crisp and Jacobsen (2000) as having at least three features: (1) it is a situation seemingly without a clear durable solution; (2) the refugees are in an organized camp setting for at least five years; and (3) the refugees caught in this type of situation have little chance of being repatriated or resettled elsewhere. Loescher and Milner (2005b) argue that this definition is too arbitrary and narrow and does not adequately reflect the nature and scope of protracted refugee situations. While the features are admittedly arbitrary, the UNHCR estimates that some 6 million people are in a protracted refugee camp situation. That is, some two-thirds of the world's refugees are now in protracted refugee camp situations.

2 See, for example, UNHCR (1982, 1983, 1993, 2000b, 2001a, 2001b, 2002) and UNSC (1998b, 1999b, 2000, 2001).

3 Exceptions include, for example, Loescher (1992, 1993), Weiner (1992/93), Terry (2002), Stedman and Tanner (2003), Barber (1997), Adelman (1998), Zolberg et al. (1989) and Anderson (1999).

4 Such as, for example, the use of Sudanese refugee camps in Ethiopia as rear bases by the southern Sudanese People's Liberation Army (UNHCR 2000a).

5 The experiences of Rwanda and the ongoing conflict in the DRC – particularly the role of the ex-Forces Armées Rwandaises (FAR, ex-Armed Forces of Rwanda) soldiers and Hutu *génocidaires* – represent a paramount example of refugee and refugee camp militarization.

6 Lischer (2000) has conducted a quantitative analysis of refugee participation in political violence. Her findings show that the proportion of refugees involved in violence declined from 60 per cent in 1987 to 32 per cent in 1998, with a sharp drop to 13 per cent in 1997. Despite the remarkable drop in the number of refugees affected, the number of receiving states reporting refugee-related violence has remained generally constant, with a slight increase since the mid-1990s. An average number of sixteen receiving states reported political violence affecting refugees between 1987 and 1991, whereas the same statistic was eighteen states between 1995 and 1998.

7 It is interesting to note that these 'liquid' or 'fluid' metaphors are similar to those used for refugee and IDP movements to begin with. Mallki (1995), Rosenau (2001) and Hyndman (2000) have also noted how refugee and IDP movements are anathema to the sedentary aspirations of states. So too with the transfer of military-style weapons, which with the exception of a few notable cases are usually expected to be retained only by states, thus ensuring their monopoly on the use of force.

8 Based on personal communications with UNHCR and other authorities in Khartoum in November 2005.

9 An extreme example of weapons build-ups outside of camps can be found in Rwanda. Arms caches were established along areas of the Zairean border controlled by the *interahamwe* (i.e. former Rwandan Hutu army and militia members who massacred several hundred thousand Tutsi and moderate Hutus in the 1994 genocide). Despite the fact that humanitarian personnel repeatedly warned the international community about these stockpiles, little

37

action was taken to address the issue and prevent the ensuing massacres; see, for example, Small Arms Survey (2001, 2002).

10 Quoting a relief worker in Tanzania, the ICG (1999) reported that 'diplomats keep coming here [Tanzania] asking questions about militarization. We don't see the training in the camps that they fear. They should be looking instead at the huge forest and savannah areas outside the camps. If they really wanted to, they could fly surveillance planes to see ... they came only focused on the militarization of these camps.'

11 See, for example, Ullman (1983), Bearman (1992) and Miles and Thränhardt (1995).

12 See, for example, Ferris (1993), Weiner (1991), Poku and Graham (2000), Dowty and Loescher (1996), Papedimittrou (1994) and Adelman (1998).

13 See, for example, Gamba and Chachiua (1999), Austin (2000) and Byman et al. (2001).

14 See, for example, Reno (2000), Keen (2000), Duffield (2005) and others.

15 See, for example, Buchanan and Muggah (2005), Muggah with Griffiths (2002).

16 In Zambia, having facilitated the flow of arms to UNITA, the government was well aware of these arms coming back into Zambia carried by Angolan refugees. Confiscated refugee arms regularly made their way into Zambian soldiers' hands, though it is not known whether they were destined for personal use or for the state armoury.

17 For the purposes of this volume, IDP militarization is similar, and refers to the 'involvement of individual (or groups) of IDPs in militaristic activities within and outside IDP camps'. The question of defining IDP militarization is potentially more complex than that for refugees because of the lack of agreed and legally binding standards for what constitutes IDP status. While the IDP Guiding Principles established in 1998 have to some extent clarified the rights of the internally displaced and responsibilities of host governments, there is still no consensus on when IDP status can be said to have begun or ended. See, for example, Phuong (2005) and Muggah (2003).

18 Armed elements include ex-combatants, soldiers who refuse to hand in their weapons after seeking asylum, rebels, militias, criminal gangs, police and armed forces of the host states, armed private security firms, and armed vigilantes and individuals.

19 See, for example, Small Arms Survey (2005, 2004, 2003, 2002 and 2001).

20 UNHCR's internal Annual Protection Reports and Global Hot Spot Briefs summarize many of the security and protection problems for each refugee-receiving state and the camps themselves. The reports consist of narrative answers to survey questions and include responses to security incidents and protection problems in the relevant countries. The USCR's annual publication, *World Refugee Survey*, provides individual reports for each country and can be used to supplement data from UNHCR.

21 A variety of methods are used to analyse the available data. Large volumes of primary data are organized into categories on the basis of themes and concepts or similar features to help identify relationships among concepts.

In addition, the data are analysed for trends and patterns, key events and critical terms. Reporting is done in a narrative form using quotes to support the concepts, arguments and relationships that are put forward (Miles and Huberman 1994).

22 Repatriation has been prevented in a variety of situations owing to the capacity of armed elements to intimidate refugees. For example, in Rwanda armed elements in Zairean camps used their position to control the information passed on to refugees and were able to indoctrinate camp members. Their hold was such that when UNAMIR air-dropped pamphlets into the camps in August 1994 (in a bid to draw attention to the favourable conditions in Rwanda for the return of Hutu refugees), this was interpreted by many as support for the new regime in Kigali. As such, it was seen as a UN-driven process of involuntary repatriation.

23 The recent attempt by a few dozen South African mercenaries to launch a coup in Equatorial Guinea is a good example of this.

24 In the former Zaire, the late president, Mobutu Sese Seko, and subsequently Laurent Kabila and his son, Joseph Kabila, used ex-FAR, while Tanzania has used Burundian refugees to achieve strategic goals. They were the most effective fighting component of the so-called Forces Armées Congolaise during the war.

25 Countries reporting political violence among refugees include Uganda, involving Rwandans and Sudanese, Zaire, involving Rwandans and Burundians, Tanzania, involving Rwandans and Burundians, Ethiopia, involving Sudanese, Guinea, involving Liberians and Sierra Leoneans, Côte d'Ivoire Coast, involving Liberians, Sierra Leone, involving Liberians, and Liberia, involving Sierra Leoneans.

26 Anderson (1999), Small Arms Survey (2001: 227), Terry (2002).

27 The demand for small arms by refugees and the presence of such arms in refugee camps can occur in a variety of scenarios: (1) whenever there are armed elements in camps, including criminal gangs; (2) where refugees support armed insurgency; (3) whenever refugee camps are used for arms storage and trafficking; and (4) whenever refugees are engaged in armed resistance. Each of these situations must be considered if the dynamics of arms flows into and out of camps are to be effectively gauged.

28 See, for example, Muggah and Berman (2001). Research undertaken in Dadaab and Kakuma camps, for example, revealed that some 75 per cent of all reported rape incidents involved one or more armed assailants.

29 For a review of DDR programmes in Africa, consult Small Arms Survey (2005) and Muggah (2006).

30 For example, following the failure of the UN Security Council and the Zairean government to respond to calls by the high commissioner and secretary-general for a greater peacekeeper presence in eastern Zaire, UNHCR was forced to hire President Mobutu's Presidential Guard to secure the Goma camps during the Rwandan refugee crisis.

31 UN Security Council Resolution S/1998/318 has made similar calls.

32 Drawing from UNSC (2001), which states that 'if [armed] elements are

found and national forces are unable or unwilling to intervene, consider the range of options ... [including] deploying regional or international military forces that are prepared to take effective measures to protect civilians. Such measures could include compelling disarmament of the combatants or armed elements.'

33 Several types of FSOs have been proposed: (1) police HSOs liaising with local police; (2) public security HSOs working with military forces of the host country; (3) humanitarian security and investigation HSOs providing expertise on criminal procedures in partnership with local judicial authorities; and (4) HSOs with expertise on discrete issues such as sexual and domestic violence.

34 ESS operates in close cooperation with the regional bureaux and coordinates UNHCR's preparedness for, and response to, emergencies, as well as the safety and security of staff and refugees. According to informants within UNHCR, ESS was to be restructured and strengthened in 2005 to address policy development and capacity building more effectively in the areas of emergency and security management.

35 In 1998 in the Burundian refugee camps in Tanzania, UNHCR started supporting some 270 Tanzanian police officers whose task was to enhance security and to assist in ensuring the camps' civilian and humanitarian character.

36 In the late 1990s, in order to respond to growing insecurity in Kakuma and Dadaab refugee camps, UNHCR supported the hiring of more than 150 informal police reservists to patrol the camps and provide security.

37 These efforts have taken place not only in Africa. For example, in 1999 in Kosovar Albanian camps in Macedonia, UNHCR arranged for the deployment of international police advisers to work in partnership with the local police; see UNHCR (2000b), Jacobsen (2000) and Crisp and Jacobsen (2000).

38 The focus is on manufacturers and suppliers, and on measures to control transfers; regulate the availability, use and storage of small arms, manage the collection and removal of surplus arms, and increase transparency and accountability. Issues such as banning the introduction of trade to 'non-state actors', 'civilian possession' and various types of regulatory measures have been 'redlined' by the United States, among others.

39 Article II.6 of the convention states: 'For reasons of security, countries of asylum shall, as far as possible, settle refugees at a reasonable distance from the frontier of their country of origin.'

40 Also under consideration is a draft protocol, encompassing weapons marking, information exchange, corruption and brokering.

41 The Nairobi Declaration, however, is an exception. Signatories from the Great Lakes and Horn of Africa have identified the movement of 'armed refugees' across national boundaries as greatly contributing to the proliferation of illicit arms and light weapons in the region. Similarly, the OAU report of African experts (OAU 2000) also identifies armed refugees as contributing to the illicit proliferation of small arms.

42 The UN Security Council has also advised that refugee camps should keep a civilian character through the separation of the civilian population from soldiers and militiamen (UNSC 1999b, 2001). The notion of the camps

as 'humanitarian sanctuaries' and the presence of 'refugee warriors' in them are a contradiction and the latter is proscribed (Zolberg et al. 1989). The tone of the law is that once in exile, political activities by refugees must be kept within bounds. The 1951 UN Convention Relating to the Status of Refugees does not explicitly deal with the issue, even though Article 2 requires refugees to conform to the laws and regulations of the host country. This requirement in itself does not prohibit host states from supporting military activities by refugees.

References

Adelman, H. (1992) 'The ethics of humanitarian intervention: the case of Kurdish refugees', *Public Affairs Quarterly*, 6(1): 61–88.

— (1998) 'Why refugee warriors are threats', *Journal of Conflict Studies*, XVIII(1): 49–69.

— (2003) 'The use and abuse of refugees in Zaire', in S. J. Stedman and F. Tanner (eds), *Refugee Manipulation: War, Politics, and the Abuse of Human Suffering*, Washington, DC: Brookings Institution Press.

Amnesty International (1995) *RWANDA: Arming the Perpetrators of the Genocide*, Report AFR 02/14/95, 13 June, <www.129.194.252.80/catfiles/2671. pdf>.

Anacleti, O. (1996) 'The regional response to the Rwandan emergency', *Journal of Refugee Studies*, 9(3): 303–11.

Anderson, B. M. (1999) *Do No Harm: How Aid Can Support Peace – Or War*, Boulder, CO and London: Lynne Rienner.

Annan, K. (1998) *The Causes of Conflict and the Promotion of Durable Peace and Sustainable Development in Africa*, New York: United Nations, <www. un.org/ecosocdev/geninfo/afrec/sgreport/repdfs/confltov.pdf>.

Austin, K. (2000) 'Open letter to the United Nations High Commissioner for Refugees, S. Ogata', accessed November 2000, <www.fundforpeace.org>.

Baldwin, D. A. (1997) 'The concept of security', *Review of International Studies*, 23(1): 5–26.

Bamako Declaration on an African Common Position on the Illicit Proliferation, Circulation and Trafficking of Small Arms and Light Weapons (2000), Adopted by the member states of the OAU, in pursuance of Decision AHG/ Dec. 137 (LXX) of 1999, Bamako, Mali, 30 November–1 December.

Barber, B. (1997) 'Feeding refugees, or war? The dilemmas of humanitarian aid', *Foreign Affairs*, July/August, pp. 8–14.

Bearman, S. (1992) *Strategic Survey 1990–1991*, London: Brassey's for the Institute of International Security Studies.

Berdal, M. (1996) *Disarmament and Demobilization after Civil Wars*, Oxford: Oxford University Press.

Betts, T. F. (1981) 'Documentary note on rural refugees in Africa', *International Migration Review*, 15(1): 213–18.

Booth, K. (1991) 'Security and emancipation', *Review of International Studies*, 17(4): 313–26.

Booth, K. and N. Wheeler (1992) 'Contending philosophies about security in Europe', in C. McInnes (ed.), *Security and Strategy in the New Europe*, London and New York: Routledge.

Boutwell, J. and M. T. Klare (1998) 'Small arms and light weapons: controlling the real instruments of war', *Arms Control Today*, August/September, available at <www.armscontrol.org/act/1998_08-09/mkas.asp>.

— (1999) *Light Weapons and Civil Violence: Policy Options for the International Community Project on World Security*, Project on World Security, Rockefeller Brothers Fund.

Brahim, J. P. (1997) 'How Tanzania was affected by the refugee crisis in the Great Lakes region and the response to it', Paper presented at a workshop on the Asylum Crisis in East and Central Africa organized by the University of Dar es Salaam and Oxfam UK and Ireland, Arusha, Tanzania.

Brauman, R. (1998) 'Refugee camps, population transfers, and NGOs', in J. Moore (ed.), *Hard Choices: Moral Dilemmas in Humanitarian Intervention*, Oxford: Rowman and Littlefield.

Brown, M. (1996) 'Introduction', in M. Brown, *The International Dimensions of Internal Conflict*, Cambridge, MA: Center for Science and International Affairs.

Buchanan, C. and R. Muggah (2005) *No Relief: Surveying the Effects of Gun Violence on Humanitarian Aid and Development Personnel*, Geneva: Centre for Humanitarian Dialogue and the Small Arms Survey, <www.smallarmsurvey.org>.

Byman, D. L. et al. (2001) *Trends in Outside Support for Insurgent Movements*, Washington, DC: RAND.

Chambers, R. (1986) 'Hidden losers? The impact of rural refugees and refugee programs on the poor hosts', *International Migration Review*, XX(2): 245–58.

Crisp, J. (2001) *Lessons Learnt from the Implementation of the Tanzania Security Package*, Geneva: UNHCR Evaluation and Policy Analysis Unit, EPAU2001/05.

Crisp, J. and K. Jacobsen (2000) 'Security in refugee populated areas', *Refugee Studies Quarterly*, special issue, vol. 19.

Dikshit, P. (1995) 'Proliferation of small arms and minor weapons', in J. Singh (ed.), *Light Weapons and International Security*, New Delhi: Pugwash, IDSA and BASIC.

Dowty, A. and G. Loescher (1996) 'Refugee flows as grounds for international action', *International Security*, 21(1): 43–71.

Duffield, M. (2005) *Global Governance and the New Wars: The Merger of Development and Security*, 3rd edn, London: Zed Books.

Durieux, J.-F. (2000) 'Preserving the civilian character of refugee camps: lessons from the Kigoma refugee programme in Tanzania', *Refugees, Conflict & Conflict Resolution*, 9(3).

Ferris, E. (1993) *Beyond Borders: Refugees, Migrants and Human Rights in the Post-Cold War Era*, Geneva: WCC Publications.

— (1994) 'Peace, security and the movement of people', *Peace and Change*, 19(4): 399–416.

Frey, B. (2001) 'The question of the trade, carrying and use of small arms and light weapons in the context of human rights and humanitarian norms', Working paper submitted in accordance with Sub-Commission Decision 2001/120 ECOSOC.

Gamba, V. and M. Chachiua (1999) 'Small arms trade in Africa', *New People Africa Feature Service*, vol. 98, August.

Gerami, A. (2001) 'Addressing the demand side of the small arms complex: ensuring balance at the 2001 UN Conference on the Illicit Trade in Small Arms and Light Weapons', *Ploughshares Monitor*, March.

Goodwin-Gill, G. S. (1996) *The Refugee in International Law*, 2nd edn, Oxford: Oxford University Press.

Gordenker, L. (1987) *Refugees in International Politics*, London and Sydney: Croom Helm.

Grahl-Madsen, A. (1966) *The Status of Refugees in International Law*, Leyden: A. W. Sijthoff.

Havinga, T. and A. Bocker (1999) 'Country of asylum by choice or chance: asylum seekers in Belgium, the Netherlands and the UK', *Journal of Ethnic Studies*, 28(1): 43–61.

Human Rights Watch (1995) *Rearming with Impunity: International Support for the Perpetrators of the Rwandan Genocide*, New York: Human Rights Watch.

— (2002a) *Playing with Fire: Weapons Proliferation, Political Violence, and Human Rights in Kenya*, New York, Washington, DC, London and Brussels: Human Rights Watch.

— (2002b) *Liberian Refugees in Guinea: Refoulement, Militarization of Camps, and Other Protection Concerns*, New York: Human Rights Watch.

Huysmans, J. (1995) 'Migrants as a security problem: dangers of "securitizing" societal issues', in Miles and Thränhardt (1995).

Hyndman, J. (2000) *Managing Displacement: Refugees and the Politics of Humanitarianism*, Minnesota: University of Minnesota.

ICG (International Crisis Group) (1999) 'Burundian refugees in Tanzania: the key factor to the Burundi peace process', ICG Central Africa Report no. 12, 30 November.

Jacobsen, K. (2000) 'A framework for exploring the political and security context of refugee populated areas', *Refugee Studies Quarterly*, special issue, vol. 19.

— (2002) 'African states and the politics of refugees: refugee assistance as political resources', Feinstein International Famine Center Working Paper no. 6.

Jefferson, K. and A. Urquhart (2002) *The Impact of Small Arms in Tanzania: Results of a Country Study*, Institute for Security Studies (ISS) Monograph Series no. 70, March.

Karin, W. (1991) 'Refugees and civil wars: only a matter of interpretation?' *International Journal of Refugee Law*, 3(3): 435–51.

Keen, D. (2000) 'Incentives and disincentives for violence', in M. Berdal and D. Malone, *Greed and Grievance: Economic Agendas in Civil Wars*, Boulder, CO: Lynne Rienner.

Klare, M. T. (1995) 'Light weapons diffusion and global violence in the post-cold war era', in J. Singh (ed.), *Light Weapons and International Security*, New Delhi: Pugwash, IDSA and BASIC.

Laurance, E. and R. Stohl (2002) *Making Global Public Policy: The Case of Small Arms and Light Weapons*, Occasional Paper no. 7, Geneva: Small Arms Survey.

Lemarchand, R. (1994) *Burundi: Ethnocide as Discourse and Practice*, New York and Cambridge: Woodrow Wilson Center Press and Cambridge University Press.

Lischer, S. K. (1999) *Militarized Refugee Populations: Humanitarian Challenges in the Former Yugoslavia*, Rosemary Rogers Working Paper Series no. 5.

— (2000) *Refugee Involvement in Political Violence: Quantitative Evidence from 1987–1998*, UNHCR Working Paper no. 1, Geneva.

— (2001) 'Refugee crises and the spread of civil war', Paper presented at the 97th Annual Meeting of the American Political Science Association, San Francisco, CA, 30 August–2 September.

Loescher, G. (1992) *Refugee Movements and International Security*, London: Brassey's for the International Institute for Strategic Studies.

— (1993) *Beyond Charity: International Cooperation and the Global Refugee Crisis*, New York and Oxford: Oxford University Press.

— (2001) *The UNHCR and World Politics: A Perilous Path*, Oxford: Oxford University Press.

Loescher, G. and J. Milner (2005a) 'The long road home: protracted refugee situations in Africa', *Survival*, 47(2).

— (2005b) 'Protracted refugee situations: domestic and international security implications', *Adelphi Paper* no. 375, London: IISS.

Loescher, G. and L. Monahan (1999) 'Introduction', in G. Loescher and L. Monahan (eds), *Refugees and International Relations*, Oxford: Clarendon Press.

Loescher, G. and J. Scanlan (1986) *Calculated Kindness: Refugees and America's Half Open Door: 1945 to the Present*, New York: Free Press.

Mallki, L. (1995) *Purity and Exile: Violence, Memory, and National Cosmology Among Hutu Refugees in Tanzania*, Chicago, IL: University of Chicago Press.

Marrus, R. M. (1985) *Unwanted: European Refugees in the Twentieth Century*, Oxford: Oxford University Press.

Mason, L. and R. Brown (1983) *Rice, Rivalry and Politics: Managing Cambodian Relief*, Notre Dame, IN: University of Notre Dame Press.

Miles, M. and A. Huberman (1994) *Qualitative Data Analysis*, California: Sage.

Miles, R. and A. Thränhardt (eds) (1995) *Migration and European Integration: The Dynamics of Inclusion and Exclusion*, London: Pinter.

Mills, K. (1998) 'United Nations intervention in refugee crises after the cold war', *International Politics*, 34(4): 391–424.

Mills, K. and R. J. Norton (2002) 'Refugees and security in the Great Lakes region of Africa', available at <www.homepage.mac.com/vicfalls/civilwars. html>.

Milner, J. (2000) *Sharing the Security Burden: Towards the Convergence of Refugee Protection and State Security*, RSC Working Paper no. 4, Oxford: Refugee Studies Centre.

Mtango, E. (1989) 'Military and armed attacks on refugee camps', in G. Loescher and L. Monahan (eds), *Refugees and International Relations*, New York: Oxford University Press.

Muggah, R. (2002) 'Why should we have a humanitarian perspective on small arms?', *Humanitarian Practice Review*, London: Overseas Development Institute (ODI).

— (2003) 'Small arms and forced migration', *Forced Migration Online*, accessed March 2005. <www.forcedmigration.org/guides/fmo002/>.

— (2005a) 'Crisis turning inward: refugee and IDP militarization in Uganda', *Humanitarian Exchange*, 29, London: ODI, <www.odihpn.org/report. asp?ID=2574>.

— (2005b) 'No magic bullet: a critical perspective on DDR and weapons reduction in post-conflict contexts', *International Journal of Commonwealth Studies. The Round Table*, 94(379): 239–52.

— (2006) 'Emerging from the shadow of war: considerations of DDR and weapons reduction in the post-conflict period', *Journal of Contemporary Security Policy*.

Muggah, R. and E. Berman (2001) *Humanitarianism under Threat: The Humanitarian Impacts of Small Arms and Light Weapons*, Geneva: Small Arms Survey.

Muggah, R. with M. Griffiths (2002) *Reconsidering the Tools of War*, Network Paper no. 39, London: ODI.

Nabuguzi, P. (1988) 'Refugees and politics in Uganda', in A. G. G. Gingyera Pinchwa (ed.), *Uganda and the Problem of Refugees*, Kampala: Makerere University Press.

Nairobi Declaration on the Problem of the Proliferation of Illicit Small Arms and Light Weapons in the Great Lakes Region and the Horn of Africa ('Nairobi Declaration') (2000) Nairobi, 15 March, <www.un.org/Depts/dda/ CAB/events.htm>.

OAU (Organization of African Unity) (2000) *Final Conference Report: Meeting of African Experts on Illicit Proliferation, Circulation and Trafficking of Small Arms Weapons, 17–19 May 2000*, Addis Ababa, Ethiopia.

Ogata, S. (1998) 'Opening statement', Presented at the Regional Meeting on Refugee Issues in the Great Lakes, sponsored by the OAU and UNHCR, Kampala, Uganda, 8–9 May.

Papedimitrou, D. (1994) 'At a crossroads: Europe and migration', in K. Hamilton (ed.), *Migration and the New Europe*, Washington, DC: Center for Strategic and International Studies.

Phuong, C. (2005) 'The international protection of internally displaced persons', *Cambridge Studies in International and Comparative Law*, 38, Cambridge: Cambridge University Press.

Poku, N. K. and T. Graham (2000) 'Introduction', in T. Graham and N. K. Poku (eds), *Migration, Globalisation and Human Security*, London and New York: Routledge.

Posen, B. (1996) 'Military responses to refugee disasters', *International Security*, 21(1): 72–111.

Prunier, G. (1995) *The Rwandan Crisis: History of a Genocide 1959–1994*, London: Hurst.

Reno, W. (1998) *Warlord Politics and African States*, Boulder, CO: Lynne Rienner.

— (2000) 'Shadow states and the political economy of civil wars', in M. Berdal and D. Malone, *Greed and Grievance: Economic Agendas in Civil Wars*, Boulder, CO: Lynne Rienner.

Reynell, J. (1989) *Political Pawns: Refugees on the Thai–Cambodian Border*, Oxford: Refugee Studies Programme.

Roberts, A. (1998) 'More refugees, less asylum: a regime in transition', *Journal of Refugee Studies*, 11(4): 375–95.

Rosenau, J. (2001) 'Stability, stasis, and change: a fragmenting world', in *The Global Century: Globalization and National Security*, vol. I, Washington, DC: National Defense University.

Sayigh, Y. (1990) *Confronting the 1990s: Security in the Developing Countries*, Adelphi Paper no. 251, London: Brassey's for the International Institute for Strategic Studies.

Shawcross, W. (2000) *Deliver Us from Evil: Peacekeepers, Warlords and the World of Endless Conflict*, New York: Simon & Schuster.

Small Arms Survey (2001) *Small Arms Survey 2001: Profiling the Problem*, Oxford: Oxford University Press.

— (2002) *Small Arms Survey 2002: Counting the Human Costs*, Oxford: Oxford University Press.

— (2003) *Small Arms Survey 2003: Development Denied*, Oxford: Oxford University Press.

— (2004) *Small Arms Survey 2004: Rights at Risk*, Oxford: Oxford University Press.

— (2005) *Small Arms Survey 2005: Weapons at War*, Oxford: Oxford University Press.

Stedman, S. J. and F. Tanner (2003) 'Refugees as resources in war', in S. J. Stedman and F. Tanner (eds), *Refugee Manipulation: War, Politics, and the Abuse of Human Suffering*, Washington, DC: Brookings Institution Press.

Surke, A. and H. Adelman (1999) *The Path of a Genocide: The Rwanda Crisis from Uganda to Zaire*, New Brunswick, NJ: Transactions.

Szutucki, J. (1999) 'Who is a refugee? The convention definition: universal or obsolete?', in F. Nicholson and T. Twomey (eds), *Refugee Rights and Realities: Evolving International Concepts and Regimes*, Cambridge: Cambridge University Press.

Terry, F. (2002) *Condemned to Repeat? The Paradox of Humanitarian Action*, Ithaca, NY, and London: Cornell University Press.

Thee, M. (1980) 'Militarism and militarisation in contemporary international relations', in E. Asborn and M. Thee (eds), *The Problem of Contemporary Militarisation*, London: Croom Helm.

Ullman, R. (1983) 'Redefining security', *International Security*, 8(1): 129–53.

UN (United Nations) (1999) *United Nations Firearms Study Database, 1999*, New York: United Nations.

UNGA (United Nations General Assembly) (1995) *Supplement to an Agenda for Peace: Position Paper of the Secretary-General on the Occasion of the Fiftieth Anniversary of the United Nations*, A/50/60-2/1995/1, 3 January.

— (1997) *Report of the Panel of Governmental Experts on Small Arms*, A/52/298, 27 August, available at <www.smallarmssurvey.org/resources/un_rep.htm>.

— (1999) *Report of the Panel of Governmental Experts on Small Arms*, A/54/258, 19 August, available at <www.smallarmssurvey.org/resources/un_rep.htm>.

Unger D. (2003) 'Ain't enough blanket: international humanitarian assistance and Cambodian political resistance', in S. J. Stedman and F. Tanner (eds), *Refugee Manipulation: War, Politics, and the Abuse of Human Suffering*, Washington, DC: Brookings Institution Press.

UNHCR (United Nations High Commissioner for Refugees) (1982) 'Military attacks on refugee camps and settlements in southern Africa and elsewhere', ExCom Conclusion no. 27 (XXXIII).

— (1983) 'Military attacks on refugee camps and settlements in southern Africa and elsewhere', ExCom Conclusion no. 32 (XXXIV).

— (1986) 'Military and armed attacks on refugee camps and settlements', ExCom Conclusion no. 45 (XXXVII).

— (1987) 'Military or armed attacks on refugee camps and settlements', ExCom Conclusion no. 48 (XXXVIII).

— (1993) 'Personal security of refugees', ExCom Conclusion no. 72 (XLIV).

— (1995) 'Impact of military personnel and the militia presence in Rwandese refugee camps and settlements', Paper presented at the OAU/UNHCR Regional Conference on Assistance to Refugees, Returnees and Displaced Persons in the Great Lakes Region, Bujumbura, Burundi, 15–17 February.

— (2000a) *The State of the World's Refugees: Fifty Years of Humanitarian Action*, Oxford: Oxford University Press.

— (2000b) *The Security, Civilian and Humanitarian Character of Refugee Camps and Settlements: Operationalizing the 'Ladder of Options'*, EC/50/SC/INF.4, 27 June.

— (2001a) *The Civilian Character of Asylum: Separating Armed Elements from Refugees*, EC/GC/01/5, 19 February, <www.unhcr.ch/prexcom/standocs/english/gc01_5e.pdf>.

— (2001b) *Maintaining the Civilian and Humanitarian Character of Asylum, Refugee Status, Camps and Other Locations*, EC/GC/01/9, 30 May.

— (2001c) *UNHCR Statistical Yearbook 2000*, Geneva: UNHCR.

— (2002) 'The civilian and humanitarian character of asylum', ExCom Conclusion no. 94 (LIII).

— (2003a) 'State concerns', Paper presented at the First Meeting of States to Consider the Implementation of the Program of Action to Prevent, Combat and Eradicate the Illicit Trade in Small Arms and Light Weapons in All Its Aspects, New York, 10 July.

— (2003b) *UNHCR Statistical Year Book: Refugees, Asylum Seekers and Others of Concern: Trends in Displacement, Protection and Solutions*, Geneva: UNHCR.

— (2003c) *Agenda for Protection*, Geneva: UNHCR, available at <www.unhcr. bg/pubs/agenda_protection/en/agenda_for_protection_en.pdf>.

— (2005) *Refugee Magazine* <www.unhcr.org/cgi-bin/texis/vtx/publ>.

UNSC (United Nations Security Council (1998a) *Final Report of the International Commission of Inquiry*, S/1998/1096, 18 November.

— (1998b) *The Situation in Africa Including Refugee Camps*, Resolution S/RES/1208, 19 November.

— (1999a) *The Security, and Civilian and Humanitarian Character of Refugee Camps and Settlements*, EC/49/SC/INF.2, 14 January.

— (1999b) *Report of the Secretary-General to the Security Council on the Protection of Civilians in Armed Conflict*, S/1999/957, 8 September, available at <domino.un.org/UNISPAL.NSF/0/62038aa80887f23a85256c85007230a4? OpenDocument>.

— (2000) *On the Protection of Civilians in Armed Conflict*, Resolution SRES/1296, 19 April.

— (2001) *Report of the Secretary-General to the Security Council on the Protection of Civilians in Armed Conflict*, S/2001/331, 30 March, available at <domino.un.org/UNISPAL.nsf/0/e8b5234d0339a2c385256c8700549672? OpenDocument>.

USCR (United States Committee for Refugees) (1986) 'Afghanistan: conflict and displacement 1978–2000', *World Refugee Survey*, Washington, DC: USCR.

— (2001) 'Afghan refugees shunned and scorned', Report, Washington, DC: Immigration and Refugee Services of America, <www.reliefweb.int/library/documents/2001/uscr_afg_01oct.pdf>.

US DOS (Department of State) (2001) *Arms and Conflict in Africa*, Department of State Fact Sheet, Bureau of Intelligence and Research, 1 July.

Weiner, M. (1991) 'Security, stability and international migration', in M. Weiner (ed.), *International Migration and Security*, Boulder, CO: Westview Press.

— (1992/93) 'Security, stability and international migration', *International Security*, 17(3): 91–126.

Yu, L. (2002) *Separating Ex-combatants and Refugees in Zongo, DRC: Peacekeepers and UNHCR's 'Ladder of Options'*, New Issues in Refugee Research Working Paper no. 60, August.

Zolberg, A. R., A. Surke and S. Aguayo (1989) *Escape from Violence: Conflict and Refugee Crisis in the Developing World*, New York and Oxford: Oxford University Press.

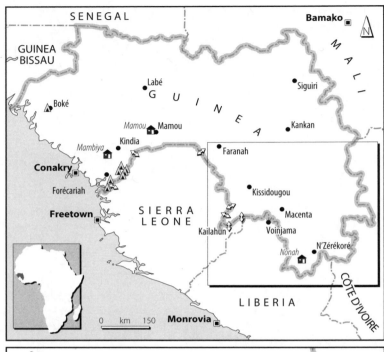

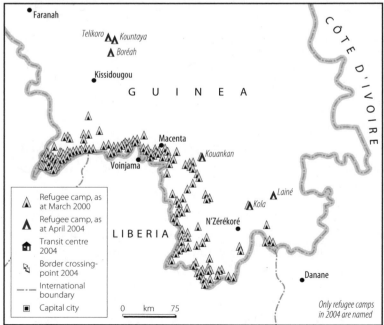

Map by **MAP*grafix***

2 | The militarization and demilitarization of refugee camps and settlements in Guinea, 1999–2004

JAMES MILNER WITH
ASTRID CHRISTOFFERSEN-DEB

Throughout the 1990s, Guinea was an island of relative stability, as conflict and warlordism engulfed its southern neighbours, Liberia and Sierra Leone.[1] From the first arrival of refugees from the Liberian civil war in 1990, through the outbreak of the Sierra Leonean conflict in 1991, the 1997 coup d'état in Freetown and the resumption of the Liberian war in 2000, Guinea provided refuge for well over 500,000 refugees during the 1990s. At the end of 1999, Guinea hosted an estimated 450,000 refugees: 350,000 from Sierra Leone and 100,000 from Liberia (USCR 2000c).[2]

The overwhelming majority of these refugees did not live in refugee camps. Most lived in refugee settlements, close to the border with Liberia and Sierra Leone. Despite their close proximity to the border, the refugees lived in relative security through most of the decade. They pursued economic self-sufficiency through agricultural production and trade with the local community.[3] This situation began to change in the late 1990s. Following a number of cross-border raids on the settlements by the Revolutionary United Front (RUF) of Sierra Leone,[4] and the reported presence of Sierra Leonean pro-government Kamajors militias in Massakoundou camp in southern Guinea,[5] the granting of asylum in Guinea became politicized. As a result, Guinea's refugee settlements lost their civilian and humanitarian character and became militarized.[6]

This situation deteriorated dramatically in 2000. The number and intensity of cross-border incursions rose significantly in the first quarter of 2000, with more sophisticated and targeted strikes against humanitarian supplies in March and April of that year. The situation deteriorated to one of full-scale conflict in September 2000, as the RUF, allegedly in conjunction with Liberian forces and Guinean dissidents, attacked major towns in southern Guinea, destroying refugee settlements, killing the UN High Commissioner for Refugees (UNHCR) head of office in Macenta, and forcing tens of thousands of refugees and Guineans to flee. Three days after a successful RUF attack on the border town of Pamalp, just 100 kilometres from the Guinean capital, Conakry, the president of Guinea, Lansana Conté, addressed the nation. In his speech, he called on Guinean citizens to defend their country by repelling the invaders and by rounding up the refugees, whom he blamed for the outbreak of violence.

The result was profound. In Conakry and across the country, refugees were detained and beaten. UNHCR estimated that as many as 6,000 refugees in Conakry alone were detained in the days following the president's speech, and countless more were evicted from their homes. At the same time, thousands of Guinean youths, many under the age of eighteen, were recruited to reinforce the poorly equipped and trained Guinean army. As many as 10,000 of these 'Young Volunteers' were armed and sent to fight at the border. At the same time, Conté is widely believed to have entered into an alliance with the newly formed group Liberians United for Reconciliation and Democracy (LURD). Based in Macenta in southern Guinea, LURD forces fought with Guinean army and militia forces to repel the incursions.

By March 2001, a tenuous calm had returned to Guinea, but the implications of the events of the previous year were significant. The country's refugee population was scattered, and the tradition of generous asylum had seemingly been irreversibly changed. LURD elements circulated freely in the remaining refugee camps, and, along with the Young Volunteers, roamed Guinea's Forest Region with impunity, using their small arms and light weapons (SALW) to threaten, rob and abuse refugees and Guineans alike.

By early 2001, it seemed as though Guinea was heading down the same path as Sierra Leone and Liberia. In March 2001, the UN Office for the Coordination of Humanitarian Activities (UNOCHA) estimated that one out of every five citizens of the Mano River Union of Guinea, Liberia and Sierra Leone was displaced by conflict: an estimated 3 million people out of a total population of 15 million (UNOCHA 2001: 5). The continuation of instability and massive displacement in these three countries prompted UN Secretary-General Kofi Annan in May 2001 to refer to the situation in the sub-region as 'one of the most serious humanitarian and political crises facing the international community today' (UNSC 2001). UNOCHA reported that 'due to heavy militarization of Southeast Guinea, a sharp increase of armed elements in the refugee camps (e.g. Nyaedou and Massakoundou) has been witnessed' (2001: 157).

In the months that followed, human rights organizations repeatedly highlighted how the presence of armed elements in the refugee camps constituted a serious threat to refugee protection, as refugees fell victim to extortion, forced recruitment, sexual violence and a range of other abuses at the hands of the armed elements.[7]

The goal of this chapter is to ask to what extent these protection concerns, especially the militarization of refugee camps, remained in Guinea four years after the initial cross-border incursions. A range of actors – including the government of Guinea, the Economic Community of West African States (ECOWAS), UN agencies, donor governments, NGOs, civil society groups and refugees themselves – have undertaken a number of initiatives in recent years to restore the civilian and humanitarian character of the refugee camps in Guinea. This chapter examines the extent to which they have been successful, and the extent to which the camps may now be described as 'demilitarized'.

Methodology

Both desk research and a field visit to Guinea were undertaken to answer these questions. A broad range of sources was consulted prior to the research in Guinea to develop the historical and political context against which the research questions are best considered.[8] The principal author of this chapter was also able to draw on his experience as a consultant with UNHCR in Guinea during 2001 to add to this background.[9]

The authors then undertook field research in Guinea from 19 September to 10 October 2004. A total of fifty meetings were held with representatives of the government of Guinea, UN agencies, NGOs, donor governments, community and business leaders, civil society representatives and refugees. Twenty-four of these interviews were conducted in Conakry, while twenty-six were conducted in the Forest Region of southern Guinea, where Guinea's six refugee camps and one transit site are located. Based in the provincial capital of N'Zérékoré, the authors visited Lainé and Kouankan refugee camps, where meetings were held with camp administrators, security personnel, the refugee committee and UNHCR's implementing partners in the camps, in addition to representatives of other refugee groups and a number of randomly selected individual refugees.

Research was also undertaken in the regional hospital in N'Zérékoré, specifically to determine the prevalence of small arms and light weapons (SALW)-related injuries in the region. The daily emergency room records for the period July 2003–July 2004 were examined to determine the number of gunshot injuries treated, and the number of refugees treated for SALW-related injuries. While this effort was meant to be comparative with previous years to identify trends, this objective could not be fulfilled, as the emergency records from the hospital for the earlier periods were either damaged beyond use or missing.

The problem of reliable and verifiable statistics encountered at the hospital in N'Zérékoré was repeated throughout the field research. A range of statistics – from local and refugee populations to medical incidents, from

53

police incidents involving small arms to details of arms seizures – were either unavailable or lacking in credibility. This problem with statistics is the result of a lack of both the necessary training of and resources available to those responsible for gathering and maintaining baseline data, and is a long-standing concern in the refugee programme in Guinea. For example, in 2002 the US Committee for Refugees (USCR) reported that the UNHCR programme in Guinea has 'long suffered from uncertainty about the numbers of refugees being assisted there' and that 'there is a high level of scepticism and uncertainty about the reliability of the figures on the part of key partners and others'. The concern was raised that many statistics relating to refugee assistance in Guinea were 'tainted by corruption' (USCR 2002: 76).

As a result, the key findings of this chapter are not derived from a statistical analysis of the nature and extent of refugee camp militarization in Guinea. Statistics contained in this research are meant to substantiate findings derived from interviews and secondary sources. The key findings of this chapter are drawn from a comparison of the situation in Guinea as experienced in 2001 and 2004. The findings are further substantiated by interviews conducted during the 2004 field visit.

Key findings

- Refugee camps were militarized during the events of 2000–03. Refugee camps and settlements were not only a key target during the attacks on Guinea between September 2000 and March 2001, but also played a significant role in the activities of LURD in northern Liberia in 2001–03.
- Regional politics and alliances significantly contributed to this militarization. The widely reported military, financial and logistical support provided by the government of Guinea to anti-Taylor groups, most notably the United Liberation Movement of Liberia for Democracy (ULIMO) and LURD, and the basing of these groups in and around the refugee camps, played a significant role in the militarization of the camps.
- Refugees and refugee camps in the Forest Region of Guinea were not militarized in 2004. All quantitative and qualitative data collected in Guinea in September/October 2004 indicated that there had been no reported presence of small arms or armed elements in the refugee camps for the preceding twelve months.
- Demilitarization of the camps by 2004 was a combined result of the change of circumstances in Liberia, the relocation of the refugee camps and the implementation of camp security arrangements. While the relocation of the refugee camps in 2001/02, the establishment of camp

security arrangements and the training of the Mixed Brigade (BMS), comprising police and gendarmerie, by the Canadian deployment all contributed significantly to the demilitarization of the camps, the fall of Taylor in Liberia was likely the single greatest factor leading to demilitarization.

- The refugee-populated areas of southern Guinea are militarized. While the refugee camps are not militarized, the presence of armed elements and the proliferation of small arms in the Forest Region as a whole are significant sources of criminality and insecurity.

- The impact of militarization on refugee protection in Guinea can be understood only in the context of refugee-populated areas, not exclusively in the context of refugee camps. Given that the boundaries between refugee camps and the surrounding villages are not enforced, given that there are significant concerns relating to militarization outside the camps, and given that these concerns have an impact on refugee security, it is better to understand refugee security in relation to the broader framework of refugee-populated areas.[10]

- The most significant sources of small arms in Guinea are internal and not related to the presence of refugees. Of the four major sources of small arms in Guinea identified during fieldwork (looting in Conakry, non-return of officially issued weapons, local production and traffic from Liberia and Côte d'Ivoire), only one source is external to Guinea, and is not related to the presence of refugees.

- The differentiation in disarmament, demobilization and reintegration (DDR) programming in Liberia and Côte d'Ivoire is creating a traffic of SALW through Guinea. As the anticipated DDR programme in Côte d'Ivoire is seen to be potentially more lucrative than that in Liberia, arms are being trafficked through southern Guinea on speculation that they will fetch a higher price in the sub-region.

- Given the fluidity of borders between countries in the sub-region, there is a need for a sub-regional approach to peace-building, conflict resolution and reconstruction.

- Between 3,000 and 10,000 Young Volunteers have yet to be disarmed and demobilized in the Forest Region of Guinea. The continued presence of these armed elements and the possibility that they may be recruited by political groups together constitute one of the greatest causes of insecurity and instability in Guinea and the sub-region, and require urgent attention by the international community.

- Camp security has improved following greater international engagement, the formation of the BMS and the Canadian deployment, but a greater scope of operations and additional material support are required. The deployment and training of the BMS has had a significant impact on ensuring the security of refugees in the camps in Guinea, but their effectiveness remains limited due both to a mandate that does not allow them to engage in local and sub-regional security planning and a lack of basic materials and equipment.

- The militarization of the refugee-populated areas and the proliferation of SALW in Guinea must be considered within the historical, social and economic context. The full implications of the presence of armed groups and the proliferation of small arms in the Forest Region are best understood in the context of the history of the regime in Guinea, the challenges to the current regime, the increasingly difficult economic climate and the growth in conflict in the Forest Region and the wider sub-region.

Background to refugee populations in Guinea

Over the past fifteen years, Guinea has hosted hundreds of thousands of refugees from Liberia, Sierra Leone and, most recently, Côte d'Ivoire. To understand the origins of the militarization of the refugee camps and settlements, it is important first to examine the various phases of arrival in Guinea, in order to understand how the features of these early arrivals contributed to the incursions of September 2000–March 2001. It is against this background, and with an understanding of the militarization of both the refugee camps and the refugee-populated areas in late 2000, that the significance of the current protection environment in Guinea is best understood. This section provides a brief introduction to these phases, while also placing the refugee question in a broader historical and political context.

Sowing the seeds of militarization 1989–99 On 24 December 1989, the National Patriotic Front of Liberia (NPFL), led by Charles Taylor, crossed into northern Liberia from Côte d'Ivoire and started one of Africa's most violent civil wars. In early January 1990, 10,000 ethnic Mano Liberians from the region fled the violence by crossing into Guinea at Yomou and settled in ethnic Mano Guinean villages. Thus began the pattern of refugee settlement in Guinea. Whereas other countries in Africa in the early 1990s responded to the mass influx of refugees by establishing isolated refugee camps, the government of Guinea allowed refugees to settle in and around Guinean villages of the same ethnicity, often resulting in the 'creation of twin villages with one single name' (Van Damme 1999: 137). This policy was in recognition not only of the long-standing social, economic and linguistic links across the border, but also of the ECOWAS legal framework, guaranteeing freedom of movement to citizens of member countries.[11]

As the NPFL advanced through Liberia in the summer of 1990, a significant number of Mandingos fled the urban trading centres of northern Liberia and sought refuge in N'Zérékoré and Macenta, two of the largest trading centres in southern Guinea. As Van Damme explains, the majority of these refugees had Guinean roots, as 'many had moved to Liberia during the 1960s and 1970s to trade' (ibid.: 37).[12] Their arrival marked the origins of the large urban refugee populations in southern Guinea, many of whom have never benefited from UNHCR assistance, but who have played a significant role in the security situation in the sub-region.

The escalation of the conflict in Liberia and its western spread into Loffa and Bong counties brought additional waves of refugees to Guinea. In June 1990 alone, 20,000 refugees fled to Yomou, 13,000 fled to the Macenta prefecture, and approximately 16,000 fled to the area around Guékédou. Like the Manos before them, these Gbande, Loma and Kpellé refugees settled in villages belonging to the same ethnicity across the border.

This pattern continued in the early 1990s, especially following the spill-over of the Liberian conflict into neighbouring Sierra Leone in early 1991 and the arrival of some 100,000 refugees, mostly Kissi and Mende from Sierra Leone (ibid.: 40). These arrivals settled in the Languette region of Guinea, a sliver of territory south of Guékédou that juts into Sierra Leone and partially borders Liberia. The Kissi refugees were able to settle in ethnically similar villages. Likewise, Kuranko refugees, who fled into the region between Kissidougou and Faranah, were also able to settle in Kuranko villages. The Mende and Gbande, however, did not have ethnic links across the border, and the first 'camp' was established at Kouloumba to house approximately 26,000 refugees (ibid.: 42).

Guékédou became the focus of the international response to successive waves of arrivals from both Sierra Leone and Liberia through the 1990s, and the UNHCR sub-office in Guékédou grew to become its largest in Africa in 1999. Table 2.1, provided by the Office of the Prefect in Guékédou, shows how the refugee population in the prefecture grew steadily through the 1990s. These refugees, mostly Sierra Leonean, lived in ninety-five refugee settlements, ranging in size from 250 to 25,000 refugees, forming a patchwork of refugee settlement throughout southern Guinea.

The overwhelming majority of refugees were concentrated in the Guékédou prefecture. The refugee population figures included in UNHCR's 2001 country operations plan, prepared by the UNHCR Guinea office in March 2000, further illustrate the concentration of almost two-thirds of the country's refugees around Guékédou.

In fact, it was not until early 1995 that refugees from Sierra Leone fled into another region of Guinea, when 24,000 Sierra Leonean refugees

57

TABLE 2.1 Population of Sierra Leonean refugee settlements in the Guékédou prefecture, 1989–2000

1989	132
1990	5,179
1991	52,721
1992	60,045
1993	76,868
1994	84,867
1995	87,439
1996	94,855
1997	97,530
1999	197,293
2000	260,619

Source: Statistics provided to UNOCHA by the prefect of Guékédou, 2003[13]

TABLE 2.2 Sierra Leonean refugees in Guinea, March 2000

Prefecture	Total
Guékédou	260,619
Kissidougou	35,474
Macenta	1,111
N'Zérékoré	955
Forécariah	22,500
Total	320,659

TABLE 2.3 Liberian refugees in Guinea, March 2000

Prefecture	Total
Guékédou	22,896
Kissidougou	1,479
Macenta	44,756
N'Zérékoré	59,992
Forécariah	1,246
Total	130,369

Source: UNHCR (2001)

from Kambia arrived in Forécariah, just 100 kilometres from Conakry. It was then that the location of refugees and their pattern of settlement became of greater concern to the government of Guinea. The May 1997 coup d'état in Freetown, Sierra Leone – which brought the Armed Forces

58

Revolutionary Council (AFRC) to power – the ECOWAS Monitoring Group (ECOMOG) intervention in February 1998 and the RUF attack on Freetown in 1999 all brought successive waves of refugees not only into southern Guinea and Forécariah, but also into Conakry. The fact that the president of Sierra Leone, Ahmed Tejan Kabbah, himself sought refuge in Conakry after the AFRC coup highlights the importance of asylum in Guinea, not to mention its political implications.

These political implications, and the perception that Guinea was using asylum as a means of supporting parties to the conflict in Sierra Leone and Liberia, became clear after the Liberian elections of July 1997. One of the main opponents of Charles Taylor was Alhaji Kromah, a Mandingo, based in southern Guinea and drawing on support from urban Liberian refugees in N'Zérékoré and Macenta. On losing the election, Kromah reverted to his armed movement against Taylor, returning his political party, ALCOP, to the United Liberation Movement of Liberia for Democracy–K (ULIMO–K), with the open support of Lansana Conté.[14] It is widely believed that LURD, formed in July 1999, is an outgrowth of ULIMO (Brabazon 2003: 22).

The overthrow of President Ahmed Tejan Kabbah of Sierra Leone in 1997, and the response of the government of Guinea, demonstrated for many the dynamics of allegiances in the sub-region around the maxim 'an enemy of my friend is my enemy'.[15] Two groupings coalesced around the mutual distrust of Conté and Taylor, originating in 1993. The first grouping consisted of the presidents of Guinea and Sierra Leone, with the support of Kamajors and ULIMO fighters. The second consisted of Charles Taylor of Liberia, with the support of the RUF and, to a lesser extent, the AFRC. As argued by the Lawyers' Committee for Human Rights, refugee protection and assistance became an important aspect of the struggle between these two groupings.[16] The distinction between refugees and rebels became blurred. This was especially the case among the Kamajoras and ULIMO fighters who assisted the Guinea military to patrol its borders and screen those seeking asylum in Guinea and assistance for refugees. In this way they indirectly bolstered the campaigns of the two groups in Sierra Leone and Liberia.

This presence resulted in the start of more targeted cross-border incursions by the RUF into Guinea as early as 1998.[17] USCR and Amnesty International both report that, on 1 September 1998, RUF elements crossed into Guinea and attacked Tomandou camp, 80 kilometres from Guékédou, killing ten people, including seven refugees (USCR 1999; Amnesty International 2001). Tomandou and Massakoundou camps, both less than 20 kilometres from the border with Sierra Leone, are alleged to have been the first camps in Guinea to have accommodated armed elements with the knowledge of the Guinean authorities.

By 1999 the refugee population in Guinea was approximately 450,000, the highest refugee population in Africa that year (USCR, 2000c).[18] Some 300,000 of these refugees were Sierra Leoneans living around Guékédou, with more than 50,000 others living in Forécariah and approximately 100,000 Liberians living in the Forest Region of Guinea between Macenta and N'Zérékoré. USCR reported in 2000 that refugee camps in the region were 'dangerously close to the border' and that 'following several deadly cross-border raids by Sierra Leonean rebels, Guinea authorities declared a midnight-to-dawn curfew in some areas' (ibid.). In response to these attacks, UNHCR began to relocate some refugees away from the border, moving some 14,000 Sierra Leonean refugees before the start of the rainy season in July.

As Sierra Leoneans were being relocated, Liberian refugees were being prepared for repatriation. UNHCR announced that assistance to Liberians in Guinea would be terminated at the end of 1999, and some 13,000 Liberians were repatriated in the first eight months of that year. The repatriation was not, however, sustainable, as over 10,000 Liberians fled to Guinea between April and August as fresh fighting erupted in northern Liberia. This violence again spilled over into Guinea when Liberian elements attacked a Guinean border town near Macenta in September 1999, leaving twenty-seven Guineans dead.[19] As a result, the border was closed and the repatriation suspended.

The year 1999 also witnessed an increase in the harassment by Guinean security forces of refugees not associated with a Conté-friendly group. Urban refugees, especially in Conakry, bore the brunt of this harassment, especially after attacks near the capital blamed on the RUF. USCR reports that in April 1999, 'following an attack on a Guinean ship, which government officials blamed on Sierra Leonean rebels, Guinean authorities rounded-up about 125 Sierra Leonean refugees in Conakry and sent them to a refugee camp in Forécariah' (ibid.).

As highlighted by this brief overview, the seeds of militarization of refugee-populated areas were sown during the late 1990s. As asylum became politicized, as alliances were formed between the government of Guinea and foreign armed groups, as these groups became based in and around refugee camps and settlements, and as the settlements became the increased target of attack by the RUF and Liberian forces, refugee-populated areas became militarized. The profound implications of this militarization became clear during the events of September 2000–March 2001.

Cross-border incursions and militarization, 2000/01[20] On 2 September 2000, the Guinea border town of Massadou, to the east of Macenta, was attacked, allegedly by Liberian elements supported by the RUF (USCR 2000c; Amnesty International 2001: 3). At least forty Guineans were killed in the attack, which marked the start of a rapid chain of events. On 4 September, Madina Woula, on the border with Sierra Leone and southeast of the regional centre of Kindia, was attacked, resulting in another forty deaths (USCR 2000c; Amnesty International 2001: 3). Two days later, on 6 September, Pamalap, the border town near Forécariah and only 100 kilometres from Conakry, was attacked and held by the RUF (IRIN 2000a, 2000b).

These seemingly coordinated attacks, spanning the length of Guinea's border with Sierra Leone and Liberia, caused panic in the capital. On 9 September 2000, President Conté addressed the nation on television and radio. Part of his speech has been translated as: 'I am giving orders that we bring together all foreigners ... and that we search and arrest all suspects ... They should go home. We know that there are rebels among the refugees. Civilians and soldiers, let's defend our country together.'[21]

According to Amnesty International, 'the President's speech is widely seen as a decisive turning point in national policy but also as implicit permission to the military, and the Guinean public, to go on the offensive against refugees in Guinea' (Amnesty International 2001: 3). Refugees in Conakry were particularly affected. Approximately 6,000 urban refugees were detained in the capital in the days following the speech. Many more were evicted from their homes and subjected to harassment and abuse, both physical and sexual, by their neighbours, the police and Young Volunteers.

The president's speech reflected the feeling within the government that the Guinean army – lacking motivation, poorly trained, and underequipped – would not be able to repel the invasion without outside support. Support was found in two groups. First, the alliance between Guinean forces and foreign groups based in Guinea was reinforced. ULIMO fighters were mobilized along with the Guinean army in the defence of Macenta and Guékédou.[22] Many of these fighters had previously been refugees in Guinea, were drawn directly from the refugee population or had family members within the refugee camps, especially Kouankan refugee camp, near Macenta.[23]

Second, thousands of young Guineans were recruited into local militias to reinforce the border defences. These Young Volunteers came primarily from prefectures along the border, were recruited by the local prefects, were armed and were sent to fight at the front line with little or no training.[24] No central registry of the Young Volunteers was kept, so it is impossible to know exactly how many were recruited, although estimates range from

7,000[25] to 30,000.[26] The prefect of N'Zérékoré confirms that 4,500 Young Volunteers were recruited in his prefecture alone.[27] In addition to fighting at the border, these Young Volunteers established roadblocks around the country and entered refugee camps and settlements to search for rebel elements.[28]

With the support of the Young Volunteers and ULIMO, the Guinean military waged a seven-month campaign against the incursions. On 17 September 2004, the town of Macenta was attacked by armed elements entering from Liberia. The attack resulted in many civilian casualties, including Mensah Kpognon, the head of the UNHCR Macenta office. A second UNHCR worker, Sapeu Laurence Djeya, was abducted and later released inside Liberia. During the attack, the UNHCR office in Macenta was looted.

Additional attacks on Macenta and Forécariah continued in September. In October and November, the fighting shifted into the Languette region of southern Guinea. By the end of November, RUF fighters had almost captured the important regional town of Kissidougou after holding the town of Yendé, south of Kissidougou, for one week. Refugee settlements were also targeted in the fighting. According to Amnesty International, 'Katkama Camp, where the RUF reportedly attempted to recruit refugees to fight, was one of the camps particularly hard hit' (Amnesty International 2001: 4).

The fighting reached Guékédou on 6 December. RUF fighters attacked from the south and west, as pro-Taylor Liberian and Guinean dissident elements reportedly joined from the east. The UNHCR sub-office in Guékédou, the base for one of the largest refugee operations in Africa, was attacked, looted and partially burned. Looted UNHCR materials from the sub-office and the regional hospital, especially Land Cruisers and communications equipment, were visibly used by both RUF and ULIMO fighters, further reinforcing the public perception of a link between the refugee population and the rebel incursions.[29] The fight for Guékédou lasted several weeks and resulted in the virtual destruction of the town. The hospital, post office and other public services were destroyed in the fighting. In addition, an estimated 100,000 Guineans fled the fighting and became internally displaced.

Fighting in the area continued until March 2001, when RUF fighters attacked the Nongoa area, 30 kilometres west of Guékédou. This was the last significant attack in the Languette, and brought to a close months of localized fighting in the Forest Region of southern Guinea – stretching from Kissidougou to N'Zérékoré – and in and around Forécariah. Government officials estimate that the conflict resulted in the death of some 1,500 Guineans and the internal displacement of well over 350,000.[30] USCR reported in 2002 that 'aid workers widely considered' the government's estimate 'to be greatly inflated', and estimated the number of displaced at the end of 2001 to be closer to 100,000 (USCR 2002: 79). During the violence, over 5,000 buildings were damaged or destroyed, mostly in Guékédou, Macenta and Forécariah.[31]

The conflict also had significant implications for the refugee population. First, tens of thousands were themselves displaced by the fighting. Following attacks on Forécariah in October, one UNHCR official estimated that some 32,000 refugees were expelled from the town.[32] The majority of the more than ninety refugee settlements in the Languette were destroyed, along with the refugees' livelihood. In the midst of the conflict, refugees were subjected to harassment, forced recruitment – both as combatants and as porters to ferry looted goods back into Sierra Leone – physical and sexual abuse, arbitrary detention and direct attacks by all sides in the conflict.[33] Finally, the killing of the UNHCR head of office in Macenta resulted in the evacuation of all UNHCR staff from Forécariah, Guékédou, N'Zérékoré and Macenta, and a consequent suspension of all UNHCR activities outside of Conakry, leaving some 400,000 refugees without assistance for months.

Restoring security to the refugee-populated areas: a review of responses, 2001–04 As the violence subsided in early 2001, UNHCR began to chart its response to the upheaval. A three-pronged strategy was developed to restore stability to the refugee population and to address the protection needs of the refugees. First, a massive relocation exercise was planned to find refugees scattered throughout southern Guinea and transport them to new refugee camps in the Albadaria and Lola prefectures, both more than 50 kilometres from the border with either Sierra Leone or Liberia. Second, a series of transit sites were constructed on the road from Kissidougou to Conakry, to facilitate the repatriation of Sierra Leonean refugees by sea to Freetown. Third, a system was designed to identify and process the estimated 30,000 refugees in need of resettlement to a third country.

The relocation of refugees from the Languette and other border areas to new refugee camps was specifically intended not only to ensure the physical security of refugees, but also to restore the civilian and humanitarian character of the refugee population. It was widely recognized that armed elements had blended with the refugees, and that the previous model of refugee settlements was no longer sustainable. Between April and May 2001, some 60,000 refugees were moved from the Languette to the newly established camps of Kountaya (13,000 refugees), Boréah (11,500) and Telikoro (7,500 refugees) near Kissidougou.[34] Sembakounya camp (7,500 refugees), near Dabola, was established to accommodate refugees relocated from Foré-cariah and Conakry.[35] Later in 2001 and into 2002, Kola and Lainé camps were established north of N'Zérékoré to accommodate refugees relocated from Yomou and Diéké. Kouankan camp, established in March 2000 before the attacks, remained open. Significantly, however, UNHCR closed Massakoundou camp near Kissidougou, in response to requests from local authorities, who had stated that the camp had become a base for rebels.

Specific activities were incorporated into the relocation exercise to help promote the civilian and humanitarian character of the new camps. First, the Guinean military, under the supervision of the Bureau National pour la Coordination des Réfugiés (BNCR), was involved in the exercise, responsible for screening the refugees and their bags for weapons before the relocation. Second, military escorts for the convoys of relocation, often including up to forty trucks, ensured the security of refugees during the relocation.[36] Third, the new camps benefited from more proactive planning for refugee security strategies. With the cooperation of the BNCR, a 'Mixed Brigade', the BMS, was formed from the police and gendarmerie to assume responsibility for security in the camps. These efforts were formalized in November 2001 with a *protocole d'accord* between UNHCR and the government of Guinea. According to one UNHCR official, 'the key strategic decision that resulted in the most significant and overall improvement of the refugees' security in Guinea was the Government's authorization and joint implementation of UNHCR's relocation proposal' (UNHCR n.d.).

Visiting the camps in February 2002, a joint mission by the Commission for Human Security and the Emergency and Security Services of UNHCR's Geneva headquarters 'quickly concluded that the general safety and security of the refugees in the six camps is incomparable to their situation in late 2000/early 2001' (ibid.). The mission found that the application of the strategies developed by UNHCR and the government of Guinea resulted in the general maintenance of law and order in the camps. In particular, it concluded that the formation of the Mixed Brigades helped focus security efforts in the camps and, along with the participation of elected refugee committees, helped ensure their civilian and humanitarian nature.

Human rights organizations and refugee advocates, however, emphasize that the establishment of the new camps was not the panacea for the problems of refugee insecurity and camp militarization. In June 2001, violence erupted in Telikoro camp, near Kissidougou, between refugees and the Mixed Brigade. Six officers were injured, 120 Sierra Leonean refugees were arrested, but the six weapons seized from the officers were never recovered. The problem of continued militarization, however, was most acute in Kouankan camp, near Macenta, where LURD elements circulated freely.

64

The NGO Action for Churches Together, managing Kouankan as UNHCR's implementing partner, was forced to withdraw in June 2001 after allegations that it was transmitting information to Monrovia on LURD activities based in the camp. Efforts to close the camp in August 2001 and relocate civilians to Kola camp were suspended owing to a lack of funding.

Moreover, while 60,000 refugees were relocated, some 75,000 chose not to relocate and remained in the Languette without UNHCR assistance (USCR 2002: 77). Many chose to remain there because they had intermarried with Guineans, wanted to remain close to the border or were distrustful of the refugee camp environment after their experience in 2000/01.[37]

POLICING REFUGEE CAMPS: THE MIXED BRIGADES AND THE CANADIAN DEPLOYMENT Working closely with the regional BCR offices, the BMS is responsible for policing within the camps, providing security for humanitarian personnel and activities, and cooperating with elected refugee committees and the Refugee Security Volunteers to promote law and order in the camps.[38] Building on the success of the 'security package' approach developed in Tanzania and Kenya, UNHCR hoped that the equipping and training of security personnel specifically responsible for the camps would ensure greater security within them.

According to the terms of the *protocole d'accord*, there was to be one BMS officer per 1,000 refugees, including a number of female officers. According to the most recent figures, this ratio has been met in all camps.

While the quantity of BMS officers met the standards outlined in the *protocole d'accord*, there was a general concern that they were not

TABLE 2.4 BMS and Refugee Security Volunteers in the refugee camps, October 2004

Camp/ transit centre	BMS	Refugee Security Volunteers	Discharged in 2004 owing to misconduct	Refugees	BMS: refugee ratio
Lainé	25	40	3	25,046	1:1,000
Kouankan	23	35	4	22,960	1:1,000
Kola	7	20	3	6,177	1:880
Nonah	4	20	3	3,979	1:975
Kuntaya	16	45	3	9,908	1:650
Telikoro	9	45	0	6,185	1:680
Boréah	7	25	7	4,063	1:580
Total	91	230	23	78,318	1:860

Source: BCR, N'Zérékoré, October 2004

operating at a sufficiently professional level.[39] Investigations of incidents were sporadic and inconsistent. Files and statistics were not being kept. Violent incidents between the BMS and refugees, on a smaller scale compared to the June 2001 incident in Telikoro camp, were documented. More disturbingly, it was found that some members of the BMS were engaged in illegal activities in the camps, including the sexual exploitation of refugee women and children. It was concluded that the BMS did not have the operational training required to police the camp populations effectively.

To address this training gap, the Canadian government reached an agreement with UNHCR to deploy two Royal Canadian Mounted Police (RCMP) officers to southern Guinea. One officer would be responsible for training the BMS in basic policing and human rights principles. The second officer would be responsible for ensuring effective coordination among UNHCR, BMS and BCR. Two officers were initially deployed to Kissidougou for twelve months in 2003. Two officers subsequently operated in N'Zérékoré for six months, starting in early 2004.

Canadian and UNHCR officials jointly undertook a mid-term review of the programme in July 2003 (Herrmann 2003). They concluded that the deployment had achieved 'mixed results'. There was concern at the lack of previous training of the BMS, and the fact that the RCMP programme had to start with the most basic principles of policing. The policy of rotating BMS officers out of the camps and back into regular duties also meant that the benefits of the training were not retained in the camps. Following the completion of the second deployment to N'Zérékoré in June 2004, the Canadian government was planning an independent review of the programme with a view to possibly replicating it elsewhere in Africa.

While gaps in the camp security arrangements remain, especially an official solution to the question of rotation, the contribution of the Canadian deployment has raised the standards of camp security in Guinea to a level unrecognizable from 2001. In fact, the improvement in camp security relative to the situation in 2001 was one of the most positive and striking findings of the 2004 field visit. More specifically, the fact that the BMS was able to provide statistics on incidents in the camps was a significant sign of progress. Furthermore, relations between the BMS and the refugees have improved significantly. Refugee committees and refugee women's committees in both Lainé and Kouankan both stated that they now have confidence in the BMS to maintain order and professionally respond to incidents in the camps.[40]

A shortcoming of the programme, however, was that it was premised on a distinction between refugee camps and refugee-populated areas. As will be argued below, this distinction is artificial in Guinea. As such, for any reinforcement of policing procedures in refugee camps to have a real impact on the protection environment of refugees, such efforts need to be replicated in the surrounding area. Moreover, the benefits of the training provided by the Canadian deployment will be fully realized only if the BMS is provided with the equipment necessary to fulfil its duties in the camps and if support is provided for further training. As of October 2004, the BMS lacked the basic equipment to effectively patrol large refugee camps such as Lainé and Kouankan. Basic communication equipment was also lacking. As a result, it can take up to two hours to respond to an incident. Finally, basic materials to support further training, such as paper and pens, are not provided for in the current budget. It is also significant to note that the statistics provided on BMS deployment in the camps showed that 10 per cent of BMS officers were discharged from their duties in 2004 owing to misconduct.

DEMOBILIZING YOUNG VOLUNTEERS The presence of child soldiers among the Young Volunteers motivated the UN Children's Fund (UNICEF) to take the lead in developing a demobilization programme. In 2002, it appealed for USD595,000 to support a programme seeking to address the reintegration needs of 5,000 Young Volunteers, arguing that a failure to reintegrate them would 'represent a serious threat to the country's stability' (UNOCHA 2002: 59). Owing to limited donor response, UNICEF was able to demobilize and train only 350 Young Volunteers from Guékédou and Kissidougou in a pilot project carried out between 2002 and 2004 (Koudougou and Idrissa 2004).

UNICEF made a further appeal in 2003 for USD936,626 to support the reintegration of an additional 500 Young Volunteers and the protection of Guinean and refugee children from kidnapping and recruitment by rebel forces, but the programme received almost no donor support. A final appeal was made in 2004 for USD778,400 to support four related objectives:

- to stop and prevent the recruitment of children by armed groups;
- to sensitize local authorities, law enforcement agents and military personnel to the provisions of the Optional Protocol on Children in armed conflict, as well as their rights;
- to develop a mechanism and a database to monitor the number of demobilized children; and
- to demobilize and reintegrate 1,000 Young Volunteers and child soldiers.

The appeal reported that the 3,879 remaining Young Volunteers have contributed to 'a phenomenon of youth gangs who intimidate and threaten the population and show complete disregard for any authority'. The appeal further stated that, with the exception of the demobilization of 350 Young Volunteers in 2002, 'little has been done to address this issue' (UNOCHA 2004: 56). It also expressed concern that this problem could be further compounded by the return of combatants from Liberia, and that this combined population could provide a fertile recruitment base for new armed groups.

While UNICEF is the only UN agency in Guinea that has been following the issue of the Young Volunteers since 2001, it has found it difficult to remain engaged in the issue for two reasons.[41] First, UNICEF is mandated only to work with children under eighteen, and many of the Young Volunteers who were children in 2001 are minors no longer. Second, there was very little funding from the donor community to support demobilization programmes. As a result, UNICEF's programmes for the Young Volunteers closed in June 2004. UNICEF has, however, had limited success in developing a response. Most importantly, it has convinced the government of Guinea of the importance of the problem, and prompted the ministries of social affairs, security and defence to form a cross-departmental working group to sustain work on the demobilization.

CONTROLLING THE BORDERS: PROPOSED ECOWAS DEPLOYMENT The 2000 attacks prompted ECOWAS to authorize the deployment of a multinational force of two battalions to monitor the border areas between Guinea and Liberia. Following initial discussions by members of the ECOWAS Mediation and Security Council meeting in Abuja in October 2000, the operation was established in December 2000, and Mali, Niger, Nigeria and Senegal offered troops (AFP 2000). Deployment never materialized, however, owing to funding constraints and lack of support from Guinea and the UN Security Council (Berman and Sams 2003: 49), contrary to earlier statements of support.[42]

It is, however, important to note that meetings in mid-January 2001 to plan the deployment coincided with renewed attacks on Guékédou (Reuters 2001). Given the delays in the deployment of the force, and concerns about its ability to fulfil its mandate if deployed, Conté grew impatient and pursued a strategy of artillery attacks on northern Sierra Leone and backing the LURD attacks on northern Liberia to create the buffer zone promised by ECOWAS. On 31 January 2001, it emerged that the Guinean army and air force had launched a series of attacks on RUF territory in northern Sierra Leone, with the tacit agreement of the government in Freetown (AFP 2001a). On 3 February 2001, the Liberian defence minister confirmed that Voinjama, the capital of Lofa county and close to the Guinean border, had been attacked by LURD forces based in Guinea (AFP 2001b). On the same day that the ECOMOG deployment was reported to be in jeopardy (ibid.), local newspapers in Sierra Leone announced the surrender of fifteen RUF commanders in Sierra Leone.[43]

As Guinea's military successes, proxy and otherwise, increased in Sierra Leone and Liberia, Conté support for the ECOWAS force faded. In fact, a deployment of ECOWAS troops after March 2001 would have hindered Guinea's objectives in Liberia, not supported them. By the time the Guinean army, supported by irregular and foreign elements, regained control of southern Guinea in March 2001, Guinea had ceased to support the ECOWAS plan, and fully pursued the defeat of the RUF and Charles Taylor through military means. This strategy seemed to work. The end to the incursions into the Forest Region coincided with the LURD capture of Voinjama. In May 2001, reports emerged that the RUF had been forced into a ceasefire by the combined pressure of the Guinean attacks and the expansion of UN Mission in Sierra Leone (UNAMSIL) activities. Finally, on 11 August 2003, Charles Taylor stepped down as president of Liberia, and went into exile in Nigeria. The following week, a peace agreement was signed in Accra, ending Liberia's civil war.

TRAINING GUINEA'S ARMED FORCES As demonstrated by the army's response to the incursions in 2000, the Guinean armed forces' ability to prevent cross-border attacks was limited, owing mostly to poor training and lack of equipment. Perhaps the exception to this rule is the Ranger battalion trained by the United States in 2002, partly in response to the incursions.[44] No lethal equipment was provided during the training, which lasted ten weeks (Berman 2002: 33). This battalion was not, however, deployed to the border region as initially planned, but has been used to address internal security concerns.[45] In 2004, Guinea had a total active force of 9,700 personnel, comprising mainly the 8,500-strong army. To these numbers should be added the 1,000 gendarmes and 1,600 Republican Guards (IISS 2004).

In addition to these regular forces, the government formed the Anti-Criminal Brigade (BAC) in January 2002.[46] Operating under the Ministry of Security, BAC is responsible for monitoring the border areas to combat small arms and narcotics trafficking. While BAC has drawn from the elite of the Gendarmerie, it is also woefully under-equipped. In October 2004, the BAC division in N'Zérékoré, for example, had only two vehicles to patrol the prefecture, both of which were being repaired.[47]

The impact of LURD activities on refugees in Guinea (2001–03) Fresh concerns were raised about the impact of LURD activities on the protection of refugees in the context of renewed fighting in northern Liberia in November 2001. As the fighting drew closer to Monrovia in February 2002, prompting Taylor to declare a state of emergency, some 26,000 Liberian refugees crossed into Guinea. Their attempt to seek asylum in Guinea was reportedly hindered significantly by LURD military objectives, as supported by the Guinean military. Human Rights Watch (HRW) reported that LURD prevented civilians from leaving their country to seek asylum in Guinea and sent asylum seekers back into Liberia from border crossings at Ouet-Kama and Tekoulo. Many of those sent back to Liberia were forced to carry supplies and arms back into Liberia from Guinea, with the knowledge of the Guinean military.[48]

These activities were based mostly in the town of Macenta and the Kouankan refugee camp. As reported by HRW, 'numerous refugees gave detailed descriptions of the presence of armed LURD combatants in the refugee camp of Kouankan, where often uniformed and sometimes armed LURD rebels moved freely in and out of the camp' (HRW 2002: 10). LURD combatants used the camp as a base for their families, as a destination for rest and relaxation and as a source of supplies, especially food and medicine. USCR reported that in 2002 'UNHCR urged Guinean officials to remove rebels from the camp and threatened to withdraw from Kouankan entirely, unless the situation improved' (USCR 2003).

Although officially denied by the government, there is ample evidence of LURD presence in the country and of tacit Guinean support for the rebel movement.[49] As reported by HRW, 'the Government of Guinea has long fuelled the Liberian conflict by providing logistical, financial and military support to the LURD rebels' (HRW 2003: 15). HRW further reported that wounded LURD fighters were evacuated to Conakry for treatment, that Guinean military officials provided technical support to LURD, and that LURD rear bases had long been established in Macenta.

Many also point to the personal link between President Conté and Sekou Conneh, the leader of LURD. It has been reported that Conneh was 'based in Guinea for most of the past 13 years and enjoys close links with Guinean President Lansana Conté' (IRIN 2003b). Conneh's wife, Aisha, is Conté's personal clairvoyant, and Conneh was consequently 'invited to become chairman of LURD because of his high-level contacts with the Guinean government' (IRIN 2003a). It is also significant to note that when Conneh returned to Liberia in late 2003 to participate in the formation of a transitional government, 'he travelled in a four-wheel-drive jeep with darkened windows and Guinea government license plates' and was accompanied by 'a fleet of Guinea government cars' (IRIN 2003b).

Of greater concern, however, is the alleged role that Guinea has played in facilitating LURD's access to arms and munitions, in violation of the UN Security Council's arms embargo on Liberia.[50] A November 2002 HRW report provides specific details of how a significant number of Liberian asylum seekers were stopped at border towns by Guinean officials and handed over to LURD commanders (HRW 2002). These asylum seekers were then forced to carry arms, ammunition and supplies across the border to LURD bases in Lofa county. Many asylum seekers reported collecting the weapons, some of which were still in their original wrapping, from Guinean military trucks, and then being forced to make the return journey up to twenty times before being allowed to seek refuge in Guinea (ibid. 15–17). At the end of 2002, the presence of armed elements in the camps, along with the remaining Young Volunteers in the areas surrounding the camps, resulted in significant protection concerns for refugees and hindered the activities of humanitarian agencies, including UNHCR.

The outbreak of violence in Côte d'Ivoire in late 2002, coupled with the arrival of thousands of Ivorian refugees and some 30,000 Guinean nationals returning from Côte d'Ivoire, added pressure to this volatile situation (USCR 2003). The government of Guinea briefly closed its border with Côte d'Ivoire, citing security concerns, but was compelled by the international donor community to reopen it by the end of 2002. There was a general concern within the humanitarian community that the combination of ongoing conflict in Liberia and the alleged involvement of refugees in the violence in Côte d'Ivoire would have serious implications for the militarization of refugee camps near N'Zérékoré. Since N'Zérékoré is Guinea's second-largest city, located less than 100 kilometres from both Liberia and Côte d'Ivoire, and the home of a thriving sub-regional market, it was feared that the new conflict would result in a dramatic increase in the flow of small arms in the Forest Region and the increased militarization of Guinea's refugee camps. Such concerns were partially legitimate.

The situation in 2004 In August 2004, UNHCR finalized a verification exercise in Guinea's six refugee camps and one transit camp, and reported that there were 78,318 UNHCR-assisted refugees in Guinea. This total of 78,318 represents a significant reduction in the refugee population from the 103,063 reported in April 2004.[51] While many refugees admitted to the authors that the statistics had been previously inflated, thereby allowing a greater number of people to benefit from UNHCR assistance, they felt that the revised statistics were too low. In Kouankan, for example, there was a feeling among the refugee committee that while the pre-verification statistic of 32,000 was inflated, the true camp population was between 27,000 and

TABLE 2.5 UNHCR-assisted refugee population in Guinea, August 2004

Prefecture	Camp	Refugees
Kissidougou	Boréah	4,063
	Kuntaya	9,908
	Telikoro	6,185
N'Zérékoré	Kola	6,177
	Lainé	25,046
	Nonah (transit centre)	3,979
Macenta	Kouankan	22,960
Total		78,318

Source: UNOCHA, *Humanitarian Situation Report: Guinea, July–August 2004*

28,000, not the 22,960 claimed by UNHCR.[52] Even the BCR argued that the camp population was higher, estimating it to be closer to 25,000.[53] Even if the statistics from the verification were taken to be a true representation of the camp-based population, the exact number of refugees in Guinea would remain unclear. The government estimates that tens of thousands of refugees remain unassisted outside the refugee camps, while UNHCR includes in its statistics only the total number of assisted refugees. For example, the prefect of N'Zérékoré stated that there are 44,000 refugees living in N'Zérékoré town, but none of them was reflected in UNHCR's numbers.[54]

While the exact numbers are contentious, it is possible to generally describe the conditions of the various refugee populations in Guinea at the end of 2004. The official repatriation programme for Sierra Leonean refugees ended in July 2004. Under the programme, over 92,000 Sierra Leoneans were repatriated from Guinea with UNHCR assistance between the emergency returns in late 2000 and the end of the organized repatriation programme. A programme is now being developed for the 1,814 remaining assisted Sierra Leonean refugees, who are currently in the camps near Kissidougou, primarily in Boréah camp. Many hundreds, if not thousands, of Sierra Leoneans remain in Conakry and in other large urban areas.[55] The majority of the Sierra Leoneans in Conakry who identify themselves as refugees claim that they cannot return to Sierra Leone, have no prospects in Guinea and consequently seek resettlement in a third country. The continued presence of these people is generally tolerated by Guinean officials, who emphasize that, as ECOWAS citizens, Sierra Leoneans benefit from additional rights.[56]

With the change in situation in Liberia since the departure of Charles Taylor in August 2003, the apparent durability of the ceasefire signed in Accra shortly after Taylor's departure and the stability of Gyude Bryant's transitional government, the facilitated repatriation of Liberian refugees began in November 2004. Notwithstanding the presidential elections in Liberia in 2005, UNHCR has not, at the time of writing, yet promoted the repatriation of refugees to Liberia. In the context of this programme, Liberian refugees remain either assisted in one of Guinea's camps, primarily around N'Zérékoré and Macenta, or unassisted in urban and rural settings. Interestingly, many of the refugees now in the camps say that they prefer their current situation over the settlements pre-2000. In a meeting with the refugee committee in Lainé camp, the members were asked which they would prefer if they could choose between living in the local community or living in the camp. All twelve committee members said that they would prefer to live in the camp.[57] In fact, conditions in the camps, especially Lainé, are significantly better than in the surrounding villages, and refugees enjoy the freedom of movement necessary to allow them to pursue economic activity outside of the camps.

Ivorian refugees in Guinea in 2004 lived in very different conditions. The 3,979 Ivorian refugees recognized in Guinea remained in the Nonah transit camp, over a year after their arrival in Guinea. Unlike in the camps where land is allocated and refugees are supported to build semi-permanent dwellings, the Ivorians in Nonah lived in large tents, housing up to fifty refugees. As a result, there were greater health concerns in the camp, with a greater number of reported skin infections and respiratory diseases compared to the other camps.[58] There were also fewer activities in Nonah, which, coupled with uncertainties related to their status, led to greater psychological problems among the refugees.

What was striking in meetings with refugee committees in Lainé and Kouankan camps was the way in which they characterized their security concerns. In 2001, many refugees expressed concerns about physical and sexual abuse, forced recruitment and theft of limited humanitarian assistance by armed elements. During the visit in September/October 2004, the refugees expressed a sense of insecurity relating to their uncertain legal status, their inability to return to their country of origin and their desire to be resettled abroad. While statistics provided by the BMS indicate that there are a number of crimes still being committed in the camps, the level of crime does not appear to be disproportionate to the size of the population and is not a significant concern for the refugee camp population.

When compared with the prevailing protection environment in 2000 and 2001, it would appear that the refugee camps may generally be considered secure. With this background in mind, the next section of this chapter provides an assessment of the current state of refugee and refugee camp militarization.

TABLE 2.6 Reported incidents in Lainé, Kounkan, Kola and Nonah refugee camps, 1 January–31 August 2004

Camp	Theft	Rape	Fist-fights	Incitement	Extortion	Child abandon-ment	Petty theft	Murder	Narcotics possession	Hunting accidents	Assault causing bodily harm
Lainé	17	3	28	5	0	4	22	0	2	2	0
Kouankan	11	3	3	0	0	1	0	0	0	0	1
Kola	16	5	23	0	3	0	0	0	0	0	0
Nonah	0	1	5	0	0	0	0	0	0	0	0
Total	44	12	59	5	3	5	22	0	2	2	1

Source: BCR/Mixed Brigade headquarters, N'Zérékoré, September 2004

Assessment of refugee and refugee camp militarization

Assessment of refugee camp militarization versus the militarization of the refugee-populated areas During the field visit to Guinea in September and October 2004, every representative interviewed from among the government of Guinea, UN agencies, NGOs, health practitioners, civil society and refugees themselves was asked a common question: 'Do you feel that the presence of small arms or armed elements in the refugee camps in southern Guinea is a cause for concern today?' In all fifty interviews, the answer was 'no'. All the representatives agreed that refugee camp militarization was no longer an issue in Guinea. Discussions with the BCR[59] and security officials[60] did not reveal any incidents related to small arms in any of the refugee camps in the twelve months preceding September 2004. This was supported by health officials in Lainé and Kouankan camps, as well as in Nonah transit camp, where no case of SALW-related injuries has been recorded since the opening of the camps.[61] Members of refugee committees said no small arms were used in reported cases of intimidation, sexual violence or abductions in and around the camps.[62]

There was, however, also consensus that while the refugee camps were free of small arms and armed elements, the Forest Region in which the camps are located is not. It was generally held that this region of southern Guinea, stretching from Kissidougou to N'Zérékoré, and containing all of Guinea's refugee camps, has a problem with SALW stemming from the events of 2000/01. There are also a number of concerns resulting from the remaining Young Volunteers, who have yet to be demobilized. As such, it is important to emphasize that while refugee camp militarization does not appear to be a cause for concern in Guinea, the militarization of the refugee-populated areas – of the towns and villages surrounding refugee camps – is a significant concern.[63]

Informants also drew attention to the prevalence of shotguns outside the camps, citing a recent case where a refugee from Kouankan camp sustained a non-fatal gunshot injury from a local using a shotgun. There is consensus on the part of government officials, UN representatives, humanitarian agencies, civil society and refugees themselves, however, that there is no link between the prolonged presence of refugees in Guinea and the proliferation or use of small arms. This lack of identification of refugees with the small-arms trade in Guinea is also evident in the absence of reported use of small arms in refugee camps.

Refugees in Guinea enjoy significant freedom of movement outside the refugee camps. Many spend considerable time outside the camps pursuing economic activities. At the same time, many Guineans come to the refugee camps to trade. Local hunters often transit through the camps on their way to the forest to hunt. Given this interaction, the distinction between the refugee camp and the local community is generally blurred. These authors consequently believe that the protection of refugees in Guinea cannot be ensured by concentrating on the conditions in the refugee camps without considering the refugee-populated areas. As such, concerns about militarization and small arms, even outside the refugee camps, can have a direct impact on the protection of refugees inside the camps.

Continued presence of armed elements While refugee camps appear to be demilitarized as of late 2004, with armed violence not a significant concern, Guinea's refugee-populated areas remain threatened by the presence of former members of the various armed groups involved in the 1999–2003 fighting. The status of these groups is discussed below.

YOUNG VOLUNTEERS Government officials openly state that Guinea was able to withstand the incursions of 2000/01 because of the masses of Young Volunteers that came forward following President Conté's 9 September 2000 appeal. More recently, however, they accept that the continued presence of the Young Volunteers and the failure of efforts to demobilize them is one of the greatest causes of insecurity in the Forest Region.[64]

The recruitment of Young Volunteers was highly decentralized. Government officials believe that each sub-prefecture recruited a minimum of 150 volunteers.[65] Given that each of Guinea's eleven prefectures comprises ten sub-prefectures, it is likely that a minimum of 16,500 Young Volunteers were recruited and armed. To this estimate, however, should be added the additional recruitment that took place in urban centres along the border and the massive recruitment that took place in Conakry. In N'Zérékoré town alone, for example, 4,500 Young Volunteers were recruited.[66] It is on this basis that estimates of the number of Young Volunteers recruited are as high as 30,000.[67]

Young Volunteers were promised future integration into the Guinean army as a reward for their service.[68] In a country with massive unemployment and few economic opportunities for young people, this was likely a strong motivating factor for volunteering. After March 2001, however, it became clear that not all Young Volunteers could be incorporated into the army, as it could not afford such an increase in its numbers and not all Young Volunteers were fit for regular military service. As an alternative to full military service, the Guinean army formed marching bands – *fanfare* – in N'Zérékoré, Yomou, Lola, Macenta, Guékédou, Kissidougou and Faranah, and filled the ranks of these bands with Young Volunteers, regardless of their musical ability.

A large number of Young Volunteers, however, were never integrated into either the army or the marching bands. A number of them remain in the Forest Region, and are still armed. The recent doubling of the price of rice, the staple food in Guinea, has led some former Young Volunteers to pick up their guns and turn to crime.[69] In the words of one humanitarian worker in Conakry, 'they are suffering, they have a gun, and they are willing to use it'.[70]

Research carried out by the Mano River Union Women's Peace Network (MRUWPN) identified 7,118 former Young Volunteers, many of whom have not been integrated, notwithstanding the army's most recent efforts to disarm them in July 2004.[71] Based on information collected on the 1,728 Young Volunteers who registered at the MRUWPN's N'Zérékoré office in 2004,[72] it appears that 94 per cent (1,630) were male, 53 per cent (990) had been integrated into the army or the *fanfare*, and 7 per cent were under eighteen during the events of 2000 – the youngest being eight.

ULIMO–K AND LURD Since the fall of Taylor in 2003, and despite Liberia's disarmament, demobilization, rehabilitation and reintegration programme, the continued presence of LURD fighters has had a significant impact on security in the Forest Region of Guinea. Given the inactivity of LURD, and the loss of a common objective for its fighters, many LURD fighters have reportedly been drifting back across the border to either benefit from humanitarian assistance or engage in criminal activity (IRIN 2004b).

LURD elements were reportedly involved in the June 2004 outbreak of violence between the Mandingo community of N'Zérékoré and the Toma and Gherze residents of the area, which lasted two days and involved the use of SALW.[73] The commandant of BAC, whose vehicle was hit by machine-gun fire during the incident, believes that LURD gunmen played a role in escalating what was initially a localized inter-group dispute.[74] The prefect of N'Zérékoré reported that more than twenty AK-47s were seized in the aftermath of the violence, but that the markings of the weapons had been tampered with so as to make it impossible to determine their origin.

RUMOURS OF OTHER PRO-TAYLOR/ANTI-CONTÉ GROUPS Rumours abound in the Forest Region about the formation of other armed groups, either pro-Taylor militias or anti-Conté factions. The Integrated Regional Information Network (IRIN) reported in September 2004 that pro-Taylor loyalists were recruiting former combatants in Liberia to travel to Guinea and train in the area around Mount Nimba (IRIN 2004d). The rumours indicate that the ex-combatants are being paid USD200 to join an armed opposition to Conté.

Associated with this opposition is the little-known Movement of the Democratic Forces of Guinea (RFDG), a group reportedly led by army officers involved in a failed 1996 coup attempt against Conté (Szajkowski 2004: 147, 298) and estimated to be 1,800 strong (IISS 2004: 375). RFDG elements reportedly fought beside the RUF and Liberian forces in the attacks on Guinea in 2000/01 (Szajkowski 2004: 298). According to the International Institute for Strategic Studies, the RFDG has now disbanded, but so little is known about the group that this is difficult, if not impossible, to confirm (IISS 2004). Government officials in Conakry, however, make frequent mention of the threat posed by exiled Guinean dissidents, and use this threat as a justification for limiting domestic political participation and protest. It is also possible that the RFDG existed in name only.

According to the International Crisis Group (ICG), the emergence of these factions, coupled with the emergence of the type of inter-communal violence witnessed in N'Zérékoré in June, illustrates the volatility of the Forest Region of southern Guinea.[75] When placed in the sub-regional context of Liberia and Côte d'Ivoire, the scale of this volatility reflects the urgent need for a sub-regional approach to disarmament and demobilization.

Cross-border and internal trade in small arms While there was general agreement that the proliferation of SALW was a significant problem in the Forest Region of Guinea, it was not possible to find any reliable statistics on the scale of the problem. Nevertheless, confidential meetings with senior government officials provided a useful overview of the various sources of illegal small arms in Guinea. Most importantly, every government official interviewed stated that there is no link in his/her mind between the continued presence of refugees in Guinea and the traffic in small arms. This view was repeated by a wide range of humanitarian and civil society representatives. While there is a common perception within the government that refugees played a role in the incursions of 2000/01 – either by providing shelter to the rebels or acting as guides during the attacks – it is now widely held that the problem of small arms in the Forest Region is not linked to the presence of refugees.[76] As reported by one official, '[t]he refugees were the first source of insecurity in Guinea before the incursions in 2000, but now there is no link and other internal sources of insecurity are more significant and more important'.[77]

Rather, the following appear to be the main sources of small arms circulating today in Guinea.

THE LOOTING OF THE CONAKRY ARMOURY In March 2001, six people died and forty-one were wounded when an ammunitions warehouse exploded at the Alpha Yaya camp in Conakry (IRIN 2001). The cause of the explosion was never reported, but it is now generally believed that the armoury was looted shortly after the blast. Arms looted from the armoury have been recovered in seizures throughout Guinea. It is generally believed that some arms, however, have remained within Guinea and are being used by criminal gangs. While this is generally regarded as the most significant source of small arms in Guinea by many officials, no details on the number or types of looted weapons are available.

YOUNG VOLUNTEERS AND RETIRED MILITARY The second-most significant cache of small arms, estimated to account for roughly 5,000 illegally circulating in Guinea, are those that were officially issued by the Guinean military but never returned at the end of service. This includes arms issued to the Young Volunteers and during the 2000/01 attacks. Yet not all Young Volunteers were armed: according to a government report, only 70 per cent of 2,380 volunteers surveyed in Guékédou handled weapons and participated in combat (Republic of Guinea 2001: 6). Several officials also explained that retiring police or army personnel are not always required to return their service weapons upon retirement. These weapons therefore routinely leak to criminal elements.

LOCAL PRODUCTION There is a significant local craft industry for the production of arms, mostly hunting rifles. This is confirmed by the BAC seizure of fifty-two 12-gauge craft shotguns between 2001 and 2003 (Republic of Guinea 2003). Hunting is an important source of income in the Forest Region, and hunting rifles are a regular sight on the main roads. There are no estimates of the scale of annual production in Guinea, and it is generally believed that these weapons are not widely used for criminal purposes.

TRAFFIC FROM LIBERIA AND CÔTE D'IVOIRE THROUGH GUINEA The most significant seizures of small arms in 2004 occurred on the border with Mali. From February to September of that year, small shipments of small arms – typically six to twelve AK-47s – were seized en route to Bamako, the capital of Mali. More prolific, however, was the traffic of weapons from Liberia to Côte d'Ivoire, fuelled by the belief that there was a differentiation between DDR programmes in the two countries. DDR programmes in Liberia offered an initial payment of USD150 for the surrender of a weapon and a further USD150 when the participant reported for reintegration support in his/her home area. The programme in northern Côte d'Ivoire was expected to offer two payments of USD450. This created a traffic of arms and combatants from Liberia to Côte d'Ivoire through southern Guinea (especially N'Zérékoré), as ex-combatants in Liberia were able to collect an additional USD150 for surrendering a weapon without ever having to participate in the reintegration elements of the programme. This traffic had a significant impact on the security environment in N'Zérékoré, as ex-combatants often engage in criminal activity during their journey.

Conclusion

Guinea's refugee population, which totalled 450,000 in the late 1990s, was severely affected by the 2000/01 cross-border attacks and the Liberian civil war. Not only did both sides target refugees during the fighting, but the infiltration of armed groups in the refugee camps caused suspicion and led to further harassment and displacement of refugees.

The full impact of militarization on refugee protection in Guinea, however, can be understood only in the context of broader refugee-populated areas. A large proportion of Guinea's refugee population, if not the majority, do not live in camps, but in nearby villages. Continued small-arms proliferation and the presence of thousands of armed and idle ex-combatants in the Forest Region demonstrate that while refugee camps have been relatively secured, significant concerns remain for the protection of refugees living elsewhere, and for civilians in general. Furthermore, as the boundaries of refugee camps are not enforced, insecurity and small-arms proliferation outside the refugee camps can have a direct impact on refugees inside the camps.

While the responses developed by national and international actors in the camps have achieved meaningful results despite very limited means, significant threats to Guinea's stability require urgent attention. The failure to mobilize sufficient funds to disarm and reintegrate the remaining 7,000 Young Volunteers has the potential to threaten the country's internal security for the years to come, especially given the uncertainty surrounding President Conté's succession. Guinea's stability also remains vulnerable to spillover effects from the conflict in neighbouring Côte d'Ivoire, including regional small-arms trafficking and the movement of armed elements. In this difficult context, increased border control and regional military cooperation stand out as prerequisites for avoiding the suffering of the past.

Notes

1 Some have argued that this stability in Guinea, relative to Sierra Leone and Liberia, masks both the political conflict that was taking place within Guinea through the decade, especially given the 1996 coup attempt in Conakry, and the active role that Guinea is widely regarded as having played in the conflict affecting its southern neighbours; see McGovern (2002).

2 Statistics from the Guinea programme, and refugee population statistics in particular, have been notoriously problematic since the late 1990s; see the discussion of statistics under 'Methodology', p. 53.

3 See Van Damme (1999).

4 Amnesty International states that 'in September 1998, UNHCR reported a RUF attack on Tomandou Camp in which ten people were killed' (Amnesty International 2001: 3).

5 See LCHR (2002: 64).

6 It is also important to note that during the same period, the United Liberation Movement of Liberia for Democracy – Kromah (ULIMO–K; see note 14), under the leadership of Alhaji Kromah, was recruiting from the predominantly Mandingo urban Liberian refugee population in N'Zérékoré and Macenta. Given that this refugee population did not live in UNHCR camps or settlements, this recruitment was largely undocumented. During the 1997 Liberian election campaign, ALCOP, the party formed by Kromah, drew the base of its support from refugees in southern Guinea – based on author's interviews with Liberian refugees in N'Zérékoré, 2001; see also Ellis (1995, 1998) and Reno (1998).

7 See Amnesty International (2001) and HRW (2001, 2002).

8 See References, this chapter.

9 The views expressed in this chapter are, however, his own, and do not necessarily reflect those of UNHCR.

10 For a detailed consideration of the term 'refugee-populated area', see Jacobsen (2000).

11 While ECOWAS treaties provide for the free movement of ECOWAS citizens between member states, especially according to the 1979 Protocol Relating to Free Movement of Persons, Residence and Free Establishment, this right is only for a temporary ninety-day period, after which the stay of the ECOWAS citizen must be regularized according to the nationality and citizenship laws of the individual member state. As of 2004, the spirit of this provision is still loosely applied to remaining Sierra Leonean refugees in Guinea, notwithstanding the length of their stay (meeting with government official, Conakry, 24 September 2004).

12 It is also important to note that many Guineans also fled the regime of Sékou Touré during this period, to escape either the regime's economic policies or its repression of real or perceived opposition. Azarya and Chazan believe that more than 2 million Guineans were living outside their country in the early 1970s, including trained professionals, unskilled and semi-skilled labourers, and political exiles, primarily in states bordering Guinea, but also in France and elsewhere; see Azarya and Chazan (1987: 118–19).

13 Original on file with author.

14 ULIMO was founded in Freetown in 1991 by Liberians who had fled the advance of Charles Taylor. The movement later split into two factions, broadly along ethnic lines. ULIMO–J included mostly Krahns under the leadership of Roosevelt Johnson and was based in Liberia and Côte d'Ivoire. ULIMO–K included mostly Mandingos under the leadership of Alhaji Kromah and was

based in southern Guinea. ULIMO was formally disbanded in 1997 under the terms of the Abuja Accords; see Ellis (1995, 1998) and Reno (1998).

15 See Kamara (2001a: 3).

16 See LCHR (2002: 55–72).

17 A number of raids across the border targeting humanitarian supplies, especially food supplies, were, however, recorded from the early 1990s.

18 Many Guinean officials believe that the refugee population at the time was, in fact, more than 1 million.

19 See FEWER (2000).

20 Details for this section are drawn from Amnesty International (2001), USCR (2001, 2002), LCHR (2002), and interviews with UNHCR and NGO staff in Geneva and Conakry.

21 See LCHR (2002: 74).

22 See HRW (2001, 2002).

23 Interviews with UN personnel, Guinea, August 2001.

24 Interviews with government officials, Conkary, 27 September and 8 October 2004.

25 Seven thousand is the figure used by UNICEF in its planning for demobilization activities for the Young Volunteers; see UNOCHA (2002, 2003a).

26 Interview with government official, Conakry, 27 September 2004.

27 Interview with prefect of N'Zérékoré, N'Zérékoré, 1 October 2004.

28 Interviews with local residents, Conakry, Macenta and N'Zérékoré, 2001, and with refugee committee, Kouankan, October 2004.

29 It is important to note that RUF fighters were more clearly identified as rebels by the Guinean population, while the status of the ULIMO fighters, as rebels or defenders, was much more ambiguous.

30 Interviews with government officials, Conakry, 24 and 27 September 2004.

31 Information gathered by UNOCHA, on file with author.

32 Interview with UNHCR official, Conakry, March 2001.

33 See Amnesty International (2001), USCR (2001, 2002), and HRW (2002).

34 It is important to note that many more refugees, some 75,000, chose not to relocate and remained in the Languette without UNHCR assistance; see USCR (2002: 77).

35 See UNOCHA (2002: 21).

36 This security was notwithstanding a number of events during the relocation, as reported by HRW; see HRW (2002).

37 Based on interviews with refugees remaining in the Languette, July 2001.

38 Refugee Security Volunteers are representatives of the refugee population who reinforce the supervisory capacity of the BMS by patrolling sectors of the refugee camps. They are not armed, but are trained to document incidents and report them to the BMS.

39 Interview with UN officials, Conakry, 23 September 2004.

40 Meetings with refugee committees in Lainé and Kouankan camps, 2 and 4 October 2004.

41 Interview with UN official, Conakry, 7 October 2004.

42 UNSC, October 2000, para. 34.

43 IRIN, 12 February 2001.

44 Another underlying motive for US assistance was to increase Guinea's military capabilities in an effort to contain Charles Taylor's Liberia.

45 Interview with US embassy staff, Conakry, 7 October 2004.

46 Interview with senior government official, Conakry, 8 October 2004.

47 Interview with BAC commandant, N'Zérékoré, 4 October 2004.

48 See HRW (2002: 11–15).

49 See UNSC (2001a: paras 174–8; 2003a: para. 68; 2003b: para. 105), ICG (2002: 11), and HRW (2002: 10; 2003: 18–25).

50 See UNSC (2001a: paras 174–8; 2003a: para. 68; 2003b: para. 105), ICG (2002: 11), and HRW (2002: 10; 2003: 18–25).

51 UNOCHA, *Humanitarian Situation Report: Guinea, March–April 2004*.

52 Meeting with refugee committee, Kouankan camp, Macenta, 4 October 2004.

53 Meeting with camp administrator, Kouankan camp, Macenta, 4 October 2004.

54 Interview with prefect of N'Zérékoré, N'Zérékoré, 1 October 2004.

55 Meeting with urban refugees, Conakry, 27 September and 8 October 2004.

56 Meeting with government official, Conakry, 24 September 2004.

57 Meeting with refugee committee, Lainé camp, 2 October 2004.

58 Meeting with refugee health NGO representatives, N'Zérékoré, 30 September 2004.

59 Meeting with camp administrators, Lainé camp, 2 October 2004, and Kouankan camp, 4 October 2004.

60 Meeting with UN staff, Conakry, 23 September 2004.

61 Meeting with NGO health representatives, N'Zérékoré, 30 September 2004; Kouankan camp, 4 October 2004; and Conakry, 24 September 2004.

62 Meeting with refugee committee, Lainé camp, 2 October 2004, and Kouankan camp, 4 October 2004; and meeting with refugee women's committee, Lainé camp, 2 October 2004.

63 For a useful overview of the prevailing security situation in the Forest Region of southern Guinea, see ICG (2003) and Melly (2003).

64 Interview with government officials in Conakry and N'Zérékoré, 24, 27 and 29 September 2004.

65 Interview with government officials, N'Zérékoré, 29 September 2004.

66 Interview with prefect of N'Zérékoré, 1 October 2004.

67 Interview with government official, Conakry, 27 September 2004.

68 Ibid.

69 The price of a 50kg sack of rice has almost doubled in the past year, from GNF50,000 to GNF90,000. This rapid rise led to rice riots in Conakry in June 2004; see IRIN (2004b).

70 Interview with humanitarian worker, Conakry, 22 September 2004.

71 Meeting with the president of the MRUWPN, Conakry, 24 September 2004.

72 It is important to note that this number represents only 38 per cent of the number of Young Volunteers reported by the prefect of N'Zérékoré.

73 See IRIN (2004a).

74 Interview with commandant of BAC, N'Zérékoré, 4 October 2004.

75 See ICG (2003).

76 As McGovern argues, the linking of refugees to the insecurity also played an important role in diverting attention to domestic political issues within Guinea during this period, especially relating to the trial of opposition leader Alpha Condé; see McGovern (2002).

77 Interview with senior government official, Conakry, 8 October 2004.

References

AFP (Agence France-Presse) (2000) 'Military observers for Guinea–Liberia–SLeone border: ECOWAS', 5 October.

— (2001a) 'S. Leone, Guinea to set up military contact group over bombings', 31 January.

— (2001b) 'Regional peacekeeping force in jeopardy: official', 6 February.

Amnesty International (2001) 'Guinea and Sierra Leone: no place of refuge', London: AI-Index AFR 05/006/2001, 24 October.

Andrews, B. L. (2003) *When is a Refugee not a Refugee? Flexible Social Categories and Host/Refugee Relations in Guinea*, New Issues in Refugee Research Working Paper no. 88, Geneva: UNHCR.

Azarya, V. and N. Chazan (1987) 'Disengagement from the state in Africa: reflections on the experience of Ghana and Guinea', *Comparative Studies in Society and History*, 29(1).

Berman, E. (2002) *French, UK, and US Policies to Support Peacekeeping in Africa: Current Status and Future Prospects*, NUPI Paper no. 622, Oslo: Norwegian Institute of International Affairs.

Berman, E. and K. Sams (2003) 'The peacekeeping potential of African regional organisations', in J. Boulden (ed.), *Dealing with Conflict in Africa: The United Nations and Regional Organisations*, New York: Palgrave Macmillan.

Brabazon, J. (2003) *Liberia, Liberians United for Reconciliation and Democracy (LURD)*, Armed Non-state Actors Project Briefing Paper no. 1, Royal Institute of International Affairs, February.

ECOWAS (Economic Community of West African States) (2001) 'ECOWAS chairman opens meeting of troop-contributing countries to Mano River Union', Press release no. 02/2001, 12 January.

Ellis, S. (1995) 'Liberia 1989–1994: a study of ethnic and spiritual violence', *African Affairs*, 94(375): April.

— (1998) 'Liberia's warlord insurgency', in C. Clapham (ed.), *African Guerrillas*, Oxford: James Currey.

Englebert, P. (2004) 'Guinea: recent history', in *Africa South of the Sahara 2004*, 33rd edn, London: Europa Publications.

FEWER (Forum on Early Warning and Early Response) (2000) 'Guinea–Conakry – causes and responses to possible conflict', Policy brief, 19 September.

Herrmann, R. (2003) *Mid-term Review of a Canadian Security Deployment to the UNHCR Programme in Guinea*, Geneva: UNHCR, Evaluation and Policy Analysis Unit, EPAU/2003/04, October.

HRW (Human Rights Watch) (2001) *Guinea: Refugees Still at Risk: Continuing Refugee Protection Concerns in Guinea*, New York: Human Rights Watch, Africa Division, July.

— (2002) 'Liberian refugees in Guinea: refoulement, militarization of camps and other protection concerns', *Human Rights Watch*, 14(8) (A), November.

— (2003) *Weapons Sanctions, Military Supplies, and Human Suffering: Illegal Arms Flows to Liberia and the June–July 2003 Shelling of Monrovia*, Human Rights Watch Briefing Paper, New York, 3 November.

— (2004) 'Small arms and conflict in West Africa: testimony of Lisa Misol, Human Rights Watch researcher, before the Congressional Human Rights Caucus', New York, 20 May.

ICG (International Crisis Group) (2002) *Liberia: The Key to Ending Regional Instability*, ICG Africa Report no. 43, Freetown/Brussels: ICG, 24 April.

— (2003) *Guinée: Incertitudes autour d'une fin de règne*, ICG Africa Report no. 74, Freetown/Brussels: ICG, 19 December.

IISS (International Institute for Strategic Studies) (2004) *The Military Balance: 2004–2005*, London: Oxford University Press for the International Institute for Strategic Studies.

IRIN (International Regional Information Networks) (2000a) 'Guinea: armed men abduct missionaries, attack garrison', 7 September.

— (2000b) 'IRIN update 800 of events in West Africa', 8 September.

— (2001) 'IRIN update 923 of events in West Africa', 5 March.

— (2003a) 'Liberia: LURD leader Sekou Conneh returns from Guinea', 24 September.

— (2003b) 'Liberia: main rebel group declares end of hostilities in Liberia', 25 September.

— (2004a) 'Guinea: ethnic tensions threaten to explode in southeast', 7 July.

— (2004b) 'Guinea: economic crisis and Liberian gunmen threaten stability', 15 July.

— (2004c) 'Refugees criss-cross a fluid and volatile border', 22 July.

— (2004d) 'Liberia: Taylor loyalists recruit Liberians to fight in Guinea – ex-combatants', 22 September.

Jacobsen, K. (2000) 'A framework for exploring the political and security context of refugee populated areas', *Refugee Survey Quarterly*, 19(1).

Kamara, T. (2001a) *Guinea: Confronting Insecurity in the Midst of Unstable Neighbours*, WRITENET Paper no. 8/2000, UNHCR, February.

— (2001b) *West Africa: Problems and Prospects for Stability in the Mano River States*, WRITENET Paper no. 02/2001, UNHCR, October.

Koudougou, S. and I. N'Diaye (2004) *Programme de formation professionelle des Jeunes Volontaires en Guinée 'Demo': Rapport de fin de formation 2003/2004*, Kissidougou: GTZ-IS/UNICEF/Government of Guinea, April.

LCHR (Lawyers' Committee for Human Rights) (2002) *Refugees, Rebels and the Quest for Justice*, New York: LCHR.

McGovern, M. (2002) 'Conflit régional et rhétorique de la contre-insurgence: Guinéens et réfugiés en septembre 2000', *Politique Africaine*, 88.

Melly, P. (2003) *Guinea: Early Warning Analysis*, WRITENET Paper no. 19/2003, UNHCR, August.

Mogire, E. and R. Muggah (2004) *Considering the Relationship between Small Arms Availability and Refugee and Refugee Camp Militarization in Africa: A Background Paper*, Geneva: Bonn International Center for Conversion (BICC) and Small Arms Survey (SAS).

OGDH (Organisation Guinéenne de Défense des Droits de l'Homme et du Citoyen) (2000) 'Declaration', 090/CD/OGDH, 13 September.

O'Neill, W. (2000) 'Conflict in West Africa: dealing with exclusion and separation', *International Journal of Refugee Law*, 12, special supplementary issue.

Reno, W. (1998) *Warlord Politics and African States*, London: Lynne Rienner.

Republic of Guinea (2001) *Rapport technique: Mission de sensibilisation et d'évaluation des Jeunes Volontaires impliqués dans la gestion des conflits armés*, Conakry: Ministry of Social Affairs, Women and Children, 24 July.

— (2003) *Statistiques des armes saisies par les services de sécurité de 2001 à 2003*, Conakry: Ministry of Security.

Reuters (2001) 'Guinea clashes force aid workers to leave refugees', 15 January.

Szajkowski, B. (ed.) (2004) *Revolutionary and Dissident Movements of the World*, 4th edn, London: John Harper.

UNEP (UN Environment Programme) (2000) *Environmental Impact of Refugees in Guinea: Report to the Secretary-General on the Findings and Recommendations of the Pre-assessment on the Environmental Impact of Refugees in Guinea*, Nairobi: UNEP Regional Office for Africa, March.

UNHCR (UN High Commissioner for Refugees) Emergency and Security Services (ESS) (n.d.) *Refugee Camp Security in Guinea: ESS Mission Report – February 2002*.

— (2001) *Plan des opérations: Guinée*, Geneva: UNHCR.

— (2004) *Plan des opérations: Guinée*, Geneva: UNHCR.

UNOCHA (UN Office for the Coordination of Humanitarian Affairs) (2001) *Consolidated Inter-agency Appeals for West Africa: 2001*, Geneva: UNOCHA.

— (2002) *Guinea: Consolidated Appeals Process*, Geneva: UNOCHA.

— (2003a) *Guinea: Consolidated Appeals Process*, Geneva: UNOCHA.

— (2003b) *Humanitarian Briefing Pack: Guinea*, Geneva: UNOCHA, RCB Africa II, March.

— (2004) *Guinea: Consolidated Appeals Process*, Geneva: UNOCHA.

UNSC (UN Security Council) (2001a) *Report of the Panel of Experts Concerning Liberia*, S/2001/1015, 26 October.

— (2001b) *Report of the Secretary-General on the Issue of Refugees and Internally Displaced Persons Pursuant to Resolution 1346 (2001)*, S/2001/513, 23 May.

— (2003a) *Report of the Panel of Experts Concerning Liberia*, S/2003/498, 24 April.

— (2003b) *Report of the Panel of Experts Concerning Liberia*, S/2003/937, 28 October.

USCR (United States Committee for Refugees) (1999) 'Country report: Guinea', *World Refugee Survey 1999*, Washington, DC: USCR.

— (2000a) 'Killings of humanitarians underscore insecurity for aid workers', *Refugee Reports*, 21(9).

— (2000b) 'Threat of widening war in West Africa: 400,000 refugees in Guinea are vulnerable', Press release, 19 October.

— (2000c) 'Country report: Guinea', *World Refugee Survey 2000*, Washington, DC: USCR.

— (2001) 'Country report: Guinea', *World Refugee Survey 2001*, Washington, DC: USCR.

— (2002) 'Country report: Guinea', *World Refugee Survey 2002*, Washington, DC: USCR.

— (2003) 'Country report: Guinea', *World Refugee Survey 2003*, Washington, DC: USCR.

Van Damme, W. (1999) 'Field reports: how Liberian and Sierra Leonean refugees settled in the forest region of Guinea (1990–96)', *Journal of Refugee Studies*, 12(1).

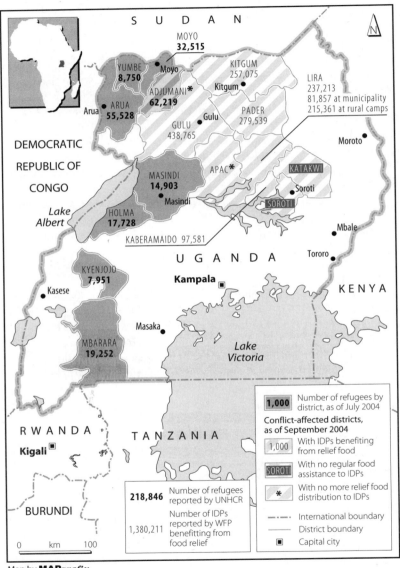

SUDAN

MOYO
32,515

YUMBE
8,750
Moyo

KITGUM
257,075
Kitgum

LIRA
237,213
81,857 at municipality
215,361 at rural camps

ADJUMANI*
62,219

ARUA
55,528
Arua

Gulu

PADER
279,539

GULU
438,765

Moroto

DEMOCRATIC

REPUBLIC OF

CONGO

MASINDI
14,903

APAC*

KATAKWI

Soroti

SOROTI

Masindi

Lake
Albert

HOLMA
17,728

Mbale

KABERAMAIDO 97,581

U G A N D A

Tororo

KYENJOJO
7,951

Kampala ▣

KENYA

Kasese

Masaka

Lake
Victoria

MBARARA
19,252

| **1,000** | Number of refugees by district, as of July 2004 |

Conflict-affected districts, as of September 2004

1,000	With IDPs benefiting from relief food
SOROTI	With no regular food assistance to IDPs
*	With no more relief food distribution to IDPs

R W A N D A

Kigali ▣

T A N Z A N I A

| 218,846 | Number of refugees reported by UNHCR |
| 1,380,211 | Number of IDPs reported by WFP benefitting from food relief |

BURUNDI

0   km   100

— · — · — International boundary
———— District boundary
▣ Capital city

Map by **MAP**grafix

3 | Protection failures: outward and inward militarization of refugee settlements and IDP camps in Uganda

ROBERT MUGGAH

Refugee settlements[1] and camps[2] for internally displaced people (IDPs) in northern Uganda are militarized. Although historically they have served as a base for armed combatants to launch attacks into neighbouring countries – referred to here as 'outward militarization' – the current experience of refugees and IDPs is also one of 'inward militarization', that is the deliberate involvement of displaced populations in their own military defence with the support of the Ugandan People's Defence Force (UPDF) and the policies of the National Revolutionary Movement (NRM) administration. In response to the deteriorating security environment caused by a nineteen-year civil war, the UPDF has supported the consolidation of refugees and IDPs into centralized settlements and camps, increased the deployment of detachments of armed militia and local defence units next to many of these population clusters, and directly drawn the civilian population into the conflict. Its stated objective is to eliminate the base – including civilian support and food production – of its primary opponent, the Lord's Resistance Army (LRA).

Although the present administration, the NRM, has advanced a series of progressive approaches to refugee settlement and camp management – including the promotion of self-reliance strategies – the physical and social security of many refugees and IDPs is perilous. Uganda continues to face a tremendous protection gap.[3] Despite the NRM's recognition that refugees constitute a vector for development, settlements – particularly Sudanese and Congolese refugee settlements in the northern and western districts – are frequently vulnerable to armed violence. IDPs, making up between 60 and 93 per cent of the total population of the northern and eastern districts, are regularly exposed to acute levels of physical and social insecurity. The policy of concentrating population groups in large camps while pursuing formal and informal military solutions to the civil war compromises the safety of IDPs. When set against a backdrop of diminishing resources for military solutions, and the recent surge of Congolese refugees into western Uganda from Ituri in the Democratic Republic of Congo (DRC), alternative strategies for protecting the displaced are urgently required.

This chapter provides a critical review of the phenomena of outward and inward militarization among Uganda's refugee settlements and IDP camps. It draws its definition of 'militarization' from Chapter 1 of this volume, encompassing the deliberate arming, recruitment and deployment of refugees and IDPs across international and municipal-administrative borders. The chapter finds that the effect of refugee militarization is, in many cases, to erode security for refugees and IDPs. In documenting the dynamics of outward and inward militarization, this chapter is designed to present a constructive overview of the current situation and possible entry points to improve protection and reduce the impact of armed violence on displaced populations. 'Protection' here refers to the statutory obligations of the United Nations High Commissioner for Refugees (UNHCR) to ensure that refugees are treated in accordance with the provisions of international refugee conventions (UN 1951; OAU 1967) and are ensured at least temporary asylum; safeguarded from forcible return; and treated according to basic human rights standards (Minear 1999). Protection is also highlighted in the IDP Guiding Principles on Internal Displacement,[4] wherein minimum physical and social guarantees for internally displaced populations are carefully articulated.[5] But unlike for refugees, there is no lead agency mandated to protect IDPs (Bagshaw and Paul 2004; Cohen and Deng 1998).

The chapter is divided into five sections. It begins with a review of the historical evolution of outward and inward militarization of refugees and IDPs in Uganda. The second section turns to a discussion of the pre-conditions of refugee and IDP militarization in the north. The third section considers the effects of militarization, touching on the physical, social, political and humanitarian dimensions. The fourth section reviews a sample of cases of refugee and IDP militarization in Gulu and Adjumani. The final section provides a number of concluding observations and recommendations.

Evolving trends in refugee and IDP militarization

The notion of refugee asylum is based upon the principle that people should be able to leave their own country when they are confronted with serious threats to life and liberty and that they should subsequently enjoy protection and security in the state that has admitted them (Crisp 2002). There is also a widely accepted norm associated with the protection and safeguarding of internally displaced people who are settled in temporary camps until they can be (voluntarily) returned or relocated (Phuong 2005; Muggah 2003). Throughout Africa, these normative safeguards are literally coming under fire.

While levels of armed violence and insecurity are not easy to measure, there is a growing consensus that protracted refugee settlement camps are becoming dangerous places. On the one hand, refugees are known voluntarily and involuntarily to participate in cross-border internal wars, referred to as 'outward militarization'. On the other, refugees and IDPs are increasingly the target of direct military attacks, coercion, intimidation, forced (involuntary) conscription into formal and militia forces, abductions, arbitrary arrest and various forms of internationally and locally motivated punishment, described here as 'inward militarization'. These phenomena together constitute refugee and IDP militarization.[6]

Displacement flows in perspective Uganda has hosted successive waves of refugees and internally displaced people since the early 1940s. The literature on the repeated migrations and displacements experienced across the country's borderlands is extensive (Lomo et al. 2001; Merkx 2002; Woodward 1991). Very generally, early refugee movements can be traced to the Second World War, when Uganda provided asylum to European refugees, and to the mid-1950s, when it provided asylum to Anglo-Egyptians. Following the independence struggles under way in Kenya and Sudan, Rwanda's first civil war in 1959 and the assassination in 1961 of Patrice Lumumba, the prime minister of then Zaire, hundreds of thousands of refugees made their way into Uganda.[7] Uganda has also been a country of expulsion since the 1970s: under the Amin and Obote regimes, Ugandan refugees fled to Sudan, Kenya, Tanzania and farther afield (Gersoney 1997; Pirouet 1988; Crisp and Ayling 1984). The costs of the civil war to oust Obote were particularly severe: more than 7 per cent of the country's population was internally displaced by 1985.[8] What is more, the successive conflicts in Uganda since the 1970s have retained a strong ethnic dimension.[9]

Although the country's alleged hospitable tendencies have recently been challenged by some academic critics,[10] policies towards refugee settlement are widely regarded as progressive by regional standards. For example, the Office of the Prime Minister (OPM), together with the UNHCR, has advanced a cluster of approaches combining long-term integration and settlement with the promotion of self-reliance since the mid-1990s (UNHCR 2004). The Ugandan cabinet has also approved a series of provisions for the care and maintenance of IDP camps. In late 2005, the OPM announced its intention to undertake a 'profiling' of northern refugee and IDP situations, with outputs expected in 2006 (East African 2005). On paper, the current policy environment appears to be remarkably positive relative to other comparator countries in the region. The extent to which the government's rhetorical commitments have actually been met, however, is open to serious criticism (IDP Database 2005; Kaiser 2000a).

	refugees (06/04)	IDPs (07/04)	Trend
	,375 (Su)	... 53,479	+
	421 (Su, *Imvempi*)	...	+
	26,414 (Su, DRC, Br, *Rhino*)		+/−
	7,249 (Su, *Madi Okollo*)		+
	8,689 (Su, *Ikafe*)		+
Gulu	...	438,000	−
Hoima	17,600 (Su, DRC, Ky, Br, *Kyangwali*)	...	+/−
Kabaermaido	...	97,561	−
Kaboraole	7,951 (DRC, *Kyaka II*)	...	+
Katakwi	...	144,945	+/−
Kitgum	...	267,078	−
Lira	...	291,762	+/−
Masindi	14,807 (Su, *Kiryandongo*)	...	+
Mbarara	14,307 (DRC, Rw, others, *Nakivale*)		
	3,948 (Rw, *Oruchinga*)	...	+
Pader	...	279,589	+/−
Soroti	...	71,462	−
Total	216,821 (19)	1,643,876 (146)	

Note: The figures do not include night commuters or drought-affected populations. They include refugees of concern to UNHCR and OCHA only, and exclude spontaneously settled refugees or IDPs. Under 'Total', the numbers of camps and settlements are given in parentheses.

* The symbol + indicates that arrivals are increasing, +/− that the situation is more or less stable, and − that current numbers are decreasing.

Key: Su (Sudanese), DRC (Democratic Republic of Congo), Br (Burundian), Ky (Kenyan), Rw (Rwandese)

Sources: OCHA, UNHCR and NGOs

The refugee decades: 1970–90 Owing in large part to the persistent instability of its neighbours – Sudan, DRC, Rwanda and Kenya – the country has experienced intense and repeated waves of outward militarization by refugees since the 1970s and 1980s. Refugees who have been involved in a combination of cross-border conflicts, training, recruitment, political mobilization and the use of small arms and light weapons have included Rwandans, returning Ugandans, Sudanese and, more recently, Congolese (Merkx 2002; Loescher 1993). By 1995, Uganda was hosting more than 300,000 refugees, with approximately five hundred arriving every day in northern Uganda as a result of the ongoing civil war in Sudan.[11] During the late 1990s and even as recently as 2005, Sudanese, Rwandese and Congolese refugees have been involved in a range of ostensibly military activities while residing on Ugandan soil.

The UNHCR, together with the OPM, has introduced a range of interventions to reduce militarization. For example, during the late 1980s and 1990s the UNHCR made an effort to distinguish Sudanese People's Liberation Army (SPLA) combatants from genuine refugees. In addition to the establishment of screening mechanisms, the government has established a number of 'reintegration centres' for former abductees and ex-combatants in Gulu.[12] Its latest application for a four-year security package in February 2004, valued at an estimated USD23 million, seeks to reinforce UPDF and police installations in refugee-affected districts only. Although the application was officially rejected in March 2004, UNHCR may be inclined to support some policing components under the self-reliance strategy (SRS). UNHCR representatives are of the opinion that the lack of a permanent police presence in settlements is strongly correlated with diminished law and order, and that these trends must be reversed (Gupta 2004).

By mid-2004 UNHCR had registered more than 216,821 refugees. Supported by the government, many were relocated to integrated settlements in Uganda's frontier districts of Adjumani, Moyo, Arua, Hoima, Massindi, Kabarale and Mbarara. In response to both the intolerable conditions in such settlements and the various pull factors elsewhere, significant numbers of refugees moved spontaneously to various urban and peri-urban centres[13] scattered throughout the country (see map).[14] The majority are Sudanese, many of them fleeing the activities of the Ugandan LRA, which is active along the border with Sudan and the DRC. Although individuals from DRC regularly crossed the border into Uganda during the late 1990s, between 2003 and 2004 there was a massive influx of over 10,000 Congolese into the western districts of Nebbi, Bundbuyo and Kasese (see map). The majority have spontaneously settled and refused to be relocated to settlements. As such, they have not been accorded refugee status. Individual refugee settlers, while benefiting from integrated services with host communities and to some extent contributing to the local economy, are nevertheless positioned in extremely volatile regions next to international and district borders.[15]

The recent policy of positioning military detachments in close proximity to settlements is double-edged. As subsequent sections make clear, while the current strategy of inward militarization potentially offers a limited degree of increased physical protection, a number of settlements continue to suffer from repeated attacks involving killings and abductions. In the northern district of Adjumani, for example, a number of these settlements have recently been relocated owing to ongoing armed conflicts between the UPDF and elements of the LRA.

The choice of physical location for refugee settlements and IDP camps has been subjected to intense criticism. Human rights activists have repeatedly accused the UPDF of using refugee settlements as buffers against international and domestic armed insurgents, though this remains an intensely controversial debate.[16] To many, it appears that the Ugandan government purposively locates settlements in strategic locales – and that the long-standing anti-Acholi bias (against both refugee and IDP populations in the north) looms large.[17] With the exception of the quiet recruitment of Sudanese by the SPLA in Adjumani and Moyo,[18] rumours of forced recruitment of Congolese refugees in the west by active insurgents in DRC,[19] and the scattered remains of Rwandan refugees from the early NRM era,[20] the current case load does not appear to be significantly outwardly militarized.[21] Even so, Sudanese refugees are subject to repeated and deliberate attacks and forced recruitment drives by both the LRA and, to a lesser extent, the SPLA.

The emergence of internal displacement: from the 1990s Although internal displacement had been commonplace under Obote and Amin (1964–85), Uganda entered into a new phase of displacement following the successive civil wars waged between the NRM and the erstwhile West Nile Bank Front (Gorogoro),[22] National Revolutionary Force (NRF II),[23] Allied Democratic Front (ADF)[24] and the LRA (Tongtong)[25] respectively (Weeks 2002; Kasozi 1998). The scale of internal displacement rose precipitously and the militarization of IDPs quickly followed. By 1996, more than 500,000 people were internally displaced in the north and north-west.[26] Tactics introduced by both the UPDF and the LRA propelled the levels of internal displacement above the 1 million mark by 2000. Despite positioning three UPDF divisions into the northern region, the LRA, with up to 75 per cent of its members estimated to be under the age of eighteen and likely fewer than 1,500 strong, contributed to the repeated displacement of refugees and IDPs alike.[27] Armed clashes between UPDF auxiliaries and LRA combatants contributed to a rapid escalation of civilian casualties.[28]

By 2004, the country was registering one of the highest rates of internal displacement in the world. As of August 2004, an estimated 1.6 to 2 million internally displaced people were in the country, located primarily in the north and eastern districts of Arua, Adjumani, Apac, Gulu, Kitgum,[29] Lira, Pader, Kabermaido, Katakwi and Soroti, and scattered throughout cities (see map). These internally displaced people are concentrated in more than 118 gazetted (government-sanctioned) and twenty-eight ungazetted (informal) camps. The socio-economic and health status of these populations – particularly the children – is poor by virtually any standard.[30] In the capital of Gulu, for example, the population swelled from 30,000 in the mid-1980s to well over 100,000 in 2003. Gulu town and areas of Kitgum and Pader also experience the notorious phenomenon of night commuters: tens of thousands of families that migrate nocturnally into temporary settlements subsidized by district authorities and international humanitarian agencies, before returning to their villages and camps in the morning. Some 40,000 were reported in Kitgum and Gulu alone in July 2004.[31]

Military responses to refugee and IDP militarization The Ugandan government has introduced a range of 'hard' interventions to address the real and perceived threats presented by the LRA and the Karamoja. Hard options include the recent deployment of three UPDF fronts in northern districts: the 3rd Division in Soroti, the 4th Division in Gulu and the 5th Division in Pader, Kitgum and Lira.[32] It has also increased the number of active paramilitaries operating in the region. The UPDF has bolstered its presence in settlements and camps themselves and claims to have doubled its numbers along the Sudanese border in order to cut off LRA camps in Juba (Sudan) from their operations in Uganda. This recent deployment, along with the introduction of the expanded amnesty in 2000, is regarded as instrumental in the apparent weakening of the LRA, now perceived to have fewer than 400–500 hard-core members, although as many as 1,500 overall (see Table 3.2). But, numbering as it does at least 42,000 in the north, it remains something of a mystery as to why the UPDF and its auxiliaries are unable to defeat militarily their comparatively small opponent.[33]

A key feature of the inward militarization of refugee settlements and IDP camps is the creation and deployment of home guards, civilian militia and local defence units (LDUs) in and around them. Although the lines between the three are porous,[34] it is generally conceded that they each fall under the purview of the Ministry for Security, even if they are managed directly by the UPDF. In response to diminishing resources and deteriorating security, and at the urging of local leaders in camps, the government has pursued a policy of arming civilians, including displaced populations. In some cases, displaced civilians are involuntarily implicated in the defence of their own communities – although the majority see little choice in the face of insecurity. With the rise of the LRA in the mid-1990s and the continued threats posed by Karamoja raiders, the UPDF trained and armed a range of civilian militia groups. Among them are the Arrow Boys[35] (estimated totel 3,000) in Teso/Soroti, the Amuka (6,000–7,000) in Lango sub-region and the Border Frontier Group (3,000) in Kitgum, among others, to allow

Box 3.1 Small arms in Uganda

Bordering five countries, Uganda is at the geographic axis of the Great Lakes and the Horn of Africa, and, as such, is a transit country par excellence. It enjoys an open corridor agreement with DRC, has various bilateral arrangements with Sudan to facilitate hot pursuits by the UPDF, and is a member of the East African Community (EAC) to facilitate shipping and transport and other multilateral mechanisms. As a result of the instability to its north and west, coupled with the complex network of political associations between state and non-state actors, it is also exposed to considerable and unregulated flows of high-powered small arms and light weapons across its frontiers (UNSC 2004). It is no surprise, then, that the Ugandan government has recently played a prominent role in regional efforts to control the illegal flow of weapons, such as the politically binding Nairobi Declaration on the Problem of Small Arms.[36]

Owing to the instability plaguing the country's neighbours and its porous borders, international flows are common. Related, the SPLA was reported to have received considerable shipments of military equipment from the NRM, just as the LRA was regularly supplied by Khartoum's National Islamic Front (NIF) and Sudanese Internal Security Services. Although agreements (in 1999, 2002 and 2004) between the two countries have sought to reduce this support, it is nevertheless known to continue. Various types of weapons including AK-47s, APM, RPG-7 and RPG-2 launchers, G2 and G3 machine guns, SMG rounds, 60mm mortars, rocket-propelled grenade (RPG) ordnance and hand grenades have been recovered from the LRA (UPDF 2004).

As in most countries, the availability of small arms is also domestically controlled and driven. Although Uganda introduced a Firearms Act in 1970, other regulatory mechanisms also exist: the National Resistance Army Statute (1992), the Police Statute (1994), the Control of Private Security Organizations Regulations (1997) and the Amnesty Act (2000).[37] Normatively, these various legislative mechanisms suffer from flaws in definition, seriously undermining the enacting of regional and international agreements (Flew and Urquhart 2004: 10–11). What is more, they do not appear to be effectively regulating domestic supplies. As early as 1979, following the ousting of Amin, and again in 1985 in the period before Museveni's NRM came to power, a considerable number of arms were looted and diverted from UPDF armouries in the West Nile and Gulu districts. An estimated 60,000 small arms were abandoned by soldiers fleeing Moroto army barracks during the ousting of Amin (Muhereza 1997). Following the overthrow of the Obote government in 1985, the Acholi-dominated UNLA also distributed weapons to Karamoja to fight the advancing NRA. After the capture of Kampala by the NRA (1986), guerrilla war persisted and a new wave of cattle rustling in Karamojang ensued. Despite the gradual increase in legislative penalties, the introduction of buy-back schemes and police-led interventions, the availability of high-powered small arms remains a dangerous threat (Pax Christi 2004).

As in other countries in East Africa, the domestic demand for and supply of weapons to combatants and civilians is driven by a variety of motivations and means (Brauer and Muggah 2006). The state-run ammunition factory at Nakasongola in central Uganda, for example, has recently gone commercial, selling small arms to private companies as well as exporting bullets to neighbouring states. The factory, trading under Luwero Industries Limited, a subsidiary of the National Enterprises Corporation (NEC), has been fabricating armoured cars, which are sold to the Ministry of Defence. At the same time, weapons are leaked into civilian circulation owing to the corrupt and poor storage and maintenance procedures of the UPDF, police, militia and LDU forces. In addition to the recycling of weapons following disarmament, demobilization and reintegration (DDR) and amnesty-related interventions, small-scale trade and leasing arrangements with criminal elements are well known. Owing to the lack of accountability in stockpile management, the relative price of weapons (or likelihood of paying a penalty) is low. Because the deliberate arming and rearming of militia factions and local defence units continues unabated, the real price of weapons also remains low. As has been argued by Brauer and Muggah (2006), demand is also conditioned by strong social and cultural preferences for arms – for dowry, status and defence – particularly among the people of the north and east.

Although the police in Adjumani and Gulu claim that cases of domestic arms smuggling are extremely rare, they also admit that they have severely constrained capacities to monitor, much less enforce, any interventions. The representative of the OPM also admitted that trade and arms smuggling by the SPLA along the Sudan–Uganda border was a real possibility and could not be ruled out. Visits to the Sudanese border and to police stations around the country by the author confirm this. For example, according to representatives of the Gulu police force, numbering some 162 members, the entire department draws on a single vehicle to carry out activities throughout the district. In Adjumani, police presence is equally limited and its capacity to protect civilians is dismissed by most. Moreover, there appears to be little communication or coordination between various district bureaus owing to limited telecommunication, institutional or logistical capacities.

communities themselves to defend their households and livelihoods (see Box 3.1 and Table 3.2).[38]

The establishment of local militia has rapidly escalated levels of inward militarization. LDUs and similar bodies such as the Joint Command Combatant (JCC) forces were set up in Gulu and Adjumani in 1997 and are now operating alongside the UPDF in virtually every refugee settlement and IDP camp. Provided with two to three months of training, living in sub-standard conditions and theoretically deployed exclusively at the sub-county level, they are supervised by the UPDF. Some are eventually integrated directly into the army. Many are known to desert with their weapons (Gomes and Mkutu 2004). The continued policy of redeploying poorly trained militia and LDU to other parts of the country against the wishes of host and IDP communities has been the source of much controversy, particularly in Acholi-dominated areas.[39] What is more, the discrepancy in pay between LDUs and UPDF for what amounts to the same post is also generating tension.[40] Most alarming, militia groups are designated in large part according to ethnic affiliation, suggesting a looming problem if not contained. Given the ethnic antagonisms between militias and the limited control by the government over the LDUs, all-out civil war is a very real possibility if the situation is left unchecked.

The Ugandan government has also increased its cross-border efforts to contain the LRA and reduce arms availability. Operations Iron Fist I (March 2002) and II (March 2004) sought to pursue LRA combatants both in Uganda and across the border in Bilinyiang, Sudan. A bilateral protocol signed between the Ugandan and Sudanese governments in March 2002 allowed for UPDF hot pursuit of LRA combatants below a red line (that is, the Torit–Nisitu–Juba road) on Sudanese territory. A new agreement between the two governments signed in March 2004 allowed the UPDF open access to the entire country.[41] A host of other low-key police-led interventions also sought to crack down on illegal weapons ownership and misuse through buy-back and coercive collection initiatives.[42] Small-scale arms markets in the Karamoja-dominated regions have also been targeted.

	Estimated strength	Multiplier**	Estimated holdings
UPDF Division 3	14,000[a]	2.25	31,500
UPDF Division 4	14,000[a]	2.25	31,500
UPDF Division 5	14,000[a]	2.25	31,500
105 Battalion	350[b]	2.25	790
Paramilitaries and auxiliaries	1,800+/−[c]	1.6	2,900
Arrow Boys	3,000	0.7	2,100
Amuka	6,000	0.7	4,200
Border Frontier Group	3,000	0.7	2,100
Local Defence Units (LDU)	15,000[d]	0.7	10,500
National police	10,000[e]	1.2	12,000
LRA	1,500	1.6	2,400
WNBF/NRM II	...	...	
ADF	100	1.6	160
Karamoja tribal fighters	20,000[f]	1.2	12,000
Criminal armed groups	...	...	Unknown
Civilian possession	...	...	Unknown
Total state	42,350		95,290
Total para-state	28,800		21,800
Total non-state	1,600 (+Karamoja)		2,560 (14,560)
Total known holdings	72,750		150,000+/−

*Northern Uganda here includes Kitgum, Pader, Gulu, Adjumani, Moyo, Nebbi, Masindi, Lira, Kotido and Katakwi **Multipliers are derived from Small Arms Survey (2003) and key informant interviews in Uganda

[a] Divisions have between three and five brigades, with a conservative average of 14,000 soldiers each   [b] Battalions traditionally have approximately 700 soldiers, but the number above is based on UPDF figures   [c] Paramilitaries and auxiliaries are divided into the Internal Security Organization, Border Defence Units, Police Air Wings and Marines (IISS 2004; key informant interviews 2004)   [d] National LDU estimate provided in IISS (2004), but it can be assumed that the numbers are unreliable   [e] The total size of the national police force was estimated to be 20,000 in 1991. It is believed that the vast majority are located in Kampala itself, so this is likely a gross overestimate   [f] According to the UPDF, some 10,686 weapons had been collected by end-2003 and these are subtracted from the total. It is not known whether the collected weapons were destroyed, though it can be assumed that many have been recycled into the UPDF, its auxiliaries or the national police.

Sources: UPDF documents/interviews, IISS (2004), Small Arms Survey (2003), and Monitor and New Vision archives.

Penalties associated with illegal arms possession, though outdated, are extremely severe.[43]

The increasingly virulent cattle raids launched by the Karamoja Graal rustlers, particularly during the dry season, remain a major concern in the eastern districts of Kotido, Moroto and Kapchowa, as well as in neighbouring Sudan and Kenya.[44] Complicating the matter are the heavily armed tribes in neighbouring Kenya (for example, Turkana and Pokot) and Sudan (for example, Dinka). Recognizing that any sustainable disarmament of the Karamoja would require complementary interventions with competing tribes, the Ugandan and Kenyan governments together launched a large-scale disarmament programme on both sides of the border. Following the enactment of a Disarmament Act by the Ugandan parliament in December 2000, the disarmament programme of the Karamoja comprised a twofold strategy: (a) first to voluntarily disarm Karamoja fighters between December 2001 and January 2002; and (b) to pursue forceful disarmament from February 2002 onwards.

The outcomes of the disarmament programme have been mixed. The UPDF claims that some 7,309 weapons were voluntarily surrendered in exchange for iron sheeting and ox ploughs, and some 2,100 forcefully or coercively collected. Although violent clashes are known to have ensued during the second phase of the operation and the UPDF ultimately pulled out with the beginning of Iron Fist II in March, some 10,686 weapons of varying quality were reportedly collected.[45] By October 2005, some 3,000 of these were reportedly destroyed in a public ceremony. The actual success of these initiatives in terms of mitigating armed violence and displacement, however, is unknown. Given the considerable secrecy associated with UPDF operations and activities, this will likely remain the case. Nevertheless, the widely reported massacres taking place in eastern Uganda and northern Kenya in mid-2005 indicate that the disarmament programmes have not had their desired effect.[46]

Though widely regarded as an economic success story, Uganda remains heavily dependent on overseas development assistance to supplement its national budget.[47] Despite the deterioration in security arising from the ongoing conflicts affecting its northern and western neighbours, its own brutal nineteen-year civil war with the LRA and the recurring attacks by Karamoja tribal raiders during the dry season, donors are not prepared to allow the government to spend more than 2 per cent of the country's GDP on national defence.[48] Unwilling to commit more resources to a military solution, donors have instead called for drastic reductions in defence spending. For example, a DDR initiative was launched in 2002 to reduce the armed forces by some 40–50 per cent, from an estimated 100,000 soldiers to approximately 60,000.[49] The Ugandan government has responded by increasing its militia presence. Though this is officially denied, the UPDF is alleged to have recently created a new Battalion 105 composed exclusively of former LRA combatants, though little is actually known about its function, and grievances between UPDF and ex-LRA members allowed to retain their official rank are notorious.[50] Although the size of the UPDF has no doubt been considerably reduced, absolute numbers cannot be verified owing to the data ban on all army records since the mid-1980s.

Soft options instead? In addition to the 'hard' tactics discussed above, the Ugandan government has introduced 'soft' interventions in order to strengthen its capacity to pursue the LRA and to protect civilians from repeated displacement and persistent violence. Soft options include the introduction of legislation, such as amnesties. Two national amnesties – one in 1987 and the other in 2000 – offer blanket immunity and freedom from criminal prosecution to low- and senior-level LRA combatants who surrender their arms. Indeed, the latest amnesty appears to have been partially successful: a recent statement by the chairman of the Amnesty Commission claims that some 13,231 combatants from the erstwhile PDA, NRF, WNBF, UNRF I /II and the LRA have been demobilized through the Commission since 1987 (Onega 2004).[51] The UPDF records several hundred combatants availing themselves of the amnesty each month.[52] Encouragingly, by early 2004 more than 1,917 LRA combatants had either taken advantage of the 2000 amnesty or had been captured, though the status of their weapons is unknown.[53] Even so, considerable shortcomings of the amnesties, including their manipulation for political purposes, have been recorded (Hovil and Lomo 2005).

Non-military approaches to improving protection also involve the disarmament and demobilization of child soldiers. Together with the Gulu Support for Child Organization (GUSCO), a locally based NGO, the UPDF has also been responsible for ensuring that rescued and deserting LRA child combatants are processed through recently established Child Protection Units (CPUs) and resettled to their communities or with relatives.[54] More than 7,000 children have been provided with personal counselling and support, the majority of them male ex-combatants. Since the renewal of the amnesty in 2000 and the launch of the UPDF's Iron Fist II, desertion and processing rates at GUSCO are alleged to have increased markedly.[55]

Another soft intervention is the introduction of the Dwog Paco, or Come Home, initiative. Launched by the Ministry of Security, and the Internal Security Organization (ISO), the intervention began in 2004 as a complement to the 2000 amnesty. It aims to attract otherwise undecided

LRA combatants to join the amnesty through programmes aired on the country's national radio station, Mega FM. Meanwhile, in order to limit the movement of unregulated small arms from DRC and Sudan, the UPDF has begun to ratchet up monitoring, surveillance and interdiction along the eastern border with DRC.[56] The police, despite limited collaboration with the UPDF, have been called back to urban centres across the country. In Gulu, as elsewhere, they are unable to police IDP camps, much less refugee settlements, and admit that most areas have not been covered since 1995.[57]

Pre-conditions for refugee and IDP militarization

The current manifestation of refugee and IDP militarization in Uganda can to some extent be attributed to political and ethnic tensions emerging in the mid-1980s (Merkx 2002; Kasozi 1998). The crisis of governance and accountability at both the centre and the periphery of Ugandan society has to some extent created the conditions for structural violence and repressive approaches to containing non-state actors in the north and east. The emergence of the LRA, as with the WNBF, NRF II and PDA, is part and parcel of long-term and sustained grievances between marginalized ethnic factions and of repressive zero-sum rule. As such, militarization should be conceived of within a historical context. In considering pre-conditions for refugee and IDP militarization, it is nevertheless possible to distil several contiguous interconnected factors: the presence of an insurgency within the hosting country; the presence of international interests in the outcomes of said insurgency; the involvement of civilians in civil defence; and the specific policies of governments towards refugee and IDP settlement.

Repeated attacks and raids launched by LRA combatants on both refugee and IDP settlements have contributed to a sustained environment of insecurity in many parts the country (OCHA 2004a, 2004b, 2004c). Among international humanitarian agencies, the UPDF and civilians alike, there is widespread paranoia about the LRA.[58] The UPDF, for its part, has pursued a policy of clearing large swaths of land to pursue its war against the LRA. It has adopted a range of extraordinary privileges and tactics to clear populated areas – thus generating settlements and camps – to achieve its aims. Thus, well over half of the entire population of the northern region is internally displaced at any given moment and temporarily settled in either camps or nocturnal shelters. Refugee settlements have been forcibly relocated and many Sudanese refugees are reported to have returned to Sudan involuntarily.

International and regional interest in the civil war is not necessarily benign, much less altruistically motivated. The Sudanese government has consistently advocated a policy of military and logistical support for the LRA in retaliation for the NRM assistance provided to the SPLA. Despite agreements between the two governments and UNSC resolutions (1375 and 1377 in 2001) and the current peace agreement between the Sudanese government and the SPLA/SPLM, the relative lawlessness of southern Sudan and northern Uganda, coupled with the common ethnic ties between the two regions, has cultivated an environment where arms can flow undeterred – especially to LRA combatants.

The LRA has also been known to launch attacks on isolated populations of refugees in retaliation for what it claims to be the Ugandan government's explicit and tacit support to the SPLA and Sudan.[59] As with its ongoing attacks on IDP communities in Gulu, Kitgum, Pader, Lira and Soroti, it is more likely that its recurring attacks against refugees are to replenish their depleting ranks of porters, sex-slaves and child soldiers as well as food.[60] What is more, collusion between military and business interests in the Ituri region of DRC and along the western border of Uganda has also contributed to arms transfers across Lake Albert and Lake Edward, and between Arua and Fort Portal (UNSC 2004). Owing to the cross-border and informal nature of these economic relations, a variety of interests are keen to ensure that armed violence continues in the region.

In theory, the UPDF has taken charge of ensuring the protection of displaced populations throughout the territory. Even so, UPDF troops, despite their considerable numbers deployed in northern Uganda – estimated to be some 42,000 – are still unable to defeat the LRA militarily.[61] Moreover, the asymmetries between district-level police forces and the LRA (such as in equipment and capacities) have led to the former's complete withdrawal from all rural areas of the region. As previously noted, the UPDF has taken the war to the LRA by proxy: by arming civilians – especially IDPs – to ensure the protection of their own camps and environs. As the individual case studies in the subsequent sections make clear, the UPDF used to deploy detachments as well as LDUs either within or in close proximity to both settlements and camps, pursuing a strategy of inward militarization. As a result, the LRA and UPDF have killed a significant number of refugees and IDPs (particularly those serving as LDUs) during armed clashes.[62] In response to the outcry from displaced populations, military units are now generally located beside settlements and camps, though killings neverthe-less continue (see Tables 3.3 and 3.4).

The UPDF's strategy of protecting displaced people relies to a large extent on relocating them into settlements and camps. Settlements and camps were initially set up as temporary measures, although most have been in existence for between one and two decades. But these same UPDF-led tactics are responsible for ratcheting up the insecurity of the very population they seek to defend. Very generally, the UPDF follows a two-pronged approach: first, to achieve military dominance by reducing food availability to the LRA; and second, to promote self-sufficiency among displaced populations. The strategy is paradoxical. On the one hand, military advantage is achieved through increased deployments, hot pursuits into Sudan and draining the proverbial sea (of food and civilians). The result has been the creation of highly compact, dependency-prone and immobile population clusters.[63] On the other hand, the pursuit of nominally progressive policies – integrated service delivery for refugees in existing national structures, the introduction of a national policy on IDPs, the promotion of self-reliance, and the location of settlements relatively far from international borders – has had unintended (and mostly negative) effects.

Government-initiated policies designed to protect refugees and IDPs have in fact increased the risk of inward militarization and insecurity. The containment of refugees and IDPs in settlements and camps, ostensibly for their own protection, has in fact invited LRA and Karamoja attacks and forced recruitment. As noted by Moro (2002: 1), the escalation of rebel assaults on refugees confined to camps in insecure parts of the country draws attention to the dangers posed to refugees by rebel groups and armed gangs.[64] The continued support to the region from a vast number of humanitarian and development agencies, while essential in preventing widespread malnutrition and destitution, also contributes to fuelling a nominal war economy.[65] Indeed, it is well known that the LRA usually attacks when food distribution is occurring or during harvest periods.

Effects of militarized refugee settlements and IDP camps

Militarized settlements and camps frustrate the mandates and operations of UNHCR, OCHA and other humanitarian and development agencies. Regardless of the bureaucratic and institutional responsibilities for refugees and IDPs or legal frameworks for protection and assistance, the most obvious outcome is physical and perceived insecurity. As the cases of Adjumani and Gulu make clear, refugees and IDPs are at an elevated risk of intentional fatal and non-fatal gunshot injury. Closely related to this is the deterioration of social security – violations of second- and third-generation human rights – for refugees and IDPs. Another critical impact relates to threats to asylum and a growing negative public perception of this critically vulnerable group – although this arguably applies more to refugees than to IDPs.[66] As a result, protection itself is potentially compromised as the rights of (existing and future) refugees and internally displaced populations to asylum and protection are diminished. Humanitarian access to both displaced populations and host communities is similarly impeded by the militarization of settlements and camps.[67]

Armed violence is a pervasive feature of militarized refugee settlements and IDP camps. The most obvious indicators of physical violence involving small arms include rates of deaths and injuries, coercion, intimidation, sexual violence and criminality. One useful approach to measuring the extent to which small-arms availability compromises the physical protection of internally displaced and refugee populations is to retrospectively assess fatal and non-fatal firearm injury rates. Indeed, the overwhelming majority of reported intentional injuries associated with armed conflict in northern and eastern Uganda appear to be a consequence of firearms. Moreover, given the sheer number of people displaced in these regions, it is perhaps unsurprising that the majority of patients in the central referral hospital are themselves displaced.[68] A comparison of injury rates (fatal and non-fatal) in four hospitals throughout Uganda is shown on the map.

Virtually all of Gulu District's population is internally displaced – some 93 per cent in 2004 according to OCHA. According to a number of surgeons working in Gulu District referral hospital, itself covering a catchment that includes all of northern Uganda, between 6 and 7 per cent of all trauma-related admissions are gunshot-related (see Tables 3.3 and 3.4; Appendix II). This persistence of these trends is echoed in other public health reports (see Accorsi et al. 2003). While landmine injuries appear to have declined since 2000,[69] small-arms-related wounds remain disturbingly common.[70] Accorsi et al. (2003) have observed that: ' ... the number of admissions related to trauma (war-related injuries) shows an upward trend over time, with a sharp increase in 1997 (with 744 cases) related to the escalation of the civil conflict ... [and] a new increase in 2002'. Given the difficulties associated with access and under-reporting, however, the tables below likely underestimate the prevalence of the problem.

Threats to the physical security of refugees in Uganda, while not as acute as for IDPs, are nevertheless severe. Although aggregated public health data on injury trends are currently unavailable, an archival review of UNHCR and OPM security incidence surveillance reports between 2002 and 2004[71] reveals a number of alarming trends. For example, on the assumption of an average denominator of 61,000 refugees in Adjumani over the three years, firearm homicide rates among the Sudanese ranged from 23 per 100,000 in 2002 to 44 per 100,000 during the first five months of 2004 (see Table 3.5; Appendix III).[72] The doubling of already disastrously high rates – equal to those of Colombia and Brazil – in less than two years is a cause of considerable concern.[73] A cursory review of security incidence

105

TABLE 3.3 Cause of injury: Gulu 2000 (*n* = 602)

Cause	Frequency	Percentage	Cumulative percentage
Traffic	191	34.4	34.4
Fall	124	22.3	56.7
Burns	102	18.4	75.1
Gunshot	36	6.5	81.6
Stab	31	5.6	87.2
Blunt injury	40	7.2	94.4
Poisoning	4	0.7	95.1
Animal bite	5	1	96.1
Other	22	3.9	100
Total	555	100	

TABLE 3.4 Cause of injury: Gulu 2001 (*n* = 1,145)

Cause	Frequency	Percentage	Cumulative percentage
Traffic	476	41.6	41.6
Fall	277	24.2	65.8
Burns	38	3.3	69.1
Gunshot	76	6.6	75.7
Stab	95	8.3	84
Blunt injury	118	10.3	94.3
Poisoning	1	0.1	94.4
Animal bite	8	0.7	95.1
Other	56	4.9	100
Total	1,145	100	

Note: Total admissions to Lacor Hospital were 17,065 in 2000 and 17,471 in 2001. See Lacor Hospital (2003)

Sources: Kobusingye et al. (2003); Small Arms Survey (2004)

reports for Moyo and other western districts revealed comparatively fewer risks to the physical security of refugees.

In order to assess the full range of impacts of militarization one has to consider not only the direct impacts (as shown by the disproportionately higher burden related to war-related injuries above), but also the indirect effects. In fact, while civilian deaths may be the direct result of military operations, increased mortality among civilians in time of conflict is usually an index of the combined effects of social disruption,[74] psycho-

TABLE 3.5 Armed violence against refugees in Adjumani District, 2002–04

Incident type	2002	2003	2004*
LRA killing of refugee	9	11	25
LRA looting of refugee household	173	81	41
LRA abduction of refugees	19	114	99
UPDF killing of refugee	1	2	2
UPDF looting of refugee household	0	15	0
Unidentified killing of refugee	4	9	0
Unidentified looting of refugee household	8	5	0
SPLA recruitment of refugee	4	3	0
Relief workers/convoy employees killed	3	21	0
Relief/commercial convoys ambushed	2	16	0
Total number of refugees killed	14	22	27
Firearm homicide rate per 100,000	22.95	36	44.46

Note: * 2004 includes February–June only
Source: Interviews and archival records from UNHCR sub-offices. See also
Appendix III

social distress, reduced access to health services, and the increased risk of communicable diseases in situations of population displacement and overcrowding in settlements and camps (Small Arms Survey 2005).

Long-term displacement and the collapse of social structures have put people at greater risk of HIV, TB, emerging infectious diseases, malnutrition and war-related injuries. Most humanitarian actors consulted during the course of this study admitted that the welfare of IDPs in northern Uganda is well below SPHERE standards.[75] For example, HIV reportedly affects between 16 and 18 per cent of the population of IDP camps, compared with the national average of 4 per cent.[76] What is more, because the disease burden associated with injuries is much greater in adult males (at higher risk of injury associated with war), the loss of productivity and the strain on social and cultural ties are severe (Kobusingye et al. 2003).

As Crisp (2002: 7) has observed, 'militarization can ... add weight to the argument that refugees are a source of insecurity, and that it is therefore legitimate for them to be excluded and/or forcibly repatriated from countries of asylum'. This appears also to be the case in Uganda. Although the NRM government strictly adheres to normative prescriptions associated with 'proper' refugee care and maintenance and IDP protection, there are growing suspicions among government officials, UPDF commanders and interest groups in the south that refugees and IDPs (read foreigners and Acholis) are responsible for the overall militarization of the north. The UPDF regularly claims that IDPs claiming to leave camps for cultivation purposes are in fact supporting the LRA with food and intelligence. This no doubt occurs on occasion, as it is widely believed that many actually purposively deposit rations on the perimeter of camps so as to deter LRA raids.[77] Alarmingly, the Minister of State Security has claimed in recent rallies that refugees and IDPs are to some extent supporting the LRA. Although the activities of SPLA-affiliated Sudanese refugees in Adjumani are quietly tolerated, the already severe restrictions on mobility may be tightened further still.

The humanitarian community has also been forced to harden itself to the widespread insecurity in northern Uganda. In response to a range of high-profile abductions and security incidents,[78] including the bombing of UNHCR compounds and the burning of sixteen UN vehicles in Adjumani District in 1996, many humanitarian and development agencies currently draw on heavily armed military escorts to IDP camps. Although the UPDF facilitates these convoys, there appear to be inadequate numbers of soldiers to ensure protection. Moreover, the costs of hiring vehicles, fuel and associated transport outlays and logistical delays are borne entirely by these same agencies.[79] There is no common policy on escorts,[80] but most international relief agencies operate with the assistance of military convoys. In Gulu, for example, OCHA (2004a, 2004c) observed that less than one-third of all camps are accessible without an escort. Kitgum and Pader are reported to be similarly insecure. The threats posed to relief workers by the Karamoja are well known (Gomes and Mkutu 2004). OCHA (2004b) has recently called for specific allocations within the Ugandan defence budget for additional military support to assist aid convoys.

Militarization: the case of Gulu and Adjumani

Gulu and Adjumani are arguably Uganda's most severely affected regions with respect to the displacement of IDPs and refugees, respectively. Although the unregulated availability of small arms may be more common along the extreme borders of the country, refugee and IDP militarization is nowhere more acute than in these two districts. In order to illustrate the patterns and dynamics of militarization, it is useful to focus on discrete cases where it is manifest *in situ*.[81] Drawing on a range of quantitative and qualitative methods, and a variety of sources, assessments were undertaken over several weeks in August 2004.[82]

Gulu District is home to most of the country's IDP population. Owing to persistent insecurity in the northern and western regions of Gulu, many of the district's forty-five IDP camps were considered too insecure to visit at the time of the assessment, even with heavily armed military escorts. As such, this assessment is affected by a selection bias that may in fact underestimate the overall degree of IDP militarization. Nevertheless, the camps of Bobi (18,000), Palenga (15,000) and Pabbo (63,181) were visited by the author in August 2004.[83] Focus groups with various residents were set up and small-scale random surveys and transect walks were held in each camp, and local UPDF representatives consulted.

Bobi IDP camp Located less than 25 kilometres from Gulu town and along the main road to Kampala, Bobi camp is considered by relief and development agencies to be extremely insecure. Established in 1996, it is the site of repeated armed incursions by the LRA and increasing reception of internally displaced people from throughout southern Gulu District.[84] Although technically ungazetted, the camp is the fastest growing in Uganda: between May and August 2003 it grew from 11,000 to more than 18,000 residents, most of whom are clustered in small huts within a 2–3-kilometre radius of the principal road. The host community numbered no more than 100 residents in the mid-1990s. Although insecurity remains, according to various residents and NGOs the LRA appears to have weakened and become more disorganized throughout 2004.

Bobi camp is heavily militarized. Owing to repeated attacks by small factions of the LRA (between twenty and twenty-five at a time) across the river on the camp's eastern border and more than a hundred abductions since 2000, a detachment of some 150 UPDF is now stationed within the camp. Some fifty to seventy UPDF are purported to patrol the eastern perimeter every night.[85] In 2003, fewer than thirty UPDF reservists were protecting the camp's comparatively smaller population. IDP residents expressed little confidence in the police and army detachments and claimed that they would acquire weapons to defend their camp if permitted.[86] According to key informants, this appears to be typical of IDP camps in northern Uganda. Moreover, at the request of the community's local leaders in early 2004, some fifteen to twenty IDPs are currently being trained as LDUs by the UPDF and equipped with AK-47s by the local detachment. IDP representatives expressed some reservations about the LDUs as many males who previously volunteered to serve as militia several years earlier were subsequently redeployed to Sudan and Congo and left the camp vulnerable. Numbers of UPDF and LDUs are nevertheless extremely difficult to verify, and even residents are unsure about precise figures.

Palenga IDP camp Palenga IDP camp is less than 20 kilometres from Gulu town and is a formal or gazetted settlement. Established in 1996, it is noticeably more developed than Bobi IDP camp; it has extensive water and electricity services, well-organized organizational committees and a considerable UPDF presence. Some 15,000 IDPs are currently residing in tightly packed semi-permanent shelters, with a school, nursery, dispensary and various market services scattered throughout. Concerns relating to criminality and intimidation (by bandits and UPDF soldiers alike) were nevertheless reported by focus group participants, and gunshots were heard regularly. Like its neighbour, it is heavily militarized.

According to the residents, there are some forty UPDF stationed permanently in barracks within the camp. Between twenty and thirty UPDF patrol the periphery of the settlement, particularly along the Ticho river. A 14mm AD gun (ZPU-1) is positioned facing outwards next to the dispensary at the easternmost point of the camp, some 100 metres from the main Kampala road.[87] Moreover, the UPDF has established at least twelve JCC from among the IDP residents, who join the army on manoeuvres and patrols. Some concerns about the lack of standardized pay for the UPDF and JCC[88] were expressed by IDP representatives during focus group discussions.

Pabbo IDP camp Pabbo enjoys an unenviable designation as one of the largest IDP camps in Uganda.[89] It is also considered to be one of its most insecure – two armed escort vehicles are required to access the camp. Located some 40 kilometres from Gulu, Pabbo hosts more than 63,118 residents. Established in 1996, it is a densely populated site with a large UPDF detachment (the 71st Battalion) recently stationed on its eastern perimeter.[90] An additional forty-six IDPs were also recently trained as LDUs and actively patrol the camp. Owing in part to its close proximity to LRA enclaves, a rear base of the LRA, it is also the site of frequent attacks. For example, in February 2004 two LRA combatants were shot during an unsuccessful raid on the camp.

In the late 1990s there were reports of some weapons being uncovered in the camp. Although some of its residents may have voluntarily joined the LRA prior to 1996, and scattered LRA combatants may have been present at the inception of the camp, it is more likely that the weapons were being transited through or used for self-defence. According to focus group participants, the physical security of the camp's residents has improved marginally since the arrival of the UPDF detachment. Many complain of continued harassment when they leave to collect firewood and supplies. Others contend that the UPDF rarely prevents or pursues LRA combatants who attack displaced households, instead resorting to a more defensive posture.

Adjumani and Moyo refugee settlements Most of the 94,800 Sudanese refugees in Adjumani and Moyo arrived between 1995 and 2000 and are clustered into sixty-four settlements throughout the two districts. Tens of thousands more self-settled and are not officially recognized by the authorities or UNHCR. They are belived to be more or less fully integrated into the host communities, sharing common ethnic and historical ties with the local residents. Although they enjoyed a productive year in 1996, the overall security situation for the district deteriorated considerably from 1997 onwards. The settlements suffered from repeated attacks between 1998 and 2003, but armed violence directed at them peaked in early 2004. Between April and June 2004, the LRA infiltrated various refugee settlements throughout the district and, in addition to killing over twenty Sudanese refugees, abducted hundreds of children. Owing to their close proximity to the adjoining Gulu District, Adjumani's refugee settlements and the surrounding communities have been severely affected.[91]

In response to these and other attacks, the UPDF deployed two battalions in 2003 and strengthened its troop strength alongside refugee settlements. Detachments are located between 100 metres and 5 kilometres from all settlements. Moreover, the government claims to have launched a concerted campaign to support the UPDF through recruitment drives, the formation of LDUs, limited community policing and additional support to internally displaced persons.[92] The UNHCR and OPM, for their part, have sought to strengthen security measures by providing the local office of the OPM and other authorities with seventeen VHF handsets and facilitating their movement by providing vehicles (one pick-up and two trucks), two motorcycles and fuel.

Mungola refugee settlement Located some 20 kilometres from Adjumani town and some 50 kilometres from the Sudanese border, Mungola settlement was at one time among the district's largest. Numbering some 11,682 in 1995, the settlement registered fewer than 2,370 residents in July 2004. Multiple attacks by the LRA in April 2004 led to massive displacement and relocation. Bombardments with RPG-7s and attacks with AK-47s by small cadres of LRA led to the evacuation of the entire settlement and the killing of several abductees and refugees. Owing in part to food insecurity and little capacity for absorption elsewhere, a few refugees had temporarily returned to the settlement at the time of the visit. Although spontaneous returns and relocations were catalysed by sporadic violence and the absence of food in other areas, the settlement is more or less deserted.

Refugees complained repeatedly of the UPDF's inability to confront the LRA and of ignoring advanced warnings by refugees. Most claimed that they are unlikely to return. As one respondent noted: '[we] saw laxity [in the UPDF] and it will continue. Until we know the LRA is handing themselves in, we won't return. Nor are the Sudanese refugees interested in forming self-defence units or acquiring weapons, as this would ... only bring more conflict.' Although outward militarization has declined since the signing of various bilateral agreements with Sudan, it is well known that Sudanese children who return to Sudan via the Kajokaji border for education are often forcibly recruited by the SPLA. This is unsurprising given their exceedingly violent experience. Even so, there is currently little evidence of designated SPLA representatives operating in Mungola and other settlements. Refugees are nevertheless known to return to Sudan frequently, often to check conditions for return. The economic relations between Kuku tribesmen on either side of the Sudan–Uganda border have remained well established since the 1950s, and trans-border movement remains common.

Kali refugee settlements Established in the comparatively calm Moyo District, Kali settlements (1, 2A, 2B, 3A, 3B, 4 and 5) are an oasis of relative safety in northern Uganda. Although at one time exposed to the activities of the now defunct WNBF, and still subject to visits by SPLA representatives, the refugees inhabiting Kali are well integrated and productive – described by local residents as 'self-reliant'. Even though located on noticeably less fertile land than that of the host communities, refugees are self-sufficient and pursue what is often called 'leja leja', or casual labour. The lines between the refugee and indigenous communities are porous. Numbering some 7,267 residents, the settlement is currently receiving up to twenty new refugees a day, most of whom are claiming to have fled from the LRA in the equatorial region of Sudan.

The security situation in Kali is fairly stable. Most crime is said to be domestic and small-scale in nature. Although a modest haul of weapons was collected by the police in 2003 and 2004 – a combination of grenades and AK-47s – the perpetrators were arrested and later prosecuted. Indeed, police posts exist in a number of refugee settlements, and some fifteen were operational throughout Kali at the time of the visit. More are planned for 2004. Patrolling is carried out by bicycle, although additional equipment (for example, weapons) and resources (such as incarceration facilities) are sparse. According to local informants, a UPDF detachment was to be deployed in late 2005.

Conclusions and recommendations

The outward and inward demilitarization of refugee settlements and IDP camps will not occur spontaneously. Any improvements in the safety and security of refugee settlements and IDP camps will depend largely on the dynamics of the region and the resolution of the ongoing internal conflict between the UPDF and the LRA. But the regional dynamics are also important – particularly in Sudan and DRC – and efforts to improve security for refugees and IDPs in Uganda rely to a disconcerting degree on neighbouring states. The fragility of the Naivasha Peace Agreement and the coalition government in DRC are cause for concern. On the other hand, the current trends in UPDF tactics and the recent surge in respondents to the amnesties suggest some tentatively encouraging changes. Indeed, the recent escalation of armed violence against refugee settlements and IDP camps indicates, perversely, that the LRA is weakening. This was confirmed by indications from the LRA leadership in late August 2004 that it was keen to sue for peace, though developments in 2005 suggest this may still be some way off. But even if the situation described above improves dramatically, a number of factors could contribute to continued refugee and IDP militarization: the establishment of armed militia and LDUs, the continued UPDF presence, widespread armed criminality and the presence of Karamoja fighters indicate that protection needs will remain great. The unregulated availability of automatic weapons remains a major concern.

Predictably, militarization will be reduced only if the causes of conflicts are addressed. The dangers associated with refugee- or IDP-centric approaches to protection and assistance are well known (Crisp 2002; Merkx 2002; Kaiser 2000a; Loescher 1993). Refugees and IDPs are living in what can only be described as an impossible security environment where they are equally at risk from UPDF and LRA, though in unequal measure. Removing them from camps may simply move rather than solve the problem. Policies that seek to strengthen protection in the interim are also important. Fortunately, it appears that current policies towards refugee settlement and IDP camps reinforce to some extent a regional and integrated approach that seeks to promote the protection of both groups, not least because most of the overall population of the north is displaced. But the continued discrepancy between the welfare of refugees and that of IDPs is pronounced and unacceptable. Moreover, their persistent recruitment – both voluntary and involuntary – is clearly in violation of well-established norms on protection.

A number of discrete strategies towards the protection and care of displaced populations need to be revisited. For one, the UPDF, OPM, UNHCR and OCHA would do well to revisit the current policy of warehousing refugees and IDPs in large settlements. With few exceptions, it is the large-scale and protracted settlements and camps which appear to be in greatest danger of internal militarization. The conventional strategy of aggregating populations into large population clusters is, at best, an approach that compromises protection, undermines livelihoods, promotes dependency, raises overall costs and increases the likelihood of attack. This strategy has contributed to a 'chronic humanitarian catastrophe' (Weeks 2002). Although it may serve a short-term military end, its long-term implications are disastrous and reinforce long-standing ethnic grievances.

UNHCR and OCHA would do well to exchange ideas and adopt common strategies on the promotion of self-reliance in settlements and camps, encourage gradual self-settlement for those who seek voluntarily to return to their place of origin, and devise mechanisms for improving integrated settlement of internally displaced populations. It appears that gestures are being made to this effect in late 2005, with the UNHCR assuming a much more prominent role in refugee and IDP protection than had previously been the case. Working in cooperation with the authorities – including the UPDF and OPM – will of course be essential to the sustainability of demilitarization. In addition to devising strategies and preparing resources for voluntary return, stakeholders should seek to reinforce the retention of settlement patterns of non-displaced populations so as to reduce congestion and exposure to armed attack. Protection will be assured only if the UPDF and OPM simultaneously consider a proactive military strategy against LRA commanders which avoids militarizing refugees and IDPs while guaranteeing their protection. The strengthening of amnesty provisions and outreach, as well as DDR for defecting LRA, is an obvious entry point.

This chapter closes with several recommendations to strengthen protection on the ground. First, refugee and IDP demilitarization could be facilitated by increased attention to the monitoring and reinforcement of borders. The strengthening of monitoring, surveillance and response to militarization of the DRC and Sudanese borders could reduce attacks on settlements and camps. Although ongoing efforts by the UPDF on the Sudanese border are notable in this regard (as are the concomitant constraints on defence capabilities noted above), relevant stakeholders need to make border control a priority. Uganda's involvement as a leading proponent of the Nairobi Declaration suggests that a degree of political will currently exists in this respect. As such, appropriate and adequate investments will be required in order to ensure adequate analysis capabilities and deployment in key areas. Regional approaches will be required, with the possible involvement of MONUC in DRC and increased operations with Kenyan authorities and the UPDF along the Sudanese border.

Efforts to ensure outreach activities to LRA combatants and others should be increased. The current efforts of the NRM government with respect to the 2000 amnesty, as well as radio programmes and the Acholi

Religious Leaders Peace Initiative (ARLPI), are to be commended, as are the programmes established to demobilize and reintegrate children via the UPDF CPU, UNICEF and GUSCO. The surge in respondents and defectors from the LRA indicates that non-violent approaches to demilitarization appear to have yielded a positive dividend. International actors should make every effort to support these locally developed programmes at the expense of military solutions.

Procedures for screening settlements and camps, as well as interning combatants, need to be strengthened. UNHCR has already elaborated screening procedures for settlements, in line with de facto international standards (Da Costa 2004). OCHA should evaluate these processes and consider establishing protocols, together with the OPM, for IDP camps. Moreover, practical, appropriate and transparent procedures for the identification, internment and demobilization of armed elements in camps need to be elaborated together with the UPDF. The current policy of demobilizing and subsequently redeploying LRA ex-combatants (Battalion 105) in the north is an extremely dangerous precedent.

The UPDF must also articulate a clear strategy for dismantling the militia, LDU and LRA. At present, the process appears ad hoc and confused. Although internal processes of DDR were undertaken in 2002 with the UPDF, and the Ugandan government has submitted to UNHCR a proposal for a security package in order to reinforce UPDF and police presence in settlements, there do not appear to be any coherent, integrated and medium-term strategies to disarm, demobilize, return or resettle ex-combatants. This should be made a priority, and included in a long-term strategy of security sector reform (SSR).

The UPDF and national police must develop a responsive and proactive approach to the protection of refugee settlements and IDP camps. Concerns were frequently registered by refugees and IDPs about the lax and in some cases predatory behaviour of the UPDF and militia in relation to refugee and IDP protection, worries that have been voiced for years (Weeks 2002). Refugee law and ExCom 94 resolutions concerning the protection of refugees articulate clear normative safeguards. In the case of IDPs, Guiding Principles 11 (2) and 21 (2) guarantee protection against rape, mutilation, torture, inhuman and degrading treatment, as well as the protection of property against pillage and direct or indiscriminate attacks. These protections should be disseminated, enforced and monitored to ensure compliance. Particular attention should be paid to self-settled or 'spontaneously settling' refugees and IDPs in ungazetted camps, and OCHA's work with the district-level Disaster Management Comittees should be continued.

Greater attention should be paid to the articulation of clear rules and regulations associated with UPDF functions and mandates in relation to protection and settlement/camp management. At present, there appears to be confusion associated with the role and mandate of the UPDF and its auxiliaries with respect to protection and management. Although perimeters are regularly established around settlement camps at nightfall, they often prove incapable of defending refugees and IDPs from attack. This is especially the case with non-recognized refugees (such as the spontaneously settled) and IDPs in ungazetted camps, many of whom are forced to search for subsistence away from the protection of UPDF and LDU forces owing to limited access to international assistance. Moreover, refugees and IDPs appear to have little negotiating strength in determining the shape and character of their own protection, despite clear norms that call for their informed consent.[93] Consultations with IDP representatives could facilitate the elaboration of appropriate benchmarks for security and protection.

Minimum benchmarks and standards of protection and care for refugees and IDPs must be adopted by all stakeholders. Although UNHCR and OCHA adhere to the principle of SPHERE standards, this approach does not appear to be shared in equal measure by OPM or UPDF with respect to camps. Application of pressure by donors and international agencies to ensure that minimum standards are devised for IDP camps and the spontaneously settled is vital. Although the likelihood of analogous standards being devised for non-settling refugees is remote, this should not be the case for IDPs, who are entitled to basic human rights under the Ugandan constitution. The establishment and deployment of international or nationally agreed protection monitors to ensure that protection and management of settlements and camps are of a minimum standard could be considered.

Preventing forced encampment and exploring concrete options for de-congestion of refugee settlements and IDP camps in conditions of safety and security is a priority. As signalled by Weeks (ibid.), the movement away from settlements and camps towards permanent settlement cannot be held hostage to the final neutralization and disbandment of the LRA. The UNHCR is already preparing the messaging, logistics and finance for voluntary repatriations from refugee settlements from 2005 onwards. Although the contexts are somewhat different, no similar strategies appear to be designed or enforced for IDP camps. Rather, the policy of forced encampment into IDP camps by the UPDF defies key norms and obligations set out in the Guiding Principles on Internal Displacement.[94] Although many IDPs would no doubt prefer to stay in camps until they perceive the security of home areas to have improved, a small minority wish to return.[95] A clear strategy for returning IDPs in conditions of safety and with dignity must be articulated, with plans and realistic financing arrangements developed in a participatory fashion.

SSR must be front and centre of any strategy to demilitarize refugee settlements and IDP camps. Strategies for SSR relate to strengthening the accountability of militia and LDU to the UPDF and civilian jurisdiction, improved training, accommodation and transparent procurement and budgeting procedures for the UPDF and its auxiliaries, and appropriate DDR activities for UPDF and LRA combatants within the context of the Multi-regional Demobilization and Reintegration Programme (MDRP) or other national processes. SSR also relates to the strengthening of the policing sector, particularly in relation to community policing in non-urban areas, improved communications infrastructure and coordination across districts, the strengthening of regulatory controls for illegal arms, the strengthening of storage and maintenance (and destruction) procedures for small arms, and other interventions. At least two committees consisting of representatives of the UPDF, national police, OPM, the Bureau for Conflict Prevention and Recovery (BCPR) and relevant international stakeholders could be established to draft a White Paper.

International agencies must also establish clear policies on the use of armed escorts. The use of military escorts to access refugee settlements and, to a greater extent, IDP camps is held to be necessary by a sizeable proportion of relief agencies operating in northern Uganda. This is particularly the case for food convoys in high-risk areas. In addition to fuelling a war economy, it sends out contradictory signals to the population it purports to assist. Greater emphasis on negotiated access and alternative approaches to service delivery should perhaps be considered. A dedicated task force, chaired by the OPM, should be established to formulate clear and unambiguous policies on the provision and guarantee of protection to relief agencies.

Finally, senior management of international and national agencies must give greater priority to the monitoring and reporting of security incidents. Although a small sample of NGOs appear to have developed approaches to gathering intelligence, and meetings are regularly held to share information, approaches are currently loose and uncoordinated. It is vital that an evidence-based approach to data collection, which gathers adequate and standardized information and is regularly updated and presented in a clear and coherent fashion, be developed. Trend analysis serves a twofold function: (a) the designation of high-priority areas so as to inform preventive interventions; and (b) the identification of likely areas of insecurity so as to reduce exposure to armed violence.

Appendix I: Comparative firearm injury rates in four hospitals

Small-arms injuries for four hospitals in Uganda

Year	Small-arm injury admissions				Injury admissions				Admissions from all causes			
	LA	MU	SO	FP	LA	MU	SO	FP	LA	MU	SO	FP
1997	238	69	16	16	915	–	–	415	15,377	66,188	6,695	7,053
1998	287	62	23	23	728	–	–	631	15,438	71,500	7,384	7,683
1999	85	14	10	25	527	–	–	528	17,649	81,093	8,891	7,648
2000	189	3	38	24	612	–	–	509	17,065	88,391	1,074	6,642
2001	65	79	39	27	549	–	891	393	17,471	94,531	7	7,805
2002	206	87	38	17	594	–	717	457	20,780		13,513	7,368
Total	1,070	517	164	132	3,925			2,933	103,780	401,170	58,610	36,551

Note: LA = Lacor, MU = Mulago, SO = Soroti, FP = Fort Portal

Source: Kobusingye et al. (2003)

General findings: There was an overall reduction in the total number of small-arm injuries between 1997 and 2002. The highest number of cases was registered in 1998, with Lacor registering the largest number of all hospitals. There was a general decline in cases in 1999 and an increase in 2000 and 2002.

Small-arms injury morbidity/mortality as a proportion of injury admissions and deaths

Year	Small arms		As a percentage of all reported external injuries	
	Injuries (Cas)	Deaths (Mor)	Admissions (Cas)	Deaths (Mor)
1997	339		–	0.11
1998	395	99	0.11	0.14
1999	263	137	0.06	0.15
2000	330	133	0.07	0.23
2001	218	181	0.04	0.52
2002	338	220	–	
Total	1,883	617		

Note: 1998 morgue data covered only the period between March and December and the 2002 morgue data covered only January and February. Cas = casualty records; Mor = morgue records

Source: Kobusingye et al. (2003)

General findings: There was a steady annual increase in the total number of small-arms injury deaths registered at the city mortuary between 1998 and 2002, representing an average percentage rate per annum as noted above

Appendix II: Security incidents directed against refugees in Adjumani, 2002–04

Reported security incidents involving refugees in Adjumani: 2002

	Jan-02	Feb-02	Mar-02	Apr-02	May-02	Jun-02	Jul-02	Aug-02	Sep-02	Oct-02	Nov-02	Dec-02
LRA killings	0	1	1	0	0	0	6	0	1	0	0	0
LRA lootings	11	2	3	0	20	1	97	1	23	2	2	0
LRA abductions	2	0	5	0	0	7	0	5	0	0	0	0
UPDF killings	0	0	0	0	0	1	0	0	0	0	0	0
UPDF lootings	0	0	0	0	2	0	1	0	0	0	0	1
Unid killings	0	0	0	0	2	0	0	0	0	0	0	4
Unid lootings	2	0	0	0	2	0	0	0	0	0	0	0
SPLA actions	0	1	1	0	2	0	0	0	0	0	0	0
Relief workers killed	0	0	1	0	0	0	0	0	0	0	2	0
Relief convoys ambushed	0	0	0	0	0	2	0	0	0	0	0	0

Reported security incidents involving refugees in Adjumani: 2003

	Jan-03	Feb-03	Mar-03	Apr-03	May-03	Jun-03	Jul-03	Aug-03	Sep-03	Oct-03	Nov-03	Dec-03
LRA killings	0	0	0	0	0	3	1	0	0	0	7	0
LRA lootings	1	0	2	18	2	31	8	0	1	0	4	4
LRA abductions	0	0	0	35	6	23	15	0	0	0	35	0
UPDF killings	0	0	0	0	0	0	0	0	0	0	0	2
UPDF lootings	0	0	0	0	6	2	0	0	3	4	0	0
Unid killings	0	0	0	0	0	0	4	0	2	0	2	0
Unid lootings	0	0	0	1	0	0	0	1	2	1	1	0
SPLA actions	1	0	0	0	2	0	1	0	0	0	1	0
Relief workers killed	0	0	0	18	0	0	3	0	0	0	0	0
Relief convoys ambushed	4	0	1	2	0	0	1	0	2	1	1	4

Reported security incidents involving refugees in Adjumani: February–June 2004

	Feb-04	Mar-04	Apr-04	May-04	Jun-04
LRA killings	4	3	13	1	5
LRA lootings	2	2	15	8	14
LRA abductions	2	12	29	19	37
UPDF killings	0	1	1	0	0
UPDF lootings	0	0	0	0	0
Unid killings	0	0	0	0	0
Unid lootings	0	0	0	0	0
SPLA actions	0	0	0	0	0
Relief workers killed	0	0	0	0	0
Relief convoys ambushed	0	0	0	0	0

Notes

1 There are two types of refugee settlements in Uganda: (a) those that are integrated with host communities (10), and (b) those that are deliberately separate from host communities (9). Interview with Juan Castro-Magluff (UNHCR) on 30 August 2004.

2 Ugandan IDP camps can also be divided into two categories: (a) those that are gazetted by the government (118) and (b) those that are ungazetted or arose spontaneously (24).

3 According to Captier (2003: 15): 'the concept of protection encompasses all activities aimed at obtaining full respect for the rights of the individual in accordance with the letter and spirit of relevant bodies of law (human rights, humanitarian and refugee law). Human rights and humanitarian actors shall conduct these activities impartially and not on the basis of race, national, or ethnic origin, language or gender'. This definition was itself developed during an ICRC workshop (January 1999) on the issue of protection.

4 Lt Gen. (ret.) Tsadkan, former chief of staff of the Ethiopian army, who fought with the UPDF and SPLA in the late 1990s against the armed forces of the Government of Sudan, has argued that UPDF forces are not well trained. Interview with John Young, February 2006. See <www.reliefweb.int/ocha_ol/pub/idp_gp/idp.html>.

5 At the outset, it should be emphasized that, while there are considerable distinctions between the legal regimes and implications for sovereignty associated with responses to refugees and IDPs, there are a number of similar causes and effects of their militarization.

6 See Chapter 1 of this volume for a review of the literature on refugee militarization in Africa.

7 The country also received refugees from Ethiopia and Somalia during this period. See Gingyera-Pinyewa (1998) and Prunier (1999).

8 In 1980, almost the entire population of the West Nile and Madi Region was forced into exile, while those living in the Luwero Triangle and in north and north-eastern Uganda were internally displaced. Though the majority of these refugees were repatriated and settled following Museveni's rise to power in 1986, a number were recruited into various rebel movements, including the LRA and WNBF, discussed in more detail below. See Lomo et al. (2001) and Kasozi (1998).

9 Under Amin (1971–79), Alur, Aringa, Lugbara, Kakwa and Madi from his home district, Arua, were prominent in the national armed forces. Following the liberation of Uganda by the Tanzanians, the Ugandan National Liberation Army (NLA) under the second Obote administration (1980–85) consisted primarily of Acholis and Langis from the districts of Adjumani, Gulu and Moyo.

10 For example, the Control of Alien Refugees Act (CARA), enacted in 1964, is widely perceived to be out of date and not in accordance with the country's current obligations under the United Nations 1951 Convention and the 1967 Protocol of the OAU Convention Governing Specific Aspects of Refugee Problems in Africa. CARA establishes a system in which refugees are to be confined to refugee settlements, prohibits their free movement without the

permission of a settlement commandment, and makes it an offence for any person to harbour a refugee outside a settlement. That said, Uganda's commitment to the aforementioned normative standards has forced the creation of a system more attuned to international standards and practice. See, for example Lomo et al. (2001) and Moro (2002).

11 Refugees then, as now, also poured into northern Uganda to evade attacks within SPLA ranks as well as by LRA forces operating within southern Sudan. Many Sudanese refugees are playing an active role in the Ugandan 2006 election, which is held to represent SPLA support for the NRM.

12 According to Jesse Bernstein, formerly with the Refugee Law Project, 'former child soldiers were occasionally detained, but this practice has pretty much ended' over the past few years. He also notes that the UPDF regularly remobilizes former child soldiers in violation of international law.

13 The OPM has primary responsibility for protecting refugees. It has evolved two methods of ensuring the civilian character of camps. The first involves third-country asylum claimants who, after reporting to the authorities (LDC, ISO, police, immigration) and being disarmed, are referred to the National Refugee Committee for Status Determination in Kampala. The second approach involves the deployment of screening teams to ascribe prima facie status to individuals from war-affected countries, register them and provide assistance. Thus, self-settled refugees such as the estimated 27,000 currently residing in Adjumani and Moyo are not formally accorded refugee status by the government.

14 The motivations underpinning spontaneous settlement in northern and western Uganda are of course much more complicated. To be sure, many so-called settlement residents also include considerable numbers of members who work in and send remittances from urban areas. These dynamics are discussed in detail by Kaiser (2005).

15 Settlements located to the west of the Nile, a natural barrier that runs north–south from the Sudan, appear to be less prone to armed violence.

16 Though rarely articulated publicly, it is also widely believed that displacement and settlement are themselves tied to the deliberate clearance of land by vested interests.

17 Although the official policy is to settle refugees more than 100 kilometres from international borders, this has rarely occurred in practice. Most refugee settlements in Moyo, Adjumani and Nebbi are less than the UNHCR's advocated 50-kilometre limit from the border with some 20 kilometres separating them from Sudan (based on field visits to Adjumani and Moyo on 26–29 August 2004).

18 The Mireyi transit camp in Adjumani is home to 1,316, primarily male, refugees. Refusing to participate in agricultural activities, they are effectively warehoused south of Adjumani town. Key informants in the region are well aware of their involvement with SPLA actors in southern Sudan.

19 Key informants within the ICRC and MONUC have speculated that the RCD-Goma is recruiting from Kyaka II refugee settlement in the west, though these remain rumours and are unsubstantiated.

20 According to Lomo et al. (2001: 5): ' ... some 3,000 (mostly Tutsi)

Rwandese soldiers had joined Museveni's 14,000 strong NRA by the time it came to power. By 1990, the size of the NRA itself had increased dramatically, the number of Rwandese in the NRA had risen to about 8,000.' See also Prunier (1999).

21 With some sixty-four discrete refugee settlements (clustered into larger units) in Adjumani and Moyo, only one transit camp close to Adjumani town is still viewed as problematic.

22 'Gorogoro' is a Swahili word referring to empty tin containers that have been converted for use at home or market (Moro 2002: 11). The WNBF emerged from erstwhile supporters of Amin's foreign minister, Juma Oris, with the support of the Sudanese government. Armed by the Sudanese army, these rebels – primarily from Kakwa and Aringa ethnic groups – waged armed violence against refugees on the west side of the Nile in north-east Uganda. The SPLA subsequently killed a number of WNBF rebels and Sudanese soldiers; and the recent decision of the Sudanese government to end its support for Ugandan rebels has improved security.

23 In 1996 the NRF II, a dissident group of the WNBF comprising 2,500 combatants and family members, returned to southern Sudan and sued for peace with the Sudanese government with an agreement signed in June of that year.

24 The Allied Democratic Front emerged in the Rwenzori region of western Uganda in 1996. According to Lomo et al. (2001: 6), by December 1999 some 120,000 residents of Bundibugyo were displaced – some 85 per cent of the total population.

25 The LRA originally consisted of Ugandan refugees from the Amin and Obote regime. The LRA is widely perceived to be an Acholi faction owing to the recruitment of Acholis within its ranks. Refugees and IDPs refer to the LRA rebels as 'Tongtong', after an insect with a painful sting, or one who chops victims to pieces. The group itself derives from Severino Lukoya, the father of Alice Lakwena (also alleged cousin of Kony), who unsuccessfully attempted to revive the struggle of the Acholi following the collapse of Lakwena's Holy Spirit Movement. See Weeks (2002).

26 Throughout the early 1990s, camps emerged spontaneously within trading centres along transport corridors throughout the north and east. By August–October 1996, the UPDF had begun concentrating these settlements in protected villages and assigning detachments. By the late 1990s between 50 and 80 per cent of all internally displaced people were encamped and the rest believed to be scattered among friends and relatives in cities. See, for example, Weeks (2002) for a detailed description of the evolution of IDP centres and protected villages.

27 UNICEF estimates that some 25,000 children have been abducted by the LRA since the mid-1990s. Lt Col. Achoke claims that the UPDF, together with the UN, has rescued more than 10,000 and that the rest are a combination of fighters, sex-slaves and porters.

28 A recent *Humanitarian Update* (OCHA 2004b) reports that UPDF operations in Sudan and northern Uganda between May and June have resulted in over 735 LRA deaths, 250 child rescues and 202 defections.

29 Kitgum was split into two, Kitgum and Pader, following national reforms in 2001.

30 Various reports issued by OCHA and the NRC have described the health, water and sanitation, food security, education and health status of IDPs since the mid-1990s.

31 According to OCHA (2004c), the total reached 45,000 per night in the towns of Gulu, Kitgum, Lira and Pader.

32 The UPDF consists of five divisions and is estimated to number some 60,000 nationally (IISS 2004: 226).

33 The questions of interests and why the government has insisted on pursuing a military rather than a negotiated solution are important ones. Some have indicated that the question of why the government, with superior equipment and massive numbers of troops, has been unable to address the insurgency satisfactorily has to be at the heart of the analysis. Discussion with Tania Kaiser, November 2004.

34 Home guards – village-level militia units – were established in the mid-1980s by the NRM under the Ministry for Internal Security for communities facing competing threats from Karamoja warriors and other forms of banditry.

35 For a detailed overview of the Arrow Boys, see Paul (2004).

36 In March 2000 government delegates from Burundi, the DRC, Djibouti, Ethiopia, Eritrea, Kenya, Rwanda, Sudan, Tanzania and Uganda signed the Nairobi Declaration on the Problem of the Proliferation of Illicit Small Arms and Light Weapons in the Great Lakes Region and the Horn of Africa. It calls for, among other things, the strengthening of multilateral cooperation on intelligence and customs, national controls, harmonizing legislation and the like. See <www.smallarmssurvey.org/source_documents/ Regional%20fora/ Africa/Nairobidecl000315.pdf>.

37 For example, arms surrendered under the Amnesty Act (2000) are to be handed to the sub-county chief of the area, although no controls exist to take such weapons out of circulation permanently.

38 UNICEF has found that a considerable number of militia members, as well as UPDF, are under the age of eighteen, and has successfully applied pressure on the army to demobilize those considered to be child combatants. The UPDF agreed and Amoka was subsequently reduced by over 1,000 recruits.

39 Between 1993 and 1994, some 12,000 Acholi residents were volunteered as militia groups to guard homesteads and protect their areas from LRA and Karamoja incursions. Despite the absence of any statutory obligations, the UPDF nevertheless conceived of the militia as auxiliaries and had them redeployed throughout the country and indeed the region, leaving the districts of Gulu, Kitgum and Pader vulnerable to further attacks. The proposed setting up of the Elephant Group, a new militia in the region, was roundly criticized by Acholi leaders owing to its ethnic connotations as well as on the basis of past experience. Owing to mounting resentment coupled with discriminatory recruitment and employment policies, Acholis are under-represented in the UPDF and current militia groups. Interview with Human Rights Focus Director, 23 August 2004.

40 LDUs make approximately UGS60,000 (USD40) per month and UPDF infantrymen some UGS165,000 (USD100). Interview with Lt Col. Achoki, 25 September 2004.

41 The International Crisis Group (ICG 2005), however, has recently claimed that southern commanders of the Sudanese armed forces are still supporting LRA rebels. This was confirmed by the author's visit to southern Sudan (Juba) in November 2005.

42 In response to a small-scale arms trade between Kitgum, Gulu and Pader in 1999, as well as a rise in organized crime, or 'Bokech' (he who prefers meat), the Ministry of Internal Affairs established a Violence Crime Crackdown Unit (VCCU) and an ARN (Anti-Robbery Unit) in 2002. Even so, some trade appears to continue between isolated UPDF forces and criminal syndicates. Interview with Mvule Richard on 24 August 2005.

43 Under provisions of the Firearms Act (1970), the Police Statute (1994) and the National Resistance Army Statute (1992), those in possession of arms ordinarily belonging to the armed forces are subject to military law and are to be sentenced to death for the misuse of, or failure to protect, war materials. Penalties for contravening the Firearms Act (1970) range from imprisonment for a term not exceeding six months or a fine not exceeding UGS20,000 (USD11 in 2005) for various offences including the purchase of ammunition without a permit and the pawning of small arms, to life imprisonment for the manufacture of small arms or for the import or export of arms that are prohibited or for which a permit has not been obtained. The fines have not been reviewed since 1970.

44 Concern about the weapons of the Karamoja are not new. Under Obote (1980–85) there were three successive attempts to disarm them, but none is alleged to have succeeded. See Mkutu (2003).

45 Very little is actually known about the process and outcomes of the Karamojan disarmament intervention, not least whether collected weapons are functional, properly stored or even destroyed. See, for example, IRIN (2004).

46 In July 2005, more than four hundred rustlers armed with assault rifles and machetes killed over seventy-five people and wounded eighteen in Marsabit District, about 150 kilometres south of the Ethiopian border. Kenyan security forces claimed to have killed some eighteen Karamoja cattle raiders from Uganda after rustlers attacked a village in Kenya's northern district of Turkana several weeks later. See BBC News (2005).

47 More than 50 per cent of the annual budget (FY04) is supplied by donors (OCHA 2004b: 10).

48 Throughout 2004 and 2005, donors demonstrated increasing impatience with President Museveni, particularly his ongoing efforts to extend his presidency. A number of major donors, including Ireland, UK and Norway, are withholding support for the budget owing to concerns with the political transition and the war in the north.

49 These estimates are drawn from a variety of sources in Kampala and outside, although they were not verified by UPDF itself. Recent media reports also note that, under the terms of the World Bank's Multi-Donor Demobiliza-

tion and Reintegration Programme, the country has also committed to redoubling its efforts to demobilize and return remaining *interahamwe*.

50 Battalion 105 is being trained in Lugore, North Gulu. According to various sources, the 350 members of the battalion will be integrated into a number of UPDF divisions in the north of the country. Interview with UPDF Intelligence, 26 April 2004.

51 This was confirmed in personal communications with Onega in early 2004.

52 See, for example, UPDF (2004).

53 These reporters, as they are colloquially known, refer to asylum grantees between October 2003 and July 2004 only (confidential document provided to the author).

54 UNICEF has also been involved in establishing the practice of protecting civilians, particularly child soldiers, in relation to the UPDF and Arrow militia.

55 A total of 1,380 LRA child combatants were received in 2003 and over 516 by mid-July 2004, more than twice the number anticipated by GUSCO representatives. Interview with the deputy director of GUSCO, 26 August 2004.

56 What is more, the introduction of joint monitoring teams from Sudan in the 1990s to survey the Sudanese refugee camps (for SPLA activity) served to defuse political tensions and reduce their explicit military support for the LRA. Interview with Lt Col. Achoke, 23 August 2004. See also Moro (2002: 6).

57 It should be noted that certain refugee settlements in Moyo do have small police posts.

58 Statements in late 2005 by the LRA that they were 'targeting white people' in response to the proceedings of the International Criminal Court (ICC), and the killing of several aid workers affiliated with Oxfam and Swiss-based NGOs in northern Uganda and southern Sudan by LRA elements, have reinforced this paranoia in the relief community.

59 For example, as recently as July 2004 the LRA raided the Zoka forest belt in Adjumani. It killed and abducted several refugees in pursuit of foodstuffs and supplies. As described in the Mungulo settlement, a large number of refugees were re-displaced. See also UNHCR (2004).

60 Weeks (2002) has documented the extraordinary psychological toll of the conflict on the population in the north and the growth of an impressive peace movement from among the Acholi religious leaders. But intriguingly, with notable exceptions, there also appears to be a complex relationship between the Acholi population and the LRA, the latter largely made up of Acholi children. This remains one of the central peculiarities of the conflict: one waged by a particular ethnic tribe against a clear enemy, but also against itself. Referring to the role of the Acholi Religious Leaders Peace Initiative, Weeks (2002: 15) has observed, '[T]here is also a very sophisticated understanding, strengthened by the realisation that the great majority of today's LRA fighters are yesterday's abducted children, that the costs to the society as a whole of retribution or of vilification would be too great.'

61 The inability of the UPDF to defeat the LRA was described to the author

as 'deliberate incompetence' by a MONUC officer in Kampala in August 2004.

62 Notable cases include Awal, Acet and Pagak, where up to 150 were killed in the late 1990s. Interview with AAH officer, August 2004.

63 As noted previously, in the early 1990s displaced people spontaneously settled in trading centres or with relatives and kin. As the situation deteriorated and the government's military strategy was ratcheted up, the UPDF began forced relocation to planned or gazetted camps initially called 'protected villages'.

64 As Moro (2002: 5–6) argues, the affluence of these camps apparently attracted the rebels, who have threatened the self-sufficiency of the camps and jeopardize the UNHCR policy of promoting refugee self-reliance. Moro insists that the UNHCR and government policies of promoting self-reliance among refugees are useless as long as refugees are placed in insecure zones where they are vulnerable to rebel attacks.

65 It is worth noting that major supply lines (such as for the secondary distribution of aid and services by large international agencies) have never been attacked by the LRA, suggesting that there is mutual recognition of the importance of these resources to all parties to the conflict.

66 In Kampala, for example, urban residents were asked by the Refugee Law Project about their impressions of refugees in the city. Many reported that the only 'refugees' in the city were people from Karamoja. Many in fact associated the term 'refugee' with the Karamojang, and then went on to describe the many difficulties such people were likely to encounter when attempting to integrate with the local population (Bernstein 2005).

67 Direct impacts relate to security threats to personnel and distribution of relief. Indirect impacts relate to constraints on access, imposed restrictions on mobility, heightened needs demonstrated by insecure populations, and reduced sustainability and return on investments. See, for example, Muggah (2005b) and Buchanan and Muggah (2005).

68 Gulu's referral hospital, Lacor, is notable for the accessibility its of quality services and application of low flat-rate fees. The composition of the hospital population makes Lacor an apt illutration of the disease burden of displaced people. In other words, distributional and urban biases are mitigated because the admission profile of Lacor is peculiar: it is located in a rural area and serves a largely poor population incapacitated by insurgency and disease, and vulnerable groups account for most of the admissions.

69 Though landmine injuries were relatively common in the mid-1990s (between 50 and 100 reported injuries per month in 1996), they have declined precipitously since 2000, with fewer than five reported each year.

70 What is more, traffic injuries have remained disproportionately high, presumably owing to fear of ambush.

71 Situation reports were drawn from UNHCR and the Office of the Prime Minister in Adjumani. Both reporting systems demonstrated clear biases and considerable gaps emerged (for example, reporting in 2004 is notably suspect – there was no reporting in January, and in the months of February to June reporting adopted a new technique excluding various categories of incidents).

Nevertheless, every effort was made to ensure that each category in Table 3.5 is mutually exclusive in order to avoid double counting.

72 At current rates, the firearm homicide rate can be expected to double, to over 90 per 100,000 by the end of the year. See Appendix III for a disaggregated accounting of security incidents between 2002 and 2004.

73 A review of health records of the twenty-three clinics operated by the African Humanitarian Agency (AHA) throughout the district revealed a comparatively low rate of gunshot injuries between 2003 and 2004, suggesting a high kill-to-injured ratio.

74 Discussions and advocacy associated with the sociocultural impacts of refugee militarization on inter-generational and gender relations, cultural assets and customary exchange systems and the like are notably absent.

75 The SPHERE project aims to improve the quality of assistance provided to people affected by disasters, and to enhance the accountability of the humanitarian system in disaster response. It includes minimum standards for water/sanitation, food, shelter and health, as well as mechanisms to ensure protection, and criteria for meeting standards for gender, children, older people, disabled people, HIV/Aids and the environment. See <www.sphereproject.org>.

76 Even so, establishing accurate figures of HIV rates is frustrated by inadequate monitoring and reporting. For example, Lacor Hospital, which is a sentinel surveillance site, recorded some 12 per cent sero-positivity. Interview with Andrew Timson, 6 September 2004.

77 Small-scale support to LRA combatants from central urban centres via motorcycle ('bodos') is more likely.

78 In 1998, personnel from Action Against Hunger (AAH) were ambushed and killed while driving to IDP camps in Gulu. Following an internal investigation, it was found that the LRA often used informants and was aware of rented truck types, travel plans and cargo manifests. When AAH and Acord used trucks previously used by the World Food Programme (WFP) (for food delivery) and the UPDF, they were attacked. Interview with Peter, AAH, 25 September 2004.

79 For example, OCHA spends approximately USD500 per month on military escorts, while WFP spends a considerably more on its daily convoys, which include Mambo and Buffalo armoured personnel carriers.

80 AAH and Médecins Sans Frontières, for example, do not use military escorts. Rather, they seek clearance from UPDF on a daily basis before driving to any location, and often triangulate with local intelligence in camps.

81 With the continuous support of OCHA, UNHCR and the OPM, field research was undertaken in four countries (Uganda, Sudan, Rwanda and DRC) and in three districts (Gulu, Adjumani and Moyo).

82 The research involved a combination of trips to IDP and refugee settlements, commissioned epidemiological research from local departments of public health and police depots, extensive interviewing with UPDF, UN, humanitarian and human rights NGO representatives, archival reviews in cooperation with the Refugee Law Project in Kampala, and other methods.

83 The researcher also visited Tetugu and Awer camps while in Gulu, though these are not discussed in this study owing to space constraints.

84 The camp had been attacked in both May and July 2004, with extensive burning of shelters and the fatal shooting of an elderly female resident.

85 IDP representatives noted that the UPDF presence nevertheless needs to be increased and that the detachment of approximately 150 soldiers should be broken up into smaller units around the camp. Interview 24 August 2004.

86 They hastened to add that the acquisition of weapons is difficult given the current presence of the UPDF and that even those who traded informally with the Karamojang in the 1980s and 1990s were often killed or captured by the UPDF. Interview 24 August 2004.

87 UPDF stationed next to the HMG report having fired it at least five times since it was acquired several months before the research visit. Interview with UPDF in Palinga IDP camp, 24 August 2004.

88 The UPDF is alleged to be paid UGS160,000 (USD100) per month while the JCC receives less than UGS60,000 (USD40).

89 It is likely that Patongo camp in Pader is the largest camp in the country. Interview with Andrew Timson, 6 September 2004.

90 Numbering some 770 soldiers, the 71st Battalion appears to have replaced the 43rd Battalion in late 2003. Local informants claim that there were two tanks, two Buffalo and one Mamba armoured personnel carrier, and at least one heavy machine gun for every detachment.

91 Refugees in Moyo, across the West Nile river, are comparatively unaffected owing to the natural barriers that have hitherto inhibited LRA incursions.

92 Refugees, however, complain that the UPDF and the police are rarely adequately represented or responsive to security threats. Interview with Alinatiwe John, Refugee Desk Officer for the Office of the Prime Minister, 27 August 2005.

93 Principle 7 of the *Guiding Principles* notes that ' ... (b) adequate measures shall be to guarantee to those to be displaced full information on the reasons and procedures for their displacement ... (c) the free and informed consent of those to be displaced shall be sought; (d) authorities concerned shall endeavour to involve those affected, particularly women, in the planning and management of their relocation ... ' See also Weeks (2002).

94 Principle 6, for example, guarantees protection against arbitrary displacement or displacement that lasts longer than required by circumstances.

95 Guiding Principle 14 sanctions liberty of movement and the right to move freely in and out of camps or other settlements, and should be condoned.

References

Accorsi, S., B. Corrado, M. Fabiani, R. Iriso, B. Nattabi, E. Ayella, M. Ogwang, P. Onek, B. Pido and S. Declich (2003) 'Competing demands and limited resources in the context of war, poverty and disease: the case of Lacor Hospital', *Health Policy and Development*, 1(1): 29–39.

Bagenda, E. and L. Hovil (2003) 'Sudanese refugees in northern Uganda: from one conflict to another', *Forced Migration Review*, 16: 14–16.

Bagshaw, S. and D. Paul (2004) *Protect or Neglect: Toward a More Effective United Nations Approach to the Protection of Internally Displaced Persons*, Washington, DC: Brookings-SAIS Project.

BBC News (2005) 'Kenya kills Uganda cattle raiders', 21 July, accessed July 2005, <http://news.bbc.co.uk/2/hi/africa/4703363.stm>.

Bernstein, J. (2005) *A Drop in the Ocean: Assistance and Protection for Forced Migrants in Kampala*, Refugee Law Project Working Paper 16, Kampala: Refugee Law Project.

Bonwick, A. (2003) 'Access to protect', *Humanitarian Exchange*, 23, March, pp. 9–12.

Brauer, J. and R. Muggah (2006) 'Completing the circle: building a theory of small arms demand', *Journal of Contemporary Security Policy*, 25(2).

Buchanan, C. and R. Muggah (2005) *No Relief: Victimisation of Humanitarian Personnel*, Geneva: Centre for Humanitarian Dialogue and the Small Arms Survey.

Captier, C. (2003) 'What does humanitarian protection really mean?', *Humanitarian Exchange*, 23, March, pp. 15–18.

Cohen, R. and F. Deng (1998) *Masses in Flight: The Global Crisis of Internal Displacement*, Washington, DC: Brookings Institution Press.

Crisp, J. (1999) *A State of Insecurity: The Political Economy of Violence in Refugee-populated Areas of Kenya*, New Issues in Refugee Research no 16, Geneva: Evaluation and Policy Analysis Unit, UNHCR.

— (2002) 'Introduction', *Refugee Survey Quarterly*, 21(1 and 2): 1–11.

Crisp, J. and R. Ayling (1984) *Ugandan Refugees in Sudan and Zaire*, London: British Refugee Council and Refugee Studies Programme.

Da Costa, R. (2004) *Maintaining the Civilian and Humanitarian Character of Asylum*, Legal and Protection Policy Research Series, Geneva: UNHCR.

East African (2005) 'Ugandan prime minister's office profiling northern IDPs', 12 November.

Flew, C. and A. Urquhart (2004) *Strengthening Small Arms Controls: An Audit of Small Arms Control Legislation in the Great Lakes Region and the Horn of Africa*, London: Saferworld and SaferAfrica.

Gersoney, R. (1997) *The Anguish of North Uganda: Results of a Field-based Assessment of the Civil Conflicts in Northern Uganda*, Kampala: USAID.

Gingyera-Pinyewa, A. (1998) *Uganda and the Problem of Refugees*, Kampala: University of Makerere Press.

Gomes, N. and K. Mkutu (2004) *Breaking the Cycle of Violence: Building Local Capacity for Peace and Development in Karamoja, Uganda*, Kampala: Pax Christi.

Gupta, H. (2004) *A Comparative Review of Refugee Security Mechanisms*, Confidential document for UNHCR, Geneva.

Hovil, L. (2001) *Refugees and the Security Situation in the Adjumani District*, Refugee Law Project Working Paper no. 2, Kampala: Refugee Law Project.

Hovil, L. and Z. Lomo (2005) *Whose Justice? Perceptions of Uganda's 2000 Amnesty Act: The Potential for Conflict-resolution and Long-term Reconciliation*, Refugee Law Project Working Paper 15, Kampala: Refugee Law Project.

HRW (Human Rights Watch) (2003) *Stolen Children: Abduction and Recruitment in Northern Uganda*, New York: HRW.

ICG (International Crisis Group) (2005) *Building a Comprehensive Peace Strategy for Northern Uganda*, Africa Briefing 27, Brussels: ICG.

IDP Database (2005) *Uganda Profile*, accessed 1 November, <www.nrc.no/ idpdatabase>.

IISS (International Institute for Strategic Studies) (2004) *The Military Balance 2003/2004*, Oxford: Oxford University Press.

IRIN (2004) 'Uganda to resume disarmament exercise in northeastern region', Reported by Xinhua News Agency, 26 July.

— (2005) 'Kampala denies arms embargo violation charge in UN report', <www.irinnews.org/print.asp?ReportID=45322>.

Kaiser, T. (2000a) 'The experiences and consequences of insecurity in a refugee populated area in northern Uganda 1996–1997', *Refugee Survey Quarterly*, 19: 38–53.

— (2000b) *UNHCR's Withdrawal from Kiryandongo: Anatomy of a Handover*, New Issues in Refugee Research no. 32, Geneva: Evaluation and Policy Analysis Unit, UNHCR.

— (2005) *We are All Stranded Here Together: The Local Settlement System, Freedom of Movement and Livelihood Opportunities in Arua and Moyo Districts*, Refugee Law Project Working Paper 14, Kampala: Refugee Law Project.

Kasozi, A. (1998) *The Social Origins of Violence in Uganda*, Kampala: Fountain Publishers.

Kobusingye, O., M. Mutto, R. Lett and B. Khingi (2003) *The Public Health Impacts of Small Arms in Uganda*, Geneva: Small Arms Survey.

Lacor Hospital (2003) *Activity Report Year 2002*, Gulu.

Lischer, S. (2000) *Refugee Involvement in Political Violence: Quantitative Evidence from 1987–1998*, New Issues in Refugee Research no. 26, Geneva: Evaluation and Policy Analysis Unit, UNHCR.

Loescher, G. (1993) *Beyond Charity: International Cooperation and the Global Refugee Crisis*, Oxford: Oxford University Press.

Lomo, Z., A. Naggaga and L. Hovil (2001) *The Phenomenon of Forced Migration in Uganda: An Overview of Policy and Practice in an Historical Context*, Working Paper no. 1, Kampala: Refugee Law Project.

Merkx, J. (2002) 'Refugee identities and relief in an Africa borderland: a study of northern Uganda and southern Sudan', *Refugee Survey Quarterly*, 21(1 and 2): 113–46.

Minear, L. (1999) *Partnerships in the Protection of Refugees and Other People at Risk: Emerging Issues and Work in Progress*, New Issues in Refugee Research no. 13, Geneva: UNHCR.

Mkutu, K. (2003) *Pastoral Conflicts and Small Arms: The Kenyan–Uganda Cross Border Region*, London: Saferworld.

Moro, L. (2002) 'Refugee camps in northern Uganda: sanctuaries or battle-grounds', Unpublished manuscript, American University of Cairo.

Muggah, R. (2003) 'Two solitudes: comparing conflict and development-induced displacement and resettlement', *Journal of International Migration*, 41(5): 1–28.

— (2005a) 'A crisis turning inwards: refugee and IDP militarisation in Uganda', *Humanitarian Exchange*, 29, <www.odihpn.org/report. asp?ID=2574>.

— (2005b) 'By targeting NGOs, they bite the hand that helps them', *Globe and Mail*, 28 October.

Muhereza, E. (1997) 'Cross border grazing and challenges for development in the dryland areas of eastern Africa: the case of Karamoja', Paper for the Ethiopian International Institute for Peace and Development, Addis Ababa.

OAU (1967) *Convention Governing the Specific Aspects of Refugee Problems in Africa*, 1001 UNTS. 45, entered into force 20 June 1974.

OCHA (UN Office for the Coordination of Humanitarian Affairs) (2004a) *Humanitarian Update: Uganda*, 5(12), January, accessed 7 July 2005, <www. reliefweb.int/rw/rwb.nsf/AllDocsByUNID/ab319f60f5ae3b4dc1256e150043 b4bb>.

— (2004b) *Humanitarian Update: Uganda*, 6(7), July, accessed 7 July, <www. reliefweb.int/rw/RWB.NSF/db900SID/HMYT-63TLKE?OpenDocument&rc=1 &cc=uga>.

— (2004c) 'Mission report: Uganda – 14 to 17 June 2004', Kampala: Regional Support Office for Central and East Africa.

— (2004d) 'Database of northern Uganda-related peace building activities', 13 August, <www.reliefweb.int/rw/dbc.nsf/doc104?OpenForm&rc=1&cc=uga>.

— (2004e) 'Assorted statistics and confidential reports, Kampala, Gulu, Kitgum', Compiled in Uganda in August.

Onega, P. (2004) 'The amnesty process: opportunities and challenges', Unpublished mimeo, Kampala.

Paul, A. 2004. 'Boys will be boys, but will states be states? Private militia groups and African state reconfiguration. A study of private militia groups in Uganda and Nigeria and their potential to initiate state formation', Unpublished dissertation.

Pax Christi (2004) *Breaking the Cycle of Violence: Building Local Capacity for Peace and Development in Karamoja, Uganda*, The Hague: Pax Christi.

Phuong, C. (2005) *The International Protection of Internally Displaced Persons. Cambridge Studies in International and Comparative Law*, Cambridge: Cambridge University Press.

Pirouet, L. (1988) 'Refugees in and from Uganda in the post-independence period', in H. Hansen and M. Twaddle (eds), *Changing Uganda: The Dimensions of Structural Adjustment and Revolutionary Change*, London: James Currey.

Prunier, G. (1999) *The Rwandan Crisis: History of a Genocide*, New York: Columbia University Press.

Refugee Law Project (2002) *Update on Repatriation of Rwandese Refugees in Uganda*, Kampala: Faculty of Law, Makerere University.

Small Arms Survey (2003) *Small Arms Survey: Development Denied*, Oxford: Oxford University Press.

— (2004) *Small Arms Survey: Rights at Risk*, Oxford: Oxford University Press.

— (2005) *Small Arms Survey: Weapons at War*, Oxford: Oxford University Press.

Stein, B. (2001) *Older Refugee Settlements in Africa*, Humanitarian Net, accessed 7 July 2005, <www.h-net.org/~africa/sources/refugee.html>.

UN (United Nations) (1951) *Convention Relating to the Status of Refugees*, accessed 7 July 2005, <www.ohchr.org/english/law/pdf/refugees.pdf>.

— (2001) *Consolidated Inter-agency Appeal 2001: Uganda*, Geneva/Kampala: UN.

UNHCR (United Nations High Commissioner for Refugees) (2004) Assorted statistics and confidential reports gathered in Kampala, Adjumani, Moyo.

UNSC (United Nations Security Council) (2004) *Report of the Group of Experts to the UN Secretary General: Monitoring the Ituri Embargo 2003–2004*, accessed 24 July 2005, <http://129.194.252.80/catfiles/3111.pdf>.

UPDF (Ugandan People's Defence Force) (2004) 'UPDF kills 113 LRA terrorists and rescues 225', *Alluta: The People's Army Bulletin*, 1(10), April.

USCR (US Committee for Refugees) (1997) *Country Report: Uganda*, accessed 7 July 2005, <www.refugees.org/countryreports.aspx?id=901>.

— (1999) *World Refugee Survey*, Washington, DC: USCR.

Van Goethem, H. (2003) 'NGOs in refugee protection: an unrecognised resource', *Humanitarian Exchange*, 23, March, pp. 12–15.

Weeks, W. (2002) *Pushing the Envelope: Moving beyond Protected Villages in Northern Uganda*, New York: OCHA.

Woodward, P. (1991) 'Uganda and southern Sudan: peripheral politics and neighbour relations', in H. Hansen and M. Twaddle (eds), *Changing Uganda: The Dimensions of Structural Adjustment and Revolutionary Change*, London: James Currey.

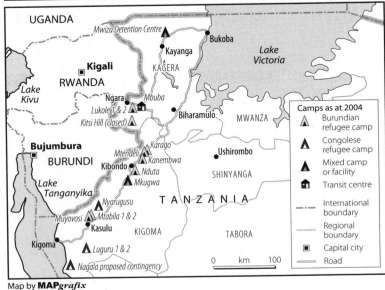

Map by **MAP**grafix

4 | Preventing or abetting: refugee militarization in Tanzania

EDWARD MOGIRE

Tanzania represents something of a paradox. In addition to being home to the continent's largest refugee case load, Tanzania is also one of the poorest countries in the world. Its Gross National Income (GNI) per capita was estimated at USD290 in 2003 by the World Bank. Tanzania qualified for full debt relief under the enhanced Heavily Indebted Poor Countries (HIPC) initiative in 2001. The north-western region of the country, where the majority of the country's refugees have been settled, is particularly impoverished owing to its remoteness and legacy of marginalization by the central authorities. Because of its comparative political stability and geographic location in the conflict-prone Great Lakes Region (GLR), and what is widely perceived to be a generous refugee policy, refugees have long turned to Tanzania for asylum. Since attaining independence in 1961, Tanzania has hosted refugees fleeing the anti-colonial struggles in southern Africa – Angola, the Comoros Islands, Namibia, Mozambique, Seychelles, South Africa and Zimbabwe – as well as refugees fleeing civil conflict in independent African states – Somalia, Rwanda, Burundi, Malawi, Uganda and Kenya.

Tanzania has the largest refugee population in Africa. According to the European Commission Humanitarian Aid Office (ECHO 2005), at the beginning of 2004 there were an estimated 476,000 UNHCR-assisted refugees. In addition, government officials stated that another 170,000 Burundians lived in permanent settlements, and 300,000 others were 'illegally' settled in Tanzanian villages (ECHO 2004: 3, 5). While UNHCR has facilitated repatriation of some Burundians since 2002, the precarious political and military situation in the GLR, in particular the simmering political and civil unrest in Burundi and the Democratic Republic of Congo (DRC), has hindered large-scale voluntary return of refugees.

This chapter examines the phenomenon of refugee militarization[1] in Tanzania, with a specific focus on Burundian refugees. Constituting the largest share of refugees in the country, the militarization of Burundians has long roots. The chapter explores the historical evolution of refugee militarization, its complex dynamics and spatial distribution, the factors that underpin it, and the relationship between militarization and small-arms proliferation. The chapter also considers the impacts of refugee militarization and arms availability on host state security and the range of policy responses that have emerged in its wake.

The chapter is itself divided into six discrete sections. It begins by assessing the legacy of refugee militarization in Tanzania. In particular, it disaggregates militarization according to specific refugee ethnicities. It finds that refugee militarization is not homogenous, but rather highly differentiated according to the particular experience of refugees themselves. The second section elaborates on this by situating the militarization of Burundian refugees in a historical context. It appraises the extent to which militarization of Burundians has changed in the intervening years. In the third section, the factors underpinning militarization are briefly considered, including the extent to which refugees receive support from the host state, the location of camps, the nature and character of the refugee population itself, regional dynamics and the like. The fourth section considers the linkages between refugees and the diffusion of illicit arms more generally. Section five provides a superficial review of the specific impacts of refugee militarization on 'protection', state and societal security and humanitarian assistance, with special emphasis on the presence and misuse of small arms. The final section concludes with an overview of the various responses undertaken by UNHCR, the Tanzanian government and refugees themselves to the particular 'problem' of refugee militarization.

A note on methodology Unlike in previous studies of refugee militarization in Tanzania[2] the findings of this particular chapter are drawn directly from a combination of secondary sources and empirical research. Archival research was undertaken in the UK, Switzerland and Tanzania, and included published and grey material as well as public archives. There is, in fact, an extensive literature on the subject, though comparatively little derived from fieldwork. The author also undertook a mission to Tanzania between June and July 2004, during which structured and semi-structured interviews were held with Tanzanian government officials[3] and representatives of development and humanitarian organizations.[4] During a field trip to northern Tanzania, a retrospective review of hospital records and prison data was also undertaken. Finally, the author commissioned a review of articles from the *Daily News*, a local newspaper.

In order to capture some of the localized dynamics of refugee militarization, refugee camps were also visited. Specifically, two camps, Mtabila and Muyovosi, hosting Burundian Hutu refugees, were selected in order to generate a more sophisticated appreciation of the dynamics at play. These camps had been visited by the author during his doctoral research several years before and were thus familiar. In addition to several informal meetings with a sample of refugees and selected refugee leaders, fourteen refugees were interviewed in Mtabila and Muyovosi refugee camps with the help of a research assistant.

As with all studies on highly complex and fluid population groups, there are a number of problems with the data cited in this chapter. A major caveat relates to data availability. Indeed, the data provided here are neither complete nor always verifiable, which renders longitudinal and comparative analysis somewhat difficult. Even where disaggregated information was made available, the method of its collection or presentation reduced its reliability and credibility. Given the scarcity and general untrustworthiness of existing data-sets, the author was compelled to generate his own data. But as a result of the small sample size from the refugee interviews and focus groups, it is impossible to render meaningful statistical analysis. The data presented in this chapter should therefore be interpreted carefully, and should be regarded as signalling indicative trends rather than statistically verifiable evidence. Clearly still more focused research will be required to substantiate the claims made herein.

A brief history of refugee militarization in Tanzania

Both refugee movements and refugee militarization in Tanzania exhibit a long history which can be traced to the 1960s. Though the phenomena came to international prominence in the 1990s as a result of the activities of Rwandese Hutu and Burundian refugees, their roots can be traced to the independence conflicts of the decolonization period. As in other countries during this period, refugees and exiles from southern Africa involved in armed resistance against former colonial powers and racist regimes in their home countries were granted asylum in Tanzania.

In fact, a number of armed liberation movements, including the Front for the Liberation of Mozambique (FRELIMO), the African National Congress (ANC), the Pan African Congress (PAC), the Zimbabwe African National Union (ZANU), the Zimbabwe African People's Union (ZAPU), the Popular Movement for the Liberation of Angola (MPLA) and the South West Africa People's Organization (SWAPO), were physically based in Tanzania. These groups received political, moral and military support from the Tanzanian government and others in their armed struggles. What is more, they were permitted to recruit and train refugees as part of their cadres, receive 'contributions' from displaced populations, and in some cases use refugee camps to conduct cross-border attacks. These armed group/refugee networks were normalized by an Organization of African Unity (OAU) resolution passed during a conference in Addis Ababa in May 1963. Moreover, successive UN General Assembly resolutions also urged member states to provide material and moral assistance to the national liberation movements under way in colonial territories – GA/Res/2189(2189(XXI) paragraph 7. Not all member states were supportive of these norms. Indeed, in the case of Tanzania, the Portuguese colonial administration actively retaliated against its enemies by conducting military raids on refugee settlements (Gasarasi 1988; Metcalfe 1971).

Rwandese Tutsi refugees, who fled to Tanzania in the early 1960s, were also rapidly militarized. The original Tutsi refugees quickly organized themselves into guerrilla cadres, which the Hutu labelled derogatively *inyenzi* (cockroaches). They staged repeated cross-border attacks into Rwanda from bases established in Uganda, Zaire and Tanzania (Adelman 1998; Prunier 1995). Many of these raids proved ineffective as the *inyezi* appeared to behave ' ... more like terrorists than guerrilla fighters, apparently not caring about the violent reprisals on the Tutsi civilian population their attacks provoked' (Prunier 1995: 54). The *inyenzi* were also largely ineffective because the Tanzanian government implemented a range of robust controls to prevent them from undertaking military operations. Prunier (ibid.) reports that, by 1964, all cross-border attacks and politicking by the Tutsi had come to an end. But this would prove to be only a temporary lull in an agonizing story.

By the late 1980s, Tutsi refugees had renewed their efforts to militarize displaced populations. By the time the civil war began in Rwanda during the early 1990s, the Rwandese Patriotic Army (RPA) – established and led by Tutsi refugees in Uganda – had begun to recruit fighters from the Rwandese diaspora in Tanzania (ibid.: 116). Following the genocide and the subsequent victory of the RPA in 1994, large-scale militarization began to be undertaken by Hutu refugees in Tanzania. Between 1994 and 1996, Rwandese Hutu refugee camps in Tanzania were controlled by armed elements including former members of the defeated Rwandese army (ex-FAR) and the *interahamwe*.[5, 6] The symptoms of refugee militarization were well documented at the time. A vast assortment of illicit arms flowed into and through the refugee camps while Hutu rebel groups began to recruit intensively from among the refugees themselves. Armed groups also began to conduct military training in the refugee camps and finally, though to a lesser extent than in eastern Zaire, began to carry out cross-border attacks from the refugee camps into Rwanda (Odhiambo 1996: 310; United Nations 1998; MSF 1995). The militarization of Rwandese refugees soon came to an end in December 1996 when, responding to internal and domestic pressures, the Tanzanian government forcefully repatriated all Rwandese refugees from its territory.

But outward refugee militarization in Tanzania is not limited to its Rwandan and Burundian neighbours. Indeed, another instance of refugee militarization manifested itself during the 1970s, when Ugandan refugees fled into Tanzania following a coup d'état and political repression led by a military junta under Idi Amin. Former President Julius Nyerere of Tanzania refused to recognize the new Ugandan government and offered 'hospitality' to deposed Ugandan president Milton Obote and his supporters. The support for Ugandan refugees was premised on the personal friendship between Nyerere and Obote as well as on legitimate political and security concerns (Mushemesha 1998: 101). Under the watchful eye of the Tanzanian authorities, camps in Tanzania were used by Obote and allies to reorganize and arm themselves in preparation for an invasion of Uganda. By 1972, Ugandan exiles had launched an invasion from their bases in Tanzania into south-western Uganda, though the attack was comprehensively repulsed by the Ugandan army and the attackers were forced to retreat back to Tanzania.[7] Cross-border attacks and Ugandan counterattacks persisted until 1979, when the military government was ultimately ousted by a combined force of Ugandan exiles and the Tanzanian defence forces (Cervenka 1977; Mushemesha 1998; Adelman 1998).

Burundian refugees in Tanzania

By far the most consistent refugee flows into Tanzania have been from neighbouring Burundi. There have been several repeated instances of refugee influxes following periods of intense violence between the Hutu majority and the Tutsi minority, in 1972, 1988, 1991, 1993 and 1996 to the present (Prunier 1995). Those refugees who fled in the 1970s – themselves numbering approximately 170,000 – have been hosted in permanent settlements (ECHO 2005: 5). By way of contrast, those fleeing the (recently ended) civil war that erupted in 1993 after the assassination of the democratically elected Hutu president Merchoir Ndadaye, and the Tutsi-led military coup in 1996, are hosted in refugee camps. Officially recognized Burundian refugees in Tanzania reached an all-time peak of 538,400 individuals in 2000 (UNHCR 2001: 89), declining to some 259,000 by August 2004. In addition, the country hosted about 300,000 'unrecognized' Burundian refugees (ECHO 2004: 3).

Tanzania has long been acknowledged as progressive when it comes to refugee settlement. Until the early 1990s, the Tanzanian government adopted a policy of hosting refugees in 'permanent' settlements, providing them with land and an array of other social services including subsidized school facilities, hospitals and clinics. The aim was ostensibly to let refugees become 'self-reliant', although the policy was also probably undertaken

TABLE 4.1 Distribution of Burundian refugees by camps, end of August 2003 and 2004

Region	Name of camp	August 2003	August 2004	Difference
Kigoma	Muyovosi	39,857	37,195	– 2,662
	Mtabila 1	17,795	16,916	– 879
	Mtabila 2	44,876	42,455	– 2,331
	Kanembwa	19,697	15, 569	– 4,128
	Mtendeli	41,334	29,115	– 1,2219
	Karago	26,508	7,485	– 19,023
	Nduta	45,523	34,281	– 11,242
Kagera	Lukole A	50,909	49,791	– 5,118
	Lukole B	32,619	30,355	– 2,264
	Mwisa	62	0	– 62
	Mbuba – transit	21	49	28
Total		319,201	263, 211	– 55,990

Source: ECHO (2004: 17)

to meet the developmental requirements of Tanzania. But against a backdrop of reduced burden sharing from donor countries, and exasperated by undiminished refugee flows, the government adopted a new policy in the early 1990s, still in force, requiring all refugees to live in designated refugee 'camps'.[8] This policy was dutifully enforced. Refugees found outside the camps without adequate documentation are regularly subject to police harassment, detention and imprisonment. At present, most Burundian refugees are hosted in eleven refugee camps located along a 250-kilometre stretch in the Kigoma and Kagera region of Tanzania's north-western border (see Map 2). Table 4.1 shows the approximate distribution of the refugee population among camps.

Militarization of Burundian refugees

The question of whether Burundian refugees and refugee camps in Tanzania were and are militarized is highly political and hotly debated. To be sure, the Burundian government has regularly condemned these populations en masse, routinely describing them as 'troublemakers' and 'terrorists'. This has contributed to fraying relations between the two countries. The Burundian government has seldom missed an opportunity to accuse Tanzania of tolerating, if not aiding and abetting, armed subversion from refugee camps (ICG 1999). For example, in April 2000 a Burundian government spokesman claimed that its armed forces were fighting against the Force pour la Défense de la Démocratie (FDD), which it claimed was attacking from bases inside refugee camps in western Tanzania (Associated Press 2001a). Others have also supported the Burundian government's grievances. Independent observers, including the UNHCR and other international aid agencies, have repeatedly accused Tanzania of insufficiently controlling the refugee camps and preventing Hutu rebels from using them to launch military attacks on Burundi. The Burundian government has also gone so far as to accuse UNHCR and international aid agencies themselves of feeding and sheltering the rebels – thus drawing out the conflict (IRIN 2000b).

Even so, the Tanzanian government and UNHCR have publicly denied that Burundian refugees and their camps are militarized. According to UNHCR, the concept of militarized refugees is itself oxymoronic – refugees who carry arms are no longer described as such, but rather as 'foreign combatants' or armed criminals. But UNHCR also bases its claims on fact. For example, in May 1997 a joint government/UNHCR field mission was deployed in the camps to assess claims of militarization. Its conclusions indicated that the camps were 'not militarized', and that no organized military preparation or training was occurring, and that no camp resident could be found carrying or possessing arms or ammunition. Subsequent joint assessment missions have reiterated these claims. It should be recalled, however, that these conclusions are based on information obtained almost exclusively from *inside* the camps and do not necessarily address recruitment from among refugee populations residing outside of the camps, spontaneously settled asylum claimants or even the indirect contributions made by refugees to support the war effort (Durieux 2000). Indeed, it appears that covert militarization and military activities in other parts of the border area actually take place on a fairly regular basis, although their exact dimensions are nearly impossible to measure with certainty (ibid; Crisp 2001: 2). The evidence presented below indicates that Burundian refugee camps are in fact still militarized, albeit less so than during the 1990s. They were and continue to be used for a number of key activities, including military mobilization, recruitment, training, cross-border attacks, fund-raising, political strategizing, arms trafficking, resource distribution, rest and recuperation and medical treatment.

Cross-border attacks Militarization of Burundian refugees in Tanzania can be traced to the early 1970s. Its origins lie in refugees who initially settled just across the border from Burundi, and who subsequently initiated guerrilla activities and staged cross-border attacks from their newly installed settlements. The Burundian government's response was swift. In 1973, it staged a bombing raid on a number of localities inside Tanzania, which resulted in the death of as many as seventy Tanzanian civilians. The Tanzanian government responded to these incursions by boycotting the handling of all Burundian cargo arriving at or leaving the ports of Kigoma and Dar es Salaam (Rutinwa 1998). A tripartite agreement between Tanzania, Burundi and Zaire aiming to constrain refugee subversion from Tanzania did not succeed in ending refugee militarization. Indeed, during the 1980s armed Hutu groups such as the Partie de Libération du Peuple Hutu (PALIPEHUTU) and the Front pour la Libération Nationale (FROLINA) carried out cross-border attacks from the camps into Burundi (Lemarchand 1994). Since the 1990s other armed Hutu groups, among them the Conseil National pour la Défense de la Démocratie (CNDD) and the Force pour la Défense de la Démocratie (FDD), have also carried out cross-border attacks from camps.

Burundian militant groups in Tanzania The chief source of refugee militarization is guerrilla groups stationed within settlements and camps. For example, PALIPEHUTU and FROLINA, the first organized Hutu armed groups, were in fact established in Burundian refugee settlements in western Tanzania during the early 1970s. These two rebel groups recruited from the refugee settlements, conducted military training and carried out small-scale cross-border attacks. While PALIPEHUTU attracted further support from followers in Rwanda and Burundi, FROLINA drew its support almost entirely from the existing refugee and local populations in Tanzania (ICG 1999: 2; Lemarchand 1994: 173). During the 1990s, PALIPEHUTU and FROLINA were joined in the refugee camps by other armed groups, among them Conseil National pour la Défense de la Démocratie (CNDD), Force pour la Défense de la Démocratie (FDD) and the military wing of another group calling itself Ubumwe Bw'Abarundi (Unity of the Burundian People) (ICG 1999: 15; Van Eck 2001: 25–35). Furthermore, some Burundian refugees who had served in the Tanzanian army or were provided with training subsequently joined guerrilla factions (HRW 1999: 19). Despite a range of efforts to contain them, various groups still maintain a presence in the refugee camps, exercise control over the refugee population, and receive support from the refugees. Their presence is indicated by the arrest in camps of 'combatants' who are then held at a special separation facility – Mwisa camp in Kagera region.[9]

Refugee recruitment Recruitment of refugees, including child soldiers, continues in western Tanzania. Tanzanian government officials have aknowledged that Hutu rebels recruit refugees who are subsequently smuggled abroad for training and arming, but hasten to add that recruitment is carried out clandestinely, without government knowledge or support (Bruns International 2000). There have been several reports in the local and international media on armed recruitment of refugees in Tanzania. For example in March 2000 the *International Tribune* reported that Jean-Bosco Ndayikengurukiye, the leader of FDD, had gone to Karago refugee camp on a recruitment mission. This report was, however, denied at the time by Paul Stromberg, the UNHCR spokesman (IRIN 2000a). There have been recent reports of recruitment of child soldiers from western Tanzania, which is said to have escalated in 2004 (Coalition to Stop the Use of Child Soldiers 2004). According to the UN secretary-general, 'despite bans on the use of child soldiers in the Arusha Accords of 2000, Burundian armed opposition groups continued to recruit children from refugee camps in western Tanzania' (UNSG 2003). For example, the Mugaborabona faction of PALIPEHUTU – FNL (Forces Nationales de Libération) and the Ndayikengurukiye faction of CNDD–FDD undertook massive child recruitment in the period leading up to the presidential elections. Possibly the main reason was to inflate their numbers so that the groups would gain recognition and bargaining power in the Burundian peace negotiations and subsequent disarmament, demobilization and reintegration (DDR) programme (Coalition to Stop the Use of Child Soldiers 2004). The Nkurunziza faction of CNDD–FDD, which has rear bases in eastern DRC, also reportedly continued to recruit and abduct children, from schools and from refugee camps in neighbouring Tanzania (Amnesty International 2003).

Owing to the clandestine nature of these recruitments, it is exceedingly difficult to determine the exact number of refugees involved. Nevertheless, a number of incidents attest to the continued recruitment of refugees. According to UNHCR (2000b: 248), by August 1998 nearly two thousand refugees had been mobilized from western Tanzania to DRC for military operations. Less than two years later, in mid-February 2000, a group of 630 refugees crossed the border from Tanzania to fight in Burundi (Skarp 2000: 37), and by May 2000 Tanzanian government officials in Kigoma had arrested 167 refugee recruits who were on their way to the DRC for military training (Guardian 2000b). Figures provided by UNICEF also highlight how Hutu rebels abducted 107 Burundian children from refugee camps in western Tanzania in 2001 to be used in the conflict as child soldiers, messengers or domestic labourers (Associated Press 2001b). The abductions occurred with the connivance of parents and other relatives, making prevention and prosecution more difficult still.

Problematically, recruitment of refugees in western Tanzania is largely voluntary. Jean-François Durieux, UNHCR head of sub-office in Kigoma between October 1997 and September 1999, states: '[d]isquieting as the thought may be, the fact is that "spontaneous" sympathy for the Hutu militant cause is widespread among the refugees. This should not come as a surprise considering the traumatic experiences, which caused their flight. Exile also reinforces feelings of Hutu "nationalism" as well as gradually dissolves the cruelty of internal conflict into an almost mythical aura of just war' (Durieux 2000).[10] Even so, involuntary recruitment, especially of child soldiers, has also been reported. Human Rights Watch (HRW 1999) was able to verify voluntary recruitment in refugee camps perpetrated by CNDD, PALIPEHUTU and their affiliated splinter groups, but was unable to generate any definitive proof of forced recruitment or active arming and training in the camps.

Military training and other indicators of militarization The militarization of Burundian refugees is also reflected in the military training within and in the vicinity of the refugee camps. A number of reports have alluded to this. For example, according to the United Nations (1995), between mid-1994 and late 1996 there existed military training camps for Burundian and Rwandan rebels in refugee camps in western Tanzania. Médecins Sans Frontières, Human Rights Watch and the International Crisis Group have also observed how Burundian refugees in western Tanzania were engaged in military training both in and outside the camps (MSF 1994; HRW 1999; ICG 1999). These reports were also confirmed by UNHCR, which reported incidents of military training involving several groups of refugees both within and in the immediate vicinity of refugee camps (UNHCR 1998a, 1998b).

Rebels are also known to use refugee resources – including food, shelter, medicines and camps themselves – for rest and recuperation. Refugees are also regularly intimidated into making financial and material contributions to guerrilla groups. According to testimonies recorded by Human Rights Watch, PALIPEHUTU imposed a TZS300 (approximately USD0.50 at prevailing rates) tax on each refugee family. CNDD did the same but, since it enjoyed greater support in the camps, contributions were allegedly voluntarily provided. Related, a food tax was also imposed, with rebels demanding a portion of newly distributed rations (HRW 1999). Alarmingly, refugees in Kigoma linked sudden surges in the incidence of child malnutrition to the payment of 'food taxes' to such armed groups (Durieux 2000).

Burundian refugee militarization is also reflected in incidents of political violence between various ethnic, partisan[11] and military factions present in the camps. Incidents of political violence involving refugees include planned riots, cross-border raids by militias based in or near refugee camps, attacks on the refugee population by the sending state, and military attacks by the receiving state on refugees or refugee-populated areas (Lischer 2000: 4). In western Tanzania, political violence has erupted as a result of rivalries between various political factions that live side by side in the camps. For example, the lingering tensions between PALIPEHUTU and CNDD have at times resulted in assassinations. In some instances people from rival parties (or presumed affiliates) have been forced to move from one area of the camp to another (Turner 1999). Reported incidents of factional violence include the conflict between PALIPEHUTU and CNDD at Kitalo Hill refugee camp in late 1996 and early 1997, conflict between CNDD and FDD at Lukole refugee camp in July 2000, and the assassination of Jean Batungwanayo, the elder brother of Leonard Nyangoma, a political leader of PALIPEHUTU, in February 2000 (Mogire 2003: 231). Between 4 and 6 March 2003 armed factions belonging to CNDD attacked Mtabila and Muyovosi refugee camps, intent on generating instability in the camps so that refugees would return to register as voters in anticipation of the general election provided for in the Arusha Agreement of 2000.[12]

Militarization of international borders Although the Burundian refugee camps have been spared any large-scale external military attacks, refugee subversion has led to the militarization of the border areas. Indeed, the threat has been considered to be sufficiently large to warrant the deployment of the Burundian and Tanzanian armed forces along their shared border. What is more, Burundi has created a 5-kilometre buffer zone on its side of the border, has proceeded to mine the frontier districts, and has adopted a policy of 'hot pursuit' of refugees and rebels attacking from Tanzania (ICG 1999: 5). For its part, in order to provide security and to address the problem of armed elements, the Tanzanian government has deployed armed police officers in the refugee camps themselves.

Explaining refugee militarization

No single factor can explain the occurrence and persistence of refugee militarization. Indeed, there are at least five interlocking factors that appear to be responsible for militarization in Tanzania. For one, there appears to have been a long tradition of *Tanzanian government support* to allow the militarization of camps to proceed. Indeed, this substantiates the claim that refugee militarization cannot in fact occur without a host government providing a sanctuary (Zolberg et al. 1989; Terry 2002). As noted above, the direct support provided by the Tanzanian government to those undertaking liberation struggles and Ugandan refugees was crucial in allowing for militarization to take place (Betts 1981). This having been said, there does not appear to have been substantial direct Tanzanian support for the militarization of Burundian refugees in recent years. Rather, Tanzania's role has been more a function of omission rather than commission. In other words, Tanzania has indirectly supported refugee militarization. In addition to allowing Burundian refugees to receive training from the Tanzanian armed forces, the Tanzanian government also allowed rebel leaders residing in the country to solicit support from governments such as Sudan and Iran[13] (HRW 1999). Others contend that Tanzania allowed refugees to become militarized out of sympathy for the Hutu cause and as part of a broader strategy to force the Burundian government into yielding concessions during the peace negotiations (Durieux 2000; Evans 1997). Some, including the International Crisis Group (ICG 1999), have gone farther, claiming that the Tanzanian government directly underwrote the militarization of Hutu refugees.

Another factor that influences refugee militarization relates to the *location of the refugee camps* in relation to a national border with the country of origin. Foreign guerrilla groups and armed factions located close to an international border can not only rapidly initiate 'lightning raids' across borders, but can just as quickly retreat into the refugee camps. Burundian refugee camps in western Tanzanian are located within walking distance of the international border;[14] in general the distance ranges from 15 to 30 kilometres – often closer than the limit now advocated by UNHCR. The location of refugee camps close to international frontiers has allowed groups of defeated or stranded Hutu insurgents to retreat into the refugee camps at regular intervals and use the camps to prepare for subsequent raids (Durieux 2000; Amnesty International 2004).

The *mixed nature of the refugee populations in camps* presents yet another major factor that at least partly explains refugee militarization. Specifically, the presence of armed factions interspersed with refugee populations can rapidly increase the likelihood of militarization. The UN secretary-general has stated that the failure to separate ' … combatants from civilians allows armed groups to take control of a camp and its population, politicizing their situation and gradually establishing a military culture within the camp' (UNSG 2001: para. 30). This is in fact what occurred in the case of the Rwandan and Burundian refugees residing in Tanzania. The then UN High Commissioner for Refugees, Sadako Ogata, stated that 'the presence of armed elements including the ex-FAR and *interahamwe* militias among Rwandese refugees who fled into Tanzania was partly responsible for the militarization of this case load' (Ogata 1998). The Burundian refugee camps were equally divided between ostensibly civilian and armed elements. This is particularly true of those coming from the DRC in the wake of the Lusaka Accord in 1996. While many armed groups emanating from Rwanda and

Burundi were disarmed and demobilized, those who did not care to disarm relocated to refugee camps in western Tanzania (Van Eck 2001: 14).[15]

A major contributing factor to the onset of refugee militarization is the *protracted nature of the refugee situation to begin with*. In the case of Burundi's refugee case load, many have been forced to adopt survival strategies, ranging from 'legitimate' subsistence livelihoods to criminality and the joining of guerrilla groups in order to cope (Goetz 2003). In western Tanzania, the sheer dearth of economic and social opportunities for Tanzanian civilians, much less young Burundian refugees, has provided a ready pool for recruitment into the ranks of Burundian guerrilla groups (Durieux 2000). According to refugees interviewed in Tanzania, membership in political parties constitutes yet another coping strategy adopted by refugees in order to share membership in a community, to acquire new friends, and to avoid feeling a sense of loss and helplessness.

Finally, the onset of refugee militarization is closely intertwined with *the conflict in Burundi itself*. Analysis of refugee behaviour in camps has revealed a strong association between the original causes of the refugees' flight and their subsequent level of political and military organization. Population displacement resulting from exclusivist and deliberate government policies of persecution, state collapse, ethnic cleansing or genocide, expulsion of unwanted populations and, above all, war is more likely to lead to armed resistance than that resulting from natural disasters, development projects or low-intensity violence (Zolberg et al. 1989: 229; Lischer 2001). Experience has shown that political refugees rarely accept their 'status' as a permanent condition, and as a result many become involved in supporting armed resistance. A good number of Burundian refugees perceive armed resistance not only as legitimate but sometimes as the only way of bringing about change in their home country. As one refugee who had been forced to seek secondary refugee in Tanzania from Zaire observed: '[F]or most of us who have been in exile for many years, we have seen many false promises and failures of peace agreements. The use of force is an option that we have to leave open if we hope to ever return to our home.'[16]

Regional factors also play a role in refugee militarization (Adelman 1998). So-called 'refugee warriors' are not so much a product of 'root causes' but of discernible failures – sometimes deliberate – in the management of conflicts and, more specifically, in the management of the plight of the refugees by neighbouring states. In the case of Burundi, the Tanzanian government supported military intervention in Burundi to end the conflict but did not receive support from regional partners. Recognizing its limited logistical, military and financial capability to act alone, the Tanzanian government opted for a political solution – namely, conflict resolution.

At the same time, the government strengthened its hand and forced a solution by allowing Hutu rebels to operate from its territory. Further, the continued influx of new refugees was not only a bitter reminder of the continuing violence in Burundi but also a source of anti-government, anti-Tutsi propaganda.

Box 4.1 The challenge of arms availability in Tanzania

There are few reliable estimates of the numbers and distribution of small arms – whether legal or illicit – in circulation in Tanzania. Though anecdote and rumour predominate, according to the home affairs minister there are nevertheless 'still too many guns in the hands of criminals' (Guardian 2004). Recent research undertaken in Tanzania reveals that Tanzanians are more concerned with the widespread presence of illegal firearms than even other urgent health-related matters, including HIV/AIDs, cholera and malnutrition (Jefferson and Urquhart 2002; Schonteich 2000). There perceptions appear to be substantiated by fact. Firearm fatalities are on the rise. Available data indicate that the use of firearms in homicides rose from 6.7 per cent of all homicides (150 out of 2,229) in 1995 (East African 2002) to 7.3 per cent (175 out of total of 2,355) in 1997 (SAS 2004: 193). It is estimated that, between 1998 and 2001, approximately 11,000 people were killed throughout the country in incidents involving the use of illegal small arms – though these figures have not been independently substantiated (East African 2002).

The Small Arms Survey estimates that there are as many as 1.3 million weapons in the country. These include some 241,000 weapons held by the armed forces, at least 42,000 held by the police, and between 500,000 and 1,000,000 in the hands of civilians (SAS 2003: 84–5). This would make Tanzania one of the more heavily armed countries in eastern Africa. Recent reports of arms seizures suggest that either the problem is growing more acute or that the police are becoming more effective. For example, between 1997 and 1999 1,313 guns and 7,113 rounds of ammunition were seized in the country, leading to the filing of 1,223 cases of trafficking of sub-machine guns, semi-automatic rifles, shotguns and handguns (UNAFEI 2001: 217). In 2003, some 850 firearms were seized and 838 suspects arrested (Guardian 2004). Between 1998 and 2001 police impounded about 3,500 firearms and 228,000 rounds of ammunition illicitly circulating in the country (East African 2002). In 2002 1,811 firearms were impounded in the refugee-hosting regions of Kigoma and Kagera. During the same year, police operations in Kagera, one of the provinces worst affected by small-arms proliferation, resulted in the recovery of a total of 1,743 firearms, 3,111 rounds of ammunition, and explosives (Potgieter and Urquhart 2003).

A country survey of small-arms issues in Tanzania by the South Africa-based Institute for Security Studies (ISS) concluded that, although firearm proliferation and crime were on the rise, they have not yet reached crisis proportions. According to this study, most respondents stated that they had seldom or never been exposed to firearm violence. In the twelve regions surveyed by the ISS, less than 25 per cent of respondents had access to firearms. In seven regions, less than 10 per cent had access to firearms, and in four less than 20 per cent. More than 25 per cent of survey respondents indicated, however, that they would like to own a firearm, with more than 30 per cent indicating willingness in nine of the twelve regions. The study also found that certain areas, especially those regions bordering on conflict zones in Rwanda, Burundi and the DRC, were more afflicted than others (Jefferson and Urquhart 2002: 45–60).

The comparatively low availability of weapons is indicated by their relatively high prices. According to the International Action Network on Small Arms (IANSA), a sub-machine gun or an AK-47 assault rifle loaded with a full magazine of ammunition was estimated to cost TZS150,000–400,000 (approximately USD150–400) (East African 2002). To fill the gap, Tanzanians have increasingly turned to improvised, home-made firearms (SAS 2003: 86).

Refugees and the diffusion of illicit firearms

As with the causes of refugee militarization, there are a number of interrelated factors that are alleged to have contributed to the diffusion of illicit small arms in Tanzania. Those mentioned in the literature include the persistence of armed conflict in neighbouring countries – or so-called 'bad neighbourhoods'; the presence of and permissive environment for illegal arms traders, brokers and trans-shipment; the presence of former freedom fighters and criminal gangs; leakages from state security forces – whether the armed forces or the police; craft production; and, controversially, refugees (SAS 2003; Mahita 2000; ICG 1999; HRW 1999). While the validity of each of these factors requires further testing, this section focuses on the role played by refugees, especially militarized refugees.

Official statements Policy-makers, politicians and the media in the region have opportunistically linked the diffusion of illicit small arms to refugee flows and camps. In some cases, these perceptions have been codified into regional agreements. For example, the preamble of the Nairobi Declaration (2000) states: 'The mass movement of armed refugees across national borders in certain countries ... [has] greatly contributed to the proliferation of illicit small arms and light weapons.' Similarly, the conference of the African Panel of Experts on the Illicit Proliferation, Circulation and Trafficking in Small Arms and Light Weapons concluded that 'in some instances, refugees are becoming "the second supply line" of small arms and light weapons' (OAU 2000). Such suggestions, particularly when not backed by adequate evidence, have potentially damaging consequences for protection and asylum.

Tanzanian government officials and politicians have publicly linked the diffusion of illicit small arms to the ebb and flow of refugees. Addressing a public gathering before the destruction of illegal firearms seized in the country, President Benjamin Mkapa echoed widespread concerns when he stated that '[t]he truth is that the proliferation of small arms is a result of refugees entering our country, a problem which is beyond our capacity to solve' (IRIN 2003). Speaking at an inter-parliamentary conference on small arms, the Tanzanian representative claimed that despite the existence of laws prohibiting the importation of small arms, refugees fleeing civil conflict in neighbouring countries brought firearms into the country (IRIN 2004). The Minister for Home Affairs (Mapuri 2003), the Inspector General of Police (Mahita 2000: 12) and the Director of Refugee Services (Brahim 1995), among other government officials, have similarly linked small-arms diffusion to the refugee influx. As is so often the case, it is frequently much easier to point to a foreign vector and source of weapons than to consider one's own backyard.

It is not only politicians or government officials who have linked the diffusion of illicit arms with refugee movements. While the absence of reliable and collated data renders an exact causal relationship unlikely, there is ample anecdotal evidence that appears to bolster the claim. Recent evidence generated by Jefferson and Urquhart (2002) suggests that refugees are a major contributing factor explaining the relatively high level of small-arms presence in Kigoma. They argue that some 25 per cent of the 418 firearms and at least 50 per cent of the 2,076 rounds of ammunition collected nationwide in 1998 were seized in the refugee-hosting region of Kigoma and Mbeya (IRIN-CEA 1999). The Director of Criminal Investigation made a similar inference, reporting that refugees were responsible for most of the 1,016 guns and 5,650 rounds of ammunition seized in Kigoma,

Kagera, Rukwa and Tabora regions between January 1998 and September 1999 (IRIN 1999). Furthermore, guns are occasionally recovered inside refugee camps by the police, who are often tipped off by locally recruited refugee 'guards' or informants (Skarp 2000). The media regularly reinforce these claims – further heightening paranoia (see Table 4.2).[17] Reports on seizures from refugees by the *Daily News* claimed that some 399 small arms, nineteen 'bombs', six hand grenades and over 5,891 rounds of ammunition were uncovered in the vicinity of camps between 1994 and 2001 (Daily News 1997a, 1997b).

TABLE 4.2 A summary of firearms and munitions alleged to have been seized in 'refugee areas' in Tanzania, 1994–2002

	Bombs	Ammunition (rounds)	Firearms	Grenades
1994	–	261	84	–
1997	19	–	111	2
1998	–	21	23	–
1999	–	3,021	1	–
2000	–	234	9	–
2001	–	178	1	–
2002	–	2,176	170	4
Total	19	5,891	399	6

Source: *Daily News* (1994–2002)

A review of prison records does appear to substantiate the claim that some refugees nevertheless have access to small arms and light weapons. Indeed, an examination of firearms-related offences – illegal possession of firearms and ammunition and armed robberies – is suggestive (see Table 4.3). For example, in February 2000 there were some 595 'refugee' inmates in Kigoma prison, fifty-eight of whom were jailed for arms-related offences. During the same period there were 457 refugee inmates in Kagera prison, sixty-eight of whom were imprisoned for arms-related offences. Even so, these trends are not necessarily constant. Prison data from Kibondo district indicate that the number of refugees in prison for arms-related offences declined over a three-year period between 1997 and 2000 (see Table 4.4).

A small-scale survey[18] conducted in Mtabila and Muyovosi refugee camps suggests that the problem of refugee militarization may not be as acute as is commonly claimed by politicians and the media. Indeed, there appear to be fewer incidents of small-arms ownership and misuse in the camps than in the past. Most refugees interviewed claimed that they seldom heard

TABLE 4.3 Refugees in Kigoma and Kagera prisons as of August 2000

Nature of crime	Kigoma	Kagera
Failing to comply	248	–
Unlawfully present in Tanzania	78	33
Unlawful assembly/rioting	15	31
Illegal movement	6	–
Unlawful possession of arms	30	41
Armed robbery	28	27
Murder/manslaughter	57	111
Stealing/housebreaking/burglary/ theft	84	97
Rape	19	22
Assault	–	8
Other	30	87
Total	595	457

Source: UNHCR Protection Unit, Kigoma, 2000

TABLE 4.4 Refugees in Kibondo District prison: 1997–2000

Nature of crime	1997	1998	1999	2000
Unlawfully present in Tanzania	11	2	9	–
Unlawful assembly/rioting	2	–	3	–
Illegal movement	9	–	5	–
Illegal firearms possession	4	3	5	1
Armed robbery	11	6	16	2
Murder/manslaughter	1	–	–	–
Theft/housebreaking/burglary/stolen goods	12	17	6	1
Rape/attempted rape/defilement	6	12	22	9
Assault/wounding	15	2	2	–
Other	13	9	20	19
Total	84	51	88	32

Source: UNHCR Protection Unit, Kibondo, 2000

gunshots in the camps, and observed fewer cases of armed robberies than had previously been the case. Many of those interviewed stated privately that it was in fact exceedingly difficult to obtain firearms. Few claimed to know of anyone who owned a firearm or claimed to have seen firearms brandished openly. Indeed, the police were widely perceived to be the sole possessors of firearms, with refugees restricted to sticks or machetes (see Appendix I).[19] Verification of respondent answers through spot checks and key informant interviews reinforced these claims.

In fact, it appears that the refugee militarization, such as it is, is more a function of 'inward' criminalization than cross-border incursions (Muggah 2005). There has been a growing concern within Tanzania's security establishment with the knock-on criminal effects of arms proliferation across its borders. The police have largely attributed this proliferation and subsequent criminal activities to refugees, though evidence is comparatively scarce. According to the Tanzanian Inspector-General of Police: 'Tanzania's long porous borders which are poorly controlled have enabled some refugees to cross through unofficial entry points with weapons which they later rent or sell to criminals who use them for criminal activities' (Mahita 2000: 10). The Kigoma Regional Refugee Coordinator explained how the arms are brought into the country:

> Refugees bearing arms do not enter the country through the official crossing points where they are searched and their arms confiscated. Rather they use the many unofficial crossing points. In some cases those bearing arms cross the borders undetected at night to hide their weapons inside Tanzania, then cross back before coming in through the official entry points after which they collect their weapons and take them into the camps. Others hide the weapons in their country close to the border, cross over to register as refugees and later leave the camps to collect them after striking a deal with a buyer.[20]

On the basis of available evidence, one conclusion that can be rendered is that refugees, especially militarized refugees, have contributed in some fashion to the availability of illicit arms in the refugee camps and surrounding camps. Indeed, there is a historical precedent that broadly informs public opinion. The active involvement of refugees in armed resistance and the lingering presence of certain armed elements in the camps have not only stimulated a domestic demand for firearms but have also facilitated the conditions for illicit trafficking into and through the camps (ICG 1999; HRW 1999). According to a UNHCR security adviser, 'the influx of firearms is inevitably linked to the presence of rebel groups and armed refugees. As a consequence the problem will remain as long as refugees continue to be militarized.'[21] On the other hand, there are also clearly broader factors that have contributed to the militarization of areas where refugees are situated, including host communities. These relate to the porous border, the predatory nature of some security forces and criminal groups in the region, and the concomitant preference for self-protection.

Impact of refugee militarization and small arms

There is little doubt that refugee militarization has adverse effects on refugees, host communities and the integrity of hosting and neighbouring states. At the most basic level, the UN secretary-general has highlighted how refugee militarization weakens the ability of host states to maintain law and order, can provoke cross-border or internal armed incursions against refugee and IDP camps, prevent humanitarian access to those affected and undermine protection, and reduce the capacity of refugees to exercise choices relating to their own future (UNSG 1998: para. 30). This next section considers the implications of refugee militarization on inter-state relations, refugee protection, safety and well-being, and humanitarian access.

Refugee subversion, real or imagined, has led to the deterioration of inter-state relations between Tanzania and Burundi. This was confirmed by Tanzania's Minister for Foreign Affairs and International Cooperation, who observed that: '[t]he presence of refugees is a source of tension in the relations between Tanzania and Burundi, and to a certain extent Rwanda, arising from the suspicion that refugees are regrouping and training for warfare for attacking the countries of origin' (Guardian 1995).

Acrimony intensified between the two countries after Burundi accused Tanzania of supporting Hutu rebel groups.[22] At the height of the tensions, the two states recalled their ambassadors, deployed troops along the frontier and in 1997 exchanged gunfire across the border (ICG 1999: 5).

The response of governments to refugee militarization has profound implications for refugee security and protection. For example, while lauded for its hospitality towards refugees and the encouragement of 'self-reliance' for the vast majority of refugees in the country, the Tanzanian government has responded to refugee militarization through a combination of forced encampment, detention, expulsions and *refoulement* (the expulsion of persons who have the right to be recognized as refugees to their country of origin or any other country where they might be subject to persecution), and security crackdowns on refugees (Mogire 2003; Rutinwa 1996c). Indeed, the phenomenon has transformed the government's refugee policy entirely. Beginning in 2003, refugees were not permitted to leave camps, and laws requiring them to remain within a 4-kilometre radius of their camp were strictly enforced.[23] One reason supplied by Tanzanian authorities for the 4-kilometre rule was that banditry linked to 'armed refugees' had increased (Amnesty International 2004: 24). Predictably, these restrictions adversely affected refugee welfare as they severely compromised the capacity of refugees to sell their labour, practise sharecropping or subsistence farming, or engage in petty trade (ibid.; USCR 2004). A World Food Programme (WFP) study in western Tanzania found that the restrictions on refugee movement and the subsequent closure of local markets resulted in deteriorating food security (Collins 2004). Elsewhere, research has shown that putting refugees in camps not only violates their freedom of movement but has also resulted in a host of other pathologies, including material deprivation, violent conflicts, sexual exploitation and psychological problems (Muggah 2003; Black 1998; Van Damme 1995).

Alarmingly, partly as a result of the popular conception linking refugees with armed violence, expulsions have increased apace (Amnesty International 2004). These forced repatriations violate the principle of non-*refoulement* – a central pillar of refugee protection. Tanzania is not alone in undertaking forced repatriation: non-*refoulement* is perhaps 'the most ignored of all rights of refugees in the Great Lakes Region where the right is neither protected under municipal laws nor in practice' (Rutinwa 1998: 21). Unfortunately, collated statistics are still unavailable, though anecdotal evidence exists. For example, following the violent conflict at Kitali Hill camp in December 1996, Tanzanian authorities forcibly expelled some 126 Burundians on 10/11 January 1997. Of those expelled at least 122 were executed immediately upon their arrival in Burundi, with Burundian authorities acknowledging that its armed forces had committed the killings (USCR 1997). Between February and May 2000, over 580 Burundian refugees were forcibly returned from Tanzania – and their whereabouts are currently unknown (Amnesty International 2000).

By far the most obvious impact of refugee militarization relates to fatal and non-fatal injuries. While there are no comprehensive public health data on fatalities caused by small arms in Tanzania, let alone among refugees, it is nevertheless possible to review indicative trends on the basis of scattered retrospective medical records and interviews with health providers in western Tanzania. In addition to the reported 11,000 firearm-related fatalities reported between 1998 and 2001 (East African 2002), there have been a number of media reports documenting arms-related injuries among both refugees and locals (Daily News 1994a, 1994b, 2001; Guardian 2000a).

Specifically, ICRC data on war-wounded refugees indicate that, between May 2001 and June 2003, some 183 refugees were treated for arms-related injuries in Kigoma region. Of these injuries, 159 were caused by bullets, seven by landmines and seventeen by grenades. Of the victims, 173 were male, 152 of whom were aged between eighteen and thirty-five (ICRC 2004). In the first three months of 2004, eight refugees were treated for arms-related injuries: four caused by bullets, three by landmines and two by grenades (ibid.). A review of admission records at the Kigoma Baptist Hospital, which was supported by the ICRC to treat war-wounded refugees, reveals that between 1996 and 2002 some thirty-one refugees and three Tanzanian nationals were treated for bullet injuries. Landmines laid along the border by the Burundian armed forces, ostensibly to prevent cross-border attacks from Tanzania, led to a number of casualties among refugees and locals alike.[24] Between 1997 and March 1999, thirty-eight refugees and ten Tanzanian civilians were injured by landmine explosives (Land Mines Monitor 2000). While these data provide illustrative trends they do not reveal the real level of risk. Indeed, there is no denominator data on which to develop frequencies, and a clear assessment of the catchment area of the hospitals and relative access has not been determined. Moreover, the data do not state where and under what the circumstances the injuries were inflicted. To judge from the cause of the injuries and the gender and age of the victims, it is likely that most of the injuries were intentional. Indeed, interviews carried out with surgeons at the Kigoma Baptist Hospital and the ICRC field hospital reveal that most victims were taken straight to the hospital from the border area. A review of the medical reports at the Muyovosi refugee camp clinic reveals very few cases of firearms injuries. In fact, most reported injuries were caused by bicycle accidents or occurred in the bush when the victim was collecting firewood.[25] Between April 2000 and June 2003 only six people were treated for gunshot injuries – two refugees and four local people[26] – while 623 people (223 refugees and 400 locals) were treated for unrelated unintentional injuries.[27] This suggests that while some 'refugees' are being injured by firearms in cross-border skirmishes, there are comparatively few firearm injuries in the camps themselves.

More generally, the influx of arms into north-western Tanzania from neighbouring countries (and leakages from the public forces) has been accompanied by an increase in the number of acts of homicide, sexual and gender-based violence, theft and armed robbery (especially highway robbery) (United Nations 1998: 48; UNHCR 1995; HRW 1999). According to the US Committee for Refugees (USCR 2002), criminal elements, members of armed militias, Tanzanian security personnel and some refugees continue to commit murder, rape and armed robberies in and around refugee camps as well as against local citizens. For example, over a three-day period in March 2003 a group of armed men, believed to be members of the CNDD–FDD, attacked Mtabila and Muyovosi camps, in the process raping several women and intimidating the Tanzanian police and the refugee security guards, as well as setting fire to several huts (Amnesty International 2004: 26). In July 2004, a group of bandits attacked Nduta and Lugufu refugee camps, stealing property and injuring one refugee with a firearm (WFP 2004a). This phenomenon of inward militarization suggests a worrying trend.

But the local response to inward militarization has also had negative knock-on effects. In the past, rebels operated a vigilante justice system in the refugee camps. There were reports that CNDD supporters operated a 'detention centre' in a home in Lukole camp, where they reportedly interrogated and applied coercive punishments against refugees whom they suspected of spying for the Burundian government.[28] Although incidents of armed crime continue to occur in camps, responses from our interviews reveal that they are very much on the decline (see Appendix II).

Unlike in neighbouring countries, refugee militarization in Tanzania has had a nominal direct impact on humanitarian relief in the country. Between 1997 and 2000, no humanitarian aid worker was killed in Tanzania as a result of refugee militarization (King 2004). More recently, however, there appears to have been an increase in criminal-related violence in and around refugee camps (Buchanan and Muggah 2005). In June 2004, for example, a Tanzanian Christian Refugee Services (TCRS) logistics officer was killed in the presence of a police escort and a UNHCR driver was hijacked but later released unharmed (WFP 2004b). Soon after, in August 2004, bandits attacked staff from the NGO Concern (WFP 2004c). These attacks seem to have been criminal in nature. The indirect impacts of refugee militarization on humanitarian aid appear to be rising, particularly as they relate to the associated costs of security. Owing to growing insecurity for refugees and aid workers, UNHCR and other NGOs have employed private guards in addition to the UNHCR deployment of police officers in the camps. According to the UNHCR's spokesperson, Ivana Unluova, the security package (see next section) was costing USD1 million annually (IRIN 2003).

Response to refugee militarization

Tanzania has long faced various forms of refugee militarization and has elaborated, in cooperation with UNHCR, a variety of mechanisms to mitigate the threat. This section briefly considers the various responses adopted by the Tanzanian government, UNHCR, UNDP and the refugees themselves to the phenomenon of refugee militarization. It finds that various interventions have, in fact, yielded some dividends but that technical solutions can have only limited impacts without concomitant transformations in the overall political and security environments.

Government responses On paper at least, the Tanzanian government does not condone or support militarization. In practice, however, its policy with respect to the Burundian refugees could best be described as ambivalent. On the one hand, Tanzania has done very little to prevent the militarization of the Burundian refugee camps because of its sympathy for the Hutu rebellion and, following the 1996 coup in Burundi, its desire to bring down the Buyoya regime (ICG 1999: 5). This is demonstrated, for example, by its rejection of an OAU proposal to send a fact-finding mission to investigate the claims of refugee militarization and instead to draw the attention of the UN Security Council to the Burundian military build-up and offensives taking place on the Burundian side of the border. In November 1999, the Security Council issued a press release on the Burundi situation calling on the states of the region 'to ensure the neutrality and civilian character of the refugee camps and to prevent the use of their territory by armed insurgents' (UNIS 1999): a clear signal to Tanzanian authorities to enact tighter border controls, regulation of the refugee camps and the prevention of their manipulation by rebels. On the other hand, Tanzanian authorities have been keen to demonstrate to all parties that they control the Burundian refugee situation in a manner compatible with both their international legal obligations and their role as mediator in the Burundian peace process (Durieux 2000). This response was at least partly catalysed by international and Burundian criticism of their handling of the refugee camps.

In order to mitigate international criticism of its handling of refugee militarization, the Tanzanian government launched a massive round-up of most Burundians living outside refugee camps or settlements. This crackdown targeted an estimated 28,000 Burundians. Both refugees and (illegal) migrants were given the 'choice' of being forced back to their country of origin or relocated to carefully contained refugee camps. The Tanzanian government's efforts followed on the heels of threats from the Burundian government that it would take action against Hutu rebels who were engaged in arms trafficking and cross-border incursions from its territory if Tanzania did not act (HRW 1999). As the then UNHCR spokesman explained, 'one reason for the security sweep was to dispel claims by Burundi's military government that Tanzania was supporting the activities of Hutu rebels in refugee camps close to the frontier' (cited in Rutinwa 1999: 27–8).

Depoliticization Another tactic adopted by the Tanzanian government and UNHCR includes the 'depoliticization' of refugees. Depoliticization in this context entails the separation of refugees from their political cause by denying them the facilities to engage in bringing changes in their home countries or in the domestic politics of the countries of asylum. Refugee policies and asylum laws in many countries both in the north and the south are inclined against political agitation and thus constrain activism, association and lobbying. Indeed, African refugees have seldom had much freedom to express their political views (OAU Article 19, 2001). Ultimately, depoliticization is based on the assumption (albeit erroneous) that politicization is synonymous with militarization. The practice of depoliticization appears to be endorsed by Article 3 of the 1969 OAU Refugee Convention. It is also often encouraged in the humanitarian assistance strategies for refugees (Holborn 1975; Metcalfe 1971). UNHCR rhetoric and practice support this policy of depoliticization. During a visit to Tanzania, Albert Peters, the UNHCR director for the African region, told Burundian refugee representatives that refugees should desist from engaging in politics while in Tanzania (*Mtanzania* 30 August 1999).[29] Finally, refugee politicization is actively discouraged in Tanzania's refugee law – Refugee Act 1998, Articles 20(2), 27 (1). On several occasions government officials have warned refugees to deist from engaging in politics.[30] The aim of this particular approach is to keep refugees insulated as far as possible from any involvement in domestic politics while at the same time preventing their pursuit of political (and potentially violent) advocacy.

In practice, however, the ban on political activities is not impartially applied or strictly adhered to. The Tanzanian government has tended to allow freedom of action to refugee groups whose interests correspond with its own, while clamping down on those that it opposes. UNHCR and camp managers are also known to engage with political leaders who make themselves known to them while taking a hard stand against those who do not come forward. Furthermore, the large size of the camps has made it virtually impossible to implement the prohibitions. Thus, 'depoliticization' appears to do little more than drive refugees' political activities underground, and has been largely ineffective in dealing with the militarization of refugees.

Separation of armed elements Separation of armed elements is another measure that has been attempted in Tanzania with varying degrees of success. Separation entails the identification, removal and maintenance of selected individuals apart from the general population of refugees. Separation has been proposed for a range of groups, including 'armed elements' (UNHCR 2001), refugees perceived as presenting a security threat (1951 UN Refugee Convention, Article 32) and political activists and intimidators (1969 OAU Refugee Convention, Article 3).

Separation of armed elements was first introduced in 1996, when the government, with the assistance of UNHCR, established the Mwisa separation camp in Kagera region initially to house those guilty or suspected of intimidating Rwandese refugees. But with the passage of the Refugee Act in 1998, it has been used to detain Burundian combatants, political intimidators and those arrested for conducting unsanctioned political activities. Separation as a measure of dealing with armed elements has been difficult to implement for a number of reasons. First, the separation facility is not properly secured. The combatants have in almost all cases managed to abscond from the camp. For example, 58 per cent of the 143 combatants in Mwisa in 2001 are alleged to have absconded (Crisp 2001: 6).

Moreover, of the 189 combatants detained in the camp in 2002, only sixty-two remained by August 2003, and by August 2004 all had left (ECHO 2004: 17). Second, difficulties have arisen over who will take care of the internees and their legal status. Third, the policy depends on successful screening and identification. For example, there have been practical problems over how to identify armed elements once they have intermingled with civilian refugees in the camps. In some instances the government's attempt to remove non-civilian elements had been met with hostility from refugees (Crisp 2001; Rutinwa 2002). Finally, separation has been hampered by lack of political will on the part of the Tanzanian government, which, as already discussed, supported some of the refugee militarization. The existence of the camp has, nevertheless, served as a deterrent, preventing known political leaders from engaging in unsanctioned political activities, in addition to its symbolic value of affirming the neutrality of the receiving state.

Tanzanian penal law does not adequately account for refugee camp militarization and dealing with armed elements. Combatants found in the border areas are charged with illegal entry or stay, but are seldom physically deported. According to Durieux (2000), existing legal efforts to reduce militarization suffer from at least two limitations. First, penalization of subversive activities is not harsh (for example, the typical jail term for illegal stay or entry is six months), and only suspends the problem before those detained are returned to the camps. The deterrent effect of police arrest and prosecution is negligible if those found guilty of acts incompatible with their refugee status are eventually released back into the camps. Second, penalization of subversive activities in some ways misses the point: the basic distinction to be made is not between law-abiding and delinquent refugees, but rather between refugees and non-refugees. Although Tanzanian law makes subversion a crime, it has not been applied to refugees.

Bilateral cooperation The signing of bilateral and multilateral agreements is another typical response to refugee militarization. Tanzania has long undertaken regional and cooperative interventions to address the issue. For example, in July 1973 Tanzania signed a tripartite agreement with Burundi and Zaire in which it pledged among other things to restrict the activities of the rebels by denying them material support, prohibiting them from holding public meetings, and transferring the refugees from the border area to faraway settlements (Rutinwa 1998: 28). Although Tanzania transferred the refugees from the border areas, other aspects of the agreement were not implemented. As noted above, it was this group of refugees which spawned the first organized armed Hutu rebel groups.

A number of ad hoc meetings have taken place between Burundi and Tanzania to discuss the problem of insecurity and refugees. In 1999, Tanzania and Burundi met to discuss insecurity, the situation in refugee camps and the issue of armed rebels in the refugee camps (Guardian 1999a). In August 2000, a meeting of the defence ministers of the two countries culminated in a joint communiqué according to which Tanzania promised to prevent Burundian rebels from using its territory as bases for launching attacks, while Burundi pledged to improve internal security and to create conducive conditions for the repatriation of refugees (IRIN 2000c). Once again, on 23 June 2001 the two states agreed to set up a joint commission to deal with the resettlement of hundreds of thousands of Burundian refugees living along Tanzania's western border (IRIN 2001). In practice, these agreements have not been implemented. Thus they remain only a statement of intention. Diplomatic bickering between the two states continues to date.

UNHCR response The official UNHCR position is that refugee camps should maintain a civilian and humanitarian character. UNHCR also holds that host states have the primary responsibility for refugee security, including the maintenance of the civilian and humanitarian character of the refugee camps and settlements. This position is underpinned by the humanitarian and non-political character of UNHCR. In practice, UNHCR's responses towards refugees were and continue to be influenced by the United Nations and the political and strategic interests of major donors and host states. From the beginning, UNHCR's response to freedom fighters was guided by the UN policy on decolonization. Several UN General Assembly resolutions recognized the legitimacy of exercising the rights to self-determination and independence (UNGA 1966, 1967). In addition, it called upon the UNHCR and other international relief organizations and specialized agencies to increase their economic, social and humanitarian assistance to the refugees from those colonial territories (UNGA 1966: para. 8). The United Nations also advised that UNHCR could validly enter into contracts with national liberation movements 'in fulfillment of its functions' (Sloane 1974). During the cold war, both East and West instrumentally used refugees as pawns in their ideological struggles and refugee assistance to disguise their support for rebels (Terry 2002; Loescher 1992). Developing states including Tanzania have also used refugees to achieve political and strategic goals – with refugees literally serving as a vector for area-based development assistance (Byman et al. 2001; Gasarasi 1988). As already seen, Tanzania has also used refugees to promote its foreign and strategic goals.

The question of UNHCR support for and recognition of freedom fighters was debated within the organization in the late 1960s and early 1970s, with two opinions emerging. One opinion held that, since the nature of UNHCR work was non-political and humanitarian, it could not protect or assist free-dom fighters who were engaged in armed struggle (UNHCR 1968). The other opinion was that since the right to struggle was recognized by the UN, the UNHCR should recognize freedom fighters as refugees (Chandappa 1970). The UNHCR official position communicated in 1974 advised that dissidents from liberation movements could be considered refugees if they fulfilled the criteria of mandate eligibility (Kelly 1974). UNHCR practice with regard to freedom fighters in Tanzania reflected this position. UNHCR provided funding for social projects for liberation movements from southern Africa but did not in any way provide military support. Indirectly, however, it freed funds for the liberation movements' armed struggle.

UNHCR has undertaken a number of measures aimed at maintaining the civilian character of refugee camps in Tanzania. As previously observed, it assisted the government in establishing the Mwisa separation facility for armed elements. UNHCR engages with those political and military leaders in the camps who make themselves known privately, but has also reported on those who do not come forward to local authorities, who in turn remove them to the separation camp (ICG 1999: 14).

Perhaps the single most important technical response to refugee milit-arization in Tanzania was the signing of the so-called security package between the UNHCR and the Ministry of Home Affairs (MHA) in August 1998. The security package is seen as a 'soft' option response in relation to the so-called 'Ladder of Options' proposed by UNHCR (2000b). The primary objective of the security package was to ensure the full-time presence of a dedicated civilian police contingent in the refugee camps with the task of maintaining the civilian and humanitarian character of the camps and law and order, and reducing sexual and gender-based violence (Crisp 2001). Under the terms of the Security Package, UNHCR would cover the mobiliza-tion and demobilization costs of the police contingent, and provide a daily subsistence allowance, basic office and accommodation structures, and logistical support (e.g. vehicles and radio equipment). The security pack-age also provided for the deployment of an international security liaison officer whose mandate was to support and advise the police contingent in its security work. The Tanzanian government, for its part, agreed to deploy 278 police officers in the camps (Skarp 2000).

Most consulted generally concede that the security package improved the general security of the refugee camps and the hosting communities. It has also yielded unexpected knock-on effects, such as improving police morale and operational effectiveness, preserving law and order in the gen-eral vicinity of the camps, and introducing police officers to the principles of refugee protection and community policing. Furthermore, it has generated some positive effects such as reinforcing the security of humanitarian personnel, averting conflict between refugees and local populations, and enhancing relations between UNHCR and Tanzanian authorities (Crisp 2001: 2).

The security package has not, however, successfully dealt with all aspects of refugee militarization. This is because it has addressed only the issue of overt militarization and applies only to the camps and their immediate vicinity. Moreover, the police contingent has been criticized for being too small and lacking adequate time, resources and knowledge to deal with 'hard' security issues such as military recruitment, subversive propaganda, power struggles between rebel factions, and infiltration by combatants. Its exclusive focus on control and repression of political activities among refugees has been widely admonished for being an inadequate response to militarization (Yu 2002: 3; Crisp 2001: 2; Durieux 2000). Furthermore, like the separation policies described above, the success of the security package is largely dependent on the Tanzanian government's political will.

Community policing UNHCR Executive Committee (ExCom), in its conclusions on the security, civilian and humanitarian character of refugee camps and settlements, has suggested that ' ... refugee populations should be encouraged to assume some responsibility for maintaining acceptable standards of order and justice in camps in a manner that conforms to the principles of community policing' (UNHCR 2000b: para. 13). In western Tanzania, this has been applied in the form of 'community policing' under which refugee guards (locally known as *sungu sungu*), appointed by UNHCR and MHA representatives, assist the police in safeguarding the security of the camps by conducting twenty-four-hour patrols in specific areas. The guards act as the eyes and ears of the police on security issues (Skarp 2000). Like the security package, community policing has succeeded in reducing general insecurity but not militarization, because of the support the Hutu rebels enjoy among the refugee population. The *sungu sungu* have their own political allegiances and are not always willing to report on the activities of their compatriots. For example, in the past they have given false information to incriminate members of rival political factions (Crisp 2001: 6).

Small-arms collection Arms collections and public sensitization campaigns are also regularly implemented to reduce small-arms ownership and misuse in refugee hosting areas. For example, the police have carried out small-arms collection campaigns in refugee camps and surrounding areas. In addition to recovering arms, this measure discourages refugees from storing small arms in the camps. Arms collection has, however, received scant attention from the humanitarian community, which has been understandably preoccupied with the provision of relief (Muggah with Griffiths 2002). In response to this failure to pay sufficient attention to the problem of small arms, the United Nations Development Programme (UNDP) has established a community-based project on collection of arms and reduction of armed violence in western Tanzania under the auspices of the Great Lakes Small Arms Reduction Programme. The project seeks to enable the police force to team up with civic and community service organizations to undertake arms recovery campaigns, as well as to provide small development grants to groups, communities and individuals that have been instrumental in arms recovery. The project duration was January–December 2004 and was budgeted to cost USD1 million (OCHA 2003: 48).

The Tanzanian government has also adopted national and regional strategies to deal with the problem of the proliferation of illicit small arms. The government has conducted a study to identify the nature and extent of small-arms proliferation in terms of supply and demand, and the existing capacity and available resources to address the problem. A national action plan has been developed, which consists of an array of projects – e.g. review of national legislation, training and capacity-building, international and regional cooperation and information exchange, public awareness and education – to be implemented jointly by the government and civil society. Since adopting the national action plan, Tanzania has also created a national focal point and established regional task forces for arms management and disarmament (Kiliba 2003).

At the regional level, Tanzania has signed a number of agreements aimed at dealing with small arms. It has signed the Nairobi Declaration on the Problem of Illicit Small Arms and Light Weapons in the Great Lakes Region and Horn of Africa, and is a member of the Southern African Regional Police Chiefs Cooperation Organization (SARPCCO), which plays a crucial role in combating illicit small-arms trafficking. It has also signed cooperation agreements with its neighbours in the areas of border security and cross-border movement of illicit small arms. It is still perhaps too early to tell what practical dividends these multilateral agreements have generated.

Conclusions

This chapter has reviewed the historical, political and security dynamics of refugee militarization in Tanzania. It has also briefly summarized the various normative and practical responses to the problem. The chapter has demonstrated that the challenges associated with refugee militarization in Tanzania are historically embedded in the country's particular experience and the geopolitical environment in the GLR. Though the Tanzanian government did not actively support militarization, it nevertheless allowed it to occur and occasionally lent it tacit support – whether political, military or moral – for a variety of reasons. The chapter has also pointed to other factors that explain the militarization of refugee camps, including the presence of armed elements among the refugee population, the protracted nature of the refugee situation, the root causes of refugee flight, and regional dynamics.

The responses adopted by the Tanzanian government, UNHCR and the refugees themselves have not always succeeded in preventing or ending incidents of refugee militarization. Nevertheless, they have successfully prevented large-scale militarization such as was witnessed in eastern Zaire. Although political, security and strategic considerations have prevented the Tanzanian government from adopting a more robust stance against militarization, the political and military leaders of Burundian rebel groups have been keen not to provoke the Tanzanian government. This has helped to stabilize the situation in the camps. UNHCR has played a seminal and constructive role in preventing further militarization through the security package, though technical interventions represent only half the solution.

More optimistically, the outward militarization of Burundian refugees appears to have recently abated. This is attributed to the signing of the Arusha Peace Accord of 2000, though the future of refugee camp militarization in the region will largely depend on its successful implementation. So far the Hutu rebels have given the political process a chance, and military activities in the camps have subsided. There is no doubt that, if the peace process breaks down, subversion from refugee camps will resume as the itinerant rebels still maintain a presence in the camps. In other words, the problem of refugee militarization will remain as long as the Burundi conflict remains unresolved.

This chapter has also challenged the perception of refugees as vectors of arms. The Tanzanian political establishment and the popular media reinforce this claim, observing how armed combatants in the refugee camps constitute primary agents that underpin the diffusion and cross-border movement of illicit small arms. These arms, it is alleged, are not only used in cross-border conflicts, but have also fuelled local criminal activity. While these claims can and should be disputed, there is little doubt that inward refugee militarization and the presence and misuse of illicit arms have had adverse effects on the physical security and protection of refugees, as well as on the security of the host populations. There appears to be a greater and more urgent need for a proactive policy of managing small arms and insecurity rather than the current reactive approach. In other words, security, and security from armed violence, should be placed at the centre of refugee care and maintenance and humanitarian assistance.

Appendix I: Surveying arms availability in refugee camps

Question	Responses	N=14
How frequently do you hear gunshots?	Very frequently	0
	Frequently	2
	Sometimes	4
	Never	8
How often are firearms used in crime?	Very often	3
	Often	3
	Sometimes	4
	Don't know	2
How often are you worried about armed crime in the camp?	Very often	2
	Often	3
	Sometimes	7
	Never	2
Have there been changes in levels of armed crimes in the last twelve months?	Decreased	7
	Unchanged	3
	Increased	1
	Don't know	2

Appendix II: Impact of armed crime on refugees

Question	Responses	N=14
Has your family been a victim of armed crime?	Yes	6
	No	9
Do you know of someone who has been the victim of armed crime?	Yes	10
	No	4
How often are firearms used in crime?	Very often	3
	Often	3
	Sometimes	4
	Don't know	2
How often are you worried about armed crime in the camp?	Very often	3
	Often	2
	Sometimes	7
	Never	2
Changes in levels of armed crime in the last twelve months	Decreased	7
	Unchanged	3
	Increased	1
	Don't know	2

Notes

1 As noted in Chapter 1, the expression 'refugee militarization' is deployed here to describe a refugee population and/or refugee camp characterized by one or a combination of the following features: (a) use of camps by rebels to launch military attacks, (b) military training, (c) recruitment, (d) presence of armed elements, (e) storage and trafficking of arms, (f) use of refugee resources by combatants, (g) violent political conflict, and (h) military or armed attacks on camps (see also Lischer 2000: 3; UNHCR 2002a).

2 An exception to the rule is Lisa Mallki's exceptional ethnographic study of two refugee communities in Tanzania. See Mallki (1995).

3 Among the government officials interviewed were the deputy director of refugee services at the Ministry of Home Affairs, the refugee coordinator for Kigoma region, the Kigoma regional criminal investigation officer, the regional planning officer, and the camp manager for Mtabila refugee camps.

4 Meetings were also held with representatives of humanitarian organizations, including the head of the UNHCR Kigoma sub-office, the UNHCR protection officer at the Kasulu field office, the UNHCR field officers in Kasulu, the International Committee of the Red Cross (ICRC) field doctor at Kigoma, Tanzanian Red Cross (TRC) doctors in charge of Muyovosi and Mtabila refugee camps, and camp managers for Mtabila and Muyovosi refugee camps.

5 *Interahamwe* – which literally means 'those who work together' – included the militias who were largely responsible for carrying out the genocide.

6 The International Commission of Inquiry – Rwanda (ICIR) estimated that 3,000–5,000 armed ex-FAR, *interahamwe* and other Rwandese militias were based in refugee camps and other areas of western Tanzania between 1994 and 1998. See, for example, United Nations (1998: paras 14–22).

7 US Library of Congress, 'Country study – Uganda', accessed 1 July 2005, <http://countrystudies.us/uganda/1.htm#Preface>.

8 The shift in refugee policy is explained by the changing political climate, the magnitude of the refugee flows, the economic and security burden of hosting refugees, and refugee 'fatigue' (for more on shifts in Tanzanian refugee policy, see Rutinwa 1999 and Mahiga 1997).

9 Indeed, Mwisa camp housed some sixty-two combatants in August 2004 (ECHO 2004: 17).

10 See also Mallki (1995) for a review of how camps can reinforce nationalist identities and shape refugee militarization.

11 Partisan violence, as distinct from criminal violence, relates primarily to acts of intimidation, harassment or outright violence undertaken in an organized fashion for political aims.

12 Interview with UNHCR protection officer for Kasulu, July 2004.

13 Both countries maintain embassies in Dar es Salaam.

14 Tanzania argues that its decision to locate camps near the border is necessary for logistical reasons, for repatriation, as well as to remind refugees of their temporary status. Political considerations, especially fear of a backlash from the local population, are another factor.

15 Furthermore, the launch of the 1996 rebellion by the Alliance of Democratic Forces for the Liberation of Congo-Zaire (ADFL) in eastern Zaire, which crushed the Hutu rebellion in the area, led to movements of Burundian refugees and rebels to refugee camps in western Tanzania, where the rebels later regrouped to mobilize their insurgency (Van Eck 2001: 14).

16 Interview with refugee leader, Mtabila refugee camp, July 2004.

17 A diverse array of reports have made similar claims. For example, some 294 firearms were discovered in refugee-hosting areas in the first eight months of 1997 (Mahita 2000: 12). Another fifty-five firearms and 1,212 rounds of ammunition were also discovered 'near camps' within one month in 1999 (Guardian 1999b). Moreover, three sub-machine guns and fifty-four rounds of ammunition were discovered in April 2000 and seven firearms and 184 rounds of ammunition between 25 August and 11 September 2000 close to refugee camps (Guardian 2000c).

18 Those interviewed include fourteen refugees and refugee leaders, camp managers of the two camps, Ministry of Home Affairs representatives, and doctors.

19 Machetes are farming tools, which is why most refugees carry them.

20 Interviews with Regional Refugee Coordinator, Kigoma, July 2004.

21 Interview with UNHCR security adviser, Kasulu, July 2004.

22 For example, in April 2000 a Burundian government spokesman claimed that its army was fighting against the FDD, which it claimed was attacking from bases inside refugee camps in western Tanzania (Associated Press 2001a; IRIN 2000b).

23 Refugees found outside the camps are arrested and sentenced to a fine of up to TZS50,000 (approximately USD50) or a prison term of up to six months, or forcibly returned to Burundi.

24 UNHCR raised concerns about this problem in April and May 2000 (UNHCR 2000c).

25 Interview, Muyovosi refugee camp hospital, July 2004.

26 The number of refugees treated is small mainly because most of the injured are taken to the ICRC partner hospital, Heri Mission Hospital in Kasulu. The Kigoma Baptist Hospital, which also used to treat the war-wounded on behalf of the ICRC, is no longer a partner of the ICRC.

27 These data were obtained from medical records, Muyovosi Hospital, July 2004.

28 This report was confirmed when Chantal Bakamiriza, a Burundian national who had come to visit her mother at the camp during her university holidays, was subsequently detained by a group of refugees that included a former bodyguard for President Ndadaye and a former captain in the Burundian army. She alleged that she was beaten and tortured. Two of her captors were arrested on 1 February 1998 when the Tanzanian police raided the home (HRW 1999).

29 UNHCR believes that depoliticization would lead to militarization. As Peters told refugee leaders, '... if you move into the political area, the next step will be the military arena' (*Mtanzania*, 30 August 1999).

30 In 1984, the then prime minister was reported to have warned Burundian refugees against engaging in the politics of their original country while in residence in Tanzania (*Daily News*, 7 July 1984). In 1985, President Nyerere, while speaking at Ulyankulu settlement scheme in Kibondo district, cautioned refugees not to involve themselves in activities to overthrow the Burundi government (ibid., 18 June 1985). During the same year the Minister for Home Affairs told parliament that refugee behaviour would not be allowed to strain existing good relationships between Tanzania and neighbouring countries (ibid., 12 July 1985). Once again, in July 1986 the Minister for Home Affairs warned against destabilization (ibid., 11 April 1986).

References

Adelman, H. (1998) 'Why refugee warriors are threats', *Journal of Conflict Studies*, 18(1): 49–69.

Amnesty International (2000) *Great Lakes Region: Refugees Denied Protection*, AI Index AFR 02/02/00, May.

— (2003) *Democratic Republic of Congo Children at War*, AI Index AFR 62/034/20039, September, <web.amnesty.org/library/index/engafr620342003>.

— (2004) *Burundi. A Critical Time: Human Rights Briefing on Burundi*, AI Index AFR 16/002/2004, 13 January.

Article 19 (2001) *Voices in Exile: African Refugees and Freedom of Expression*, London: Article 19.

Associated Press (2001a) 'Burundi army rebels fight', 1 April.

— (2001b) 'UNICEF-Hutu rebels abduct 107 Burundi children from refugee camps in Tanzania', 13 November.

Berber, B. (1997) 'Feeding refugees, or war? The dilemmas of humanitarian aid', *Foreign Affairs*, 76(4): 8–14.

Betts, F. T. (1981) 'Documentary note: rural refugees in Africa', *International Migration Review*, 15(53/54): 213–18.

Black, R. (1998) 'Putting refugees in camps', *Forced Migration Review*, 2, August, pp. 4–7.

Brahim, J. P. (1995) 'How Tanzania was affected by the refugee crisis in the Great Lakes Region and her response to it', Report of an Oxfam-sponsored research project, presented at the International Workshop on the Refugee Crisis in the Great Lakes Region, Arusha, Tanzania, 16–19 August.

Bruns International (2000) 'Burundian rebels recruiting from refugee camps', 20 January, accessed 1 July 2005, <www.unb.ca/web/bruns/9900/issue15/intnews/burundy.html>.

Buchanan, C. and R. Muggah (2005) *No Relief: Victimisation of Humanitarian Personnel*, Geneva: Centre for Humanitarian Dialogue and the Small Arms Survey.

Byman, D. L., P. Chalk, B. Hoffman, W. Rosenau and D. Brannan (2001) *Trends in Outside Support for Insurgent Movements*, Santa Monica, CA: RAND Corporation.

Cervenka, Z. (1977) *The Unfinished Quest for Unity*, London: J. Friedmann.

Chandappa, J. F. R. (1970) 'Freedom fighters – branch office memorandum no. 26, 1968-A – re-assessment', UNHCR internal memo, Geneva, 24 June.

Coalition to Stop the Use of Child Soldiers (2004) 'Child soldiers use 2003', Briefing for the 4th UN Security Council Open Debate on Children and Armed Conflict, New York, 16 January, accessed 2 July 2005, <www.child-soldiers.org/document_get.php?id=705>.

Collins, G. (2004) *The Coping Strategies Index (CSI) Baseline Survey. World Food Programme Assisted Refugees in Western Tanzania*, Prepared for WFP Tanzania, June/July, accessed 2 July 2005, <www.refugees.org/data/warehousing/tanzania/docs/csi_wfp_tanzania.pdf>.

Crisp, J. (2001) 'Lessons learnt from the implementation of the Tanzania security package', Geneva: Evaluation and Policy Analysis Unit, UNHCR.

Daily News (Dar es Salaam) (1994a) 'Four of 85 pupil bomb victims in critical condition', 10 September.

— (1994b) 'Hutu militia kill Rwanda refugees in Karagwe', 3 October.

— (1995) 'Refugee clashes leave 57 dead', 19 July.

— (1997a) '161 armed Zairian soldiers in Kigoma', 15 February.

— (1997b) 'Kigoma police impound grenades and ammunition', 24 July.

— (2001) 'Bandits kill refugee who had no money', 2 August.

Durieux, J. F. (2000) 'Preserving the civilian character of refugee camps – lessons from the Kigoma refugee programme in Tanzania', *Track Two*, 9(3), accessed 2 July 2005, <http://ccrweb.ccr.uct.ac.za/archive/two/9_3/p25_preserving_civilian.html>.

East African (Nairobi) (2002) 'Arms spiral a threat to TZ's security', 10–16 June.

ECHO (European Commission Humanitarian Aid Office) (2004) *Global Reach in the World, Humanitarian Funding by Country/Region*, <http://europa.eu.int/comm/echo/pdf_files/annual_reviews/2004_globalreach_en.pdf>.

— (2005) *Humanitarian Aid for Refugees in the United Republic of Tanzania: Global Plan 2005*, ECHO/TZA/BUD/2005/01000, Brussels: European Commission, accessed 2 July 2005. <http://europa.eu.int/comm/echo/pdf_files/decisions/2005/dec_tanzania_01000_en.pdf>.

Evans, G. (1997) *Responding to Crises in the African Great Lakes*, Adelphi Paper no. 311, London: Oxford University Press for International Strategic Studies.

Gamba, V. and M. Chachiua (1999) 'Small arms trade in Africa: arms bazaar', *New People Africa Feature Service*, 98, August.

Gasarasi, C. (1988) 'The effect of Africa's exiles/refugees upon inter-African state relations: conflict and cooperation 1958–1988', PhD thesis, New Orleans, LA: Department of Politics, Tulane University.

Goetz, H. N. (2003) *Lessons from a Protracted Refugee Situation*, Working Paper no. 74, La Jolla: Center for Comparative Immigration Studies, University of California-San Diego, April.

Government of Tanzania (1995) *The Tanzanian Refugee Policy, Implementations Record and the Tanzanian Position of the Rwanda and Burundi Refugee Related Problems*, Dar es Salaam: Ministry of Foreign Affairs.

— (2004) *Report on Situation in Refugee Camps*, Dar es Salaam: Ministry of Home Affairs.

Guardian (Dar es Salaam) (1995) 'Border closure triggers debate', 19 July.

— (1999) 'Burundi and Tanzania agree to upgrade relations', 18 February.

— (2000a) 'Refugee family perishes in grenade attack', 23 February.

— (2000b) 'Burundian combatants arrested', 23 May.

— (2000c) 'Police seize seven guns, 184 bullets from Burundi refugees', 18 September.

— (2004) 'Too many guns in hands of criminals, says Mapuri', 7 October.

Holborn, L. (1975) *Refugees a Problem of Our Time: The Work of the United Nations High Commissioner for Refugees*, Metuchen, NJ: Scarecrow Press.

HRW (Human Rights Watch) (1995) *Rearming with Impunity: International Support for the Perpetrators of the Rwandan Genocide*, New York: HRW.

— (1999) 'Tanzania: in the name of security: forced round-ups of refugees', *Human Rights Watch*, 11(4), accessed 2 July 2005, <http://hrw.org/reports/1999/tanzania.>

IANSA (International Action Network on Small Arms) (2005) 'Tanzania', accessed 2 July 2005, <http://www.iansa.org/regions/cafrica/cafrica.htm#tanzania>.

ICG (International Crisis Group) (1999) *Burundian Refugees in Tanzania: The Key Factor to the Burundi Peace Process*, Central Africa Report no. 12, Brussels: ICG, 30 November.

ICRC (International Committee of the Red Cross) (2004) 'War wounded statistics names of patients treated 2001 to 20 June 2003', Kigoma: War Wounded Programme, ICRC Kigoma Medical Department.

IRIN (Integrated Regional Information Network, Nairobi) (1999) 'Police detail refugee arms problem', 28 December.

— (2000a) 'Burundi tense, rebels recruit?', 24 March.

— (2000b) 'Thousands displaced, few leaving', 5 May.

— (2000c) 'Burundi: defence minister visits Tanzania', 6 July.

— (2001) 'Defence minister meets Tanzanian counterpart on refugees', 29 June.

— (2003) 'President ties rise in small arms to refugee inflows', 1 September.

— (2004) 'Great Lakes: light arms a scourge for peaceful development', 6 February.

IRIN-CEA (Integrated Regional Information Network for Central and Eastern Africa) (1999) 'Tanzania: high proportion of weapons seized in west', Update 713, 13 July.

Jefferson, C. and A. Urquhart (2002) *The Impact of Small Arms in Tanzania: Results of a Country Survey*, Monograph Series no. 70, Pretoria: Institute of Strategic Studies.

Kelly, J. D. R. (1974) 'UNHCR attitude with regard to dissidents and deserters from liberation movements', Internal memo, 12 February, Geneva: UNHCR.

Kiliba, K. (2003) 'Statement by the representative of the United Republic of Tanzania at the Biennial Meeting of States to Consider Action Programme on Illicit Small Arms Trade', Press release DC 2875, Geneva: United Nations, 9 July.

King, D. (2004) 'Chronology of humanitarian aid workers killed in 1997–2003', 15 January, accessed 2 July 2005, <http://vranet.com/Govt1027/Docs/chron1997-2003.html>.

Land Mines Monitor (2000) *Country Report Tanzania. Toward a Mine-free World 2000*, New York: HRW, accessed 2 July 2005, <http://www.icbl.org/lm/2000/>.

Lemarchand, R. (1994) *Burundi: Ethnocide as Discourse and Practice*, New York and Cambridge: Woodrow Wilson Center Press and Cambridge University Press.

Lischer, K. S. (2000) *Refugee Involvement in Political Violence: Quantitative Evidence from 1987–1998*, Working Paper no. 1, Geneva: UNHCR.

— (2001) 'Refugees and the spread of civil war', Paper presented at the 97th annual meeting of the American Political Science Association, San Francisco, CA, 20 August–2 September.

Loescher, G. (1992) *Refugee Movements and International Security*, Adelphi Paper 268, London: Nuffield Press for International Institute for Strategic Studies.

Mahiga, A. (1997) 'Change in direction for Tanzania', *Refugees*, 110.

Mahita, I. O. (2000) 'Keynote address: Tanzanian inspector general of police', in A. McLean, *Meeting Report: Tackling Small Arms in the Great Lakes Region and the Horn of Africa*, London: Saferworld.

Mallki L. (1995) *Purity and Exile: Violence, Memory, and National Cosmology among Hutu Refugees in Tanzania*, Chicago, IL: University of Chicago Press.

Mapuri, O. R. (2003) Tanzanian Minister for Home Affairs' keynote address at a workshop on 'The UN Programme of Action on Small Arms and Light Weapons: Building Capacity and Partnerships for Implementation', Bonn, 28/29 April.

Metcalfe, G. L. (1971) 'Effects of refugees on the national state', in H. C. Brooks and Y. El-Ayouty (eds), *An African Dilemma: Refugees South of the Sahara*, West Port, CT: Negro University Press.

Mills, K. and R. J. Norton (2002) 'Refugees and security in the Great Lakes Region of Africa', accessed 4 May 2004, <http://homepage.mac.com/vicfalls/civilwars.html>.

Mogire, E. (2003) 'Refugees in East Africa: implications for host state security. a critical re-conceptualization of refugees and security studies using empirical case studies in Kenya and Tanzania', PhD thesis, Department of Peace Studies, Bradford University.

— (2004) *A Preliminary Exploration of the Linkage between Refugees and Small Arms*, BICC Paper 35, Bonn: Bonn International Center for Conversion.

MSF (Médecins Sans Frontières) (1994) *Breaking the Cycle: MSF Calls for Action in the Rwandese Refugee Camps in Tanzania and Zaire*, 10 November, accessed 2 July 2005, <http://www.msf.fr/documents/base/1994-11-01-MSF.pdf>.

— (1995) *Deadlock in the Rwandan Refugee Crisis: Virtual Standstill on Repatriation*, accessed 2 July 2005, <http://129.194.252.80/catfiles/0109.pdf>.

Mtanzania (Dar es Salaam) (1999) 'Keep away from politics' (author's translation), 30 August.

Muggah, R. (2003) 'Two solitudes: comparing conflict and development-induced displacement and resettlement', *Journal of International Migration*, 41(5): 1–28.

— (2005) 'A crisis turning inwards: refugee and IDP militarisation in Uganda', *Humanitarian Exchange*, 29, <http://www.odihpn.org/report.asp?ID=2574>.

Muggah, R. with M. Griffiths (2002) 'Reconsidering the tools of war', Network Paper 39, London: ODI.

Mushemesha, D. E. (1998) 'Refugees and international relations: the case of Uganda and her neighbours, 1960–90', in A. G. G. Gingyera Pinychwa (ed.), *Uganda and the Problem of Refugees*, Kampala: Makerere University Press.

Nairobi Declaration on the Problems of the Proliferation of Illicit Small Arms and Light Weapons in the Great Lakes Region and in the Horn of Africa (2000) Nairobi, March, accessed 2 July 2005, <http://www.smallarmssurvey.org/source_documents/Regional%20ofora/Africa/Nairobidecl000315.pdf>.

OAU (Organization of African Unity) (1969) *Convention Governing the Specific Aspects of Refugee Problems in Africa*, Addis Ababa: OAU, 6–10 September, accessed 15 July 2005, <www.afrol.com/archive/documents/refugees_convention.htm>.

— (2000) *International Consultation on the Illicit Proliferation, Circulation and Trafficking in Small Arms and Light Weapons*, Final meeting report, Addis Ababa, 22/23 June, accessed 2 July 2005, <www.smallarmssurvey.org/source_documents/Regional%20ofora/Africa/Addis%20Ababa%20June%202000.pdf>.

OAU/UNHCR (1998) *Refugee Protection and Security in the Great Lakes Region*, Regional meeting report, Kampala, 8/9 May.

OCHA (United Nations Office for the Coordination of Humanitarian Affairs) (2003) *Tanzania 2004: Consolidated Appeal Process*, New York and Geneva: OCHA.

Odhiambo, A. (1996) 'The Regional Response to the Rwandan Emergency', *Journal of Refugee Studies*, 9(3): 303–11.

Ogata, S. (1997) Remarks by Mrs Sadako Ogata, United Nations High Commissioner for Refugees, on a Humanitarian Response and the Prevention of Deadly Conflict, Conference of the Carnegie Commission on the Prevention of Deadly Conflict and UNHCR, Geneva, 17 February.

— (1998) Opening Statement at Regional Meeting on Refugee Issues in the Great Lakes Sponsored by the Organization of African Unity and the United Nations High Commissioner for Refugees, Kampala, 8/9 May.

Otunnu, A. (1987) *Politics and the Military in Uganda, 1890–1985*, New York: St Martin's Press.

Ottunu, O. (1998) 'An historical analysis of the invasion by the Rwanda patriotic army (RPA)', in H. Adelman and A. Suhrke (eds), *The Path of Genocide: The Rwandese Crisis from Uganda to Zaire*, New Brunswick, NJ: Transaction.

Potgieter, J. and A. Urquhart (2003) *Resolving Small Arms Proliferation: The Development of National Action Plans on Arms Management and Disarmament*, Midrand: Safer Africa, accessed 2 July 2005, <www.saferafrica. org/DocumentsCentre/Monographs/RSAP/Index.asp>.

Prunier, G. (1995) *The Rwandan Crisis: History of a Genocide 1959–1994*, London: Hurst & Co.

Rajabu, A. (2002) 'The implementation of the National Plan of Action', Paper presented by Mr Adadi Rajabu, Director of Criminal Investigation, Tanzanian Commissioner of Police, at the National NGOs Conference on Small Arms and Light Weapons, Dar es Salaam, 30/31 May.

Reuters (1997) 'Tanzania holds thousands of illegal aliens – UNHCR', 14 November.

Rutinwa, B. (1996a) 'Refugee protection and security in East Africa', *Refugee Participation Network*, 22, October, accessed 2 July 2005, <www.fmreview. org/rpn225.htm#topofpage>.

— (1996b) 'The Tanzanian government response to the Rwandan emergency', *Journal of Refugee Studies,* 9(3): 291–302.

— (1996c) 'Beyond durable solutions: an appraisal of the new proposals for prevention and solution of the refugee crisis in the Great Lakes Region', *Journal of Refugee Studies*, 9(3): 312–25.

— (1998) 'Forced displacement and refugee rights in the Great Lakes region', *African Journal of International Affairs*, 1(2): 11–41.

— (1999) *The End of Asylum? The Changing Nature of Refugee Policies in Africa*, Working Paper no. 5, Geneva: Centre for Documentation and Research, UNHCR.

— (2002) 'Screening in mass influxes: the challenge of exclusion and separation', *Forced Migration Review*, 13, June, pp. 35–7.

Salim, S. A. (1997) 'Key Note Address', in Evans (1997).

SAS (Small Arms Survey) (2003) *Small Arms Survey 2003: Development Denied*, Oxford: Oxford University Press.

— (2004) *Small Arms Survey 2004: Rights at Risk*, Oxford: Oxford University Press.

Schonteich, M. (2000) 'South Africa's position in Africa's crime rankings', *African Security Review*, 9(4), accessed 2 July 2005, <www.iss.co.za/pubs/ ASR/9No4/Schonteich.html>.

Skarp, C. (2000) 'Refugees and security – a case-study of refugee issues in western Tanzania', in A. McLean (ed.), *Tackling Small Arms in the Great Lakes Region and the Horn of Africa: Strengthening the Capacity of Sub-regional Organizations*, Meeting report, Dar es Salaam: Institute for Security Studies, 7/8 May.

Sloane, B. (1974) 'Contracting with liberation movements', Letter from the Director General of Legal Division, Office of Legal Affairs, United Nations, to Mr Emmanuel K. Dadzie, Director of Protection Unit, UNHCR, Geneva, 26 March.

Terry, F. (2002) *Condemned to Repeat: The Paradox of Humanitarian Action*, Ithaca, NY, and London: Cornell University Press.

Turner, S. (1999) *Angry Young Men in Camps: Gender, Age, and Class Relations among Burundi Refugees in Tanzania*, New Issues in Refugee Research, Working Paper no. 9, Geneva: UNHCR.

Uhuru (Dar es Salaam) (2000) 'Refugees arrested with 3 SMG firearms' (author's translation from Swahili), 27 April.

UNAFEI (United Nations Asia and Far East Institute for the Prevention of Crime and the Treatment of Offenders) (2001) 'Current situation of illegal firearms trafficking and human (women, children, and migrants) trafficking presented', Resource Material Series no. 58, Tokyo, December, accessed 2 July 2005, <www.unafei.or.jp/english/pdf/PDF_rms/no58/58-17.pdf>.

UNGA (United Nations General Assembly) (1966) *Implementation of the Declaration on the Granting of Independence to Colonial Countries and Peoples*, GA/Res. 2189 (XXI), 13 December.

— (1967) *Implementation of the Declaration of Independence to Colonial Countries and Peoples*, GA/Res. 2326 (XXII), 16 December.

UNHCR (United Nations High Commissioner for Refugees) (1968) 'Question of "freedom fighters" and liberation organization in Africa', Internal memo UNHCR/IOM/22/68/ UNHCR/BOM/68, Geneva: UNHCR.

— (1995) 'Impact of military personnel and the militia presence in Rwandese refugee camps and settlements', Paper presented at the OAU/UNHCR Regional Conference on Assistance to Refugees, Returnees and Displaced Persons in the Great Lakes Region, Bujumbura, Burundi, 15–17 February.

— (1998a) 'Military training in the Lukole A camp', Internal reports NGA/Sec/HCR/058/98, Ngara, Tanzania: UNHCR.

— (1998b) 'Security situation in Lukole camps', Internal reports NGA/Sec/HCR/053/98, Geneva: UNHCR.

— (2000a) *State of the World's Refugees: Fifty Years of Humanitarian Action*, Oxford: Oxford University Press.

— (2000b) *The Security, Civilian and Humanitarian Character of Refugee Camps and Settlements: Operationalizing the Ladder of Options*, UN Doc. EC/50/SC/INF.4, 27 June.

— (2000c) 'Tanzania: UNHCR concern at mine accounts', Briefing note, 28 April.

— (2001) *The Civilian Character of Asylum: Separating Armed Elements from Refugees*, UN Doc. EC/GC/01/5, 19 February.

— (2002a) Executive Committee (ExCom) Conclusion 94 (LIII), Geneva: UNHCR.

— (2002b) *UNHCR Statistical Year Book 2001: Refugees, Asylum Seekers and Others of Concern – Trends in Displacement, Protection and Solutions*, Geneva: UNHCR.

— (2004) *UNHCR Statistical Yearbook 2002: Trends in Displacement, Protection and Solutions*, Geneva: UNHCR.

UNIS (United Nations Information Service) (1999) 'Security Council calls on parties to end violence in Burundi, pursue negotiations; murder of United Nations personnel is condemned', UNIS/SC/1160, New York, 15 November, accessed 2 July 2005, <www.unis.unvienna.org/unis/pressrels/1999/sc1160. html>.

United Nations (1994) *Statement by the President of the Security Council*, S/PRST/1994/75, 30 November.

— (1995) *Report of the Secretary-General on the Implementation of Paragraph 6 of Security Council Resolution 997 (1995) of 9 June*, S/995/552, 9 July.

— (1998) *Final Report of the International Commission of Inquiry about Illicit Arms Transfers in the Great Lakes Region*, S/1998/1096, 18 November.

— (1999) *Firearms Study Database–1999*, Geneva: UN.

UNSG (United Nations Secretary-General) (1998) *The Causes of Conflict and the Promotion of Durable Peace and Sustainable Development in Africa*, A/52/871–S/1998/318, 13 April.

— (2001) *Report on the Protection of Civilians in Armed Conflict*, S/2001/331, 30 March.

— (2003) *Report of the Secretary-General on Children and Armed Conflict*, A/58/546–S/2003/1053, 10 November.

USCR (United States Committee for Refugees) (1997) 'Tanzania's expulsion of Burundian refugees should cease; executions prove Burundi remains extremely dangerous', Press release, Washington, DC, 15 January.

— (2002) *Country Report: Tanzania 2002*, accessed 2 July 2005, <www.refugees. org/countryreports.aspx?id=1252>.

— (2004) *Tanzania's Mission Findings and Recommendations*, Washington, DC: USCR, August.

Van Damme, W. (1995) 'Do refugees belong in camps? Experiences from Goma and Guinea', *Lancet*, 346: 360–62.

Van Eck, J. (2001) 'Polarisation of parties into "win power" and "keep power" camps threatens the collapse of peace process', Unpublished manuscript, Pretoria: Centre for International Policy Studies, University of Pretoria.

Weiner, M. (1993) 'Security, stability and international migration', *International Security*, 17(3): 91–126.

WFP (World Food Programme) (2004a) *Emergency Report No. 30*, WFP Tanzania, 23 June.

— (2004b) *Emergency Report No. 34*, WFP Tanzania, 13 August.

— (2004c) *Emergency Report No. 37*, WFP Tanzania, 10 September.

Yu, L. (2002) *Separating Ex-combatants and Refugees in Zongo, DRC: Peacekeepers and UNHCR's 'Ladder of Options'*, New Issues in Refugee Research, Working Paper no. 60, Belfast: Queen's University.

Zolberg, A., A. Suhrke and S. Aguayo (1989) *Escape from Violence: Conflict and the Refugee Crisis in the Developing World*, Oxford: Oxford University Press.

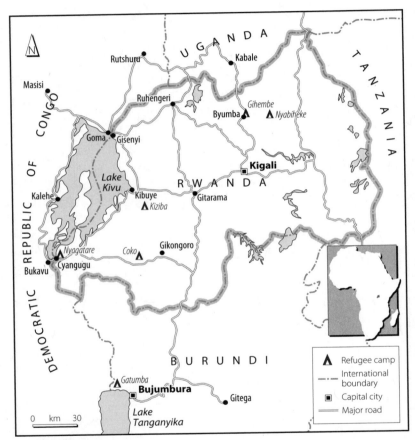

5 | The wheel turns again: militarization and Rwanda's Congolese refugees

GREGORY MTHEMBU-SALTER

The primary focus of this chapter is the nature and extent of the militarization of Rwanda's Congolese refugees. 'Militarization' has been used as an umbrella term for a range of related activities, including the recruitment of refugees into military structures, the use of refugee or camp resources to support military action, and the continued involvement of refugees in the conflict of their homeland, all of which are examined in this chapter. The literature on events in the Great Lakes Region during and since the 1994 genocide is enormous and growing. This chapter limits itself to a brief summary of the regional and historical context of the Congolese refugee presence in Rwanda, and then considers the different roles played by the refugees and their political leadership on the one hand, and the other key domestic, regional and international actors on the other, ending with some conclusions and recommendations.

Refugee militarization in Rwanda is a controversial issue, which has pitted a UN panel of experts investigating compliance with the ongoing arms embargo imposed on the Democratic Republic of Congo (DRC) against the Rwandan government and a dissident researcher from within the UN's own investigative team. Humanitarian agencies have been caught uncomfortably in the middle, unwilling to go on record about developments they suspect but cannot conclusively prove.

Just over a decade ago, after the 1994 genocide in Rwanda, camps for over 2 million Rwandan refugees were established in eastern DRC – then Zaire. During the period 1994–96, leaders of the just-defeated Rwandan government, commanders of the Forces Armées Rwandaises (FAR) and leaders of the *interahamwe* militia, who had just coordinated the mass murder of up to 1 million people, worked together in the camps with the Zairean government and armed forces. The ex-FAR and *interahamwe* made full use of the camps' ample humanitarian supplies and the fact that humanitarian agencies maintained a presence only during the day, and eventually succeeded in militarizing the Bukavu and Goma refugee camps to the point that they were well-armed bases for the ex-FAR and *interahamwe*'s attempted military reconquest of Rwanda.

All this was despite, yet assisted by, the massive presence of UNHCR and other humanitarian agencies, and the massive absence of UN military personnel. The Kivu camps were later destroyed by the Rwandan Defence Force (RDF) and its Congolese allies, launching a war that engulfed the whole of the DRC and culminated with the fall of President Mobutu Sese Seko.

A decade later the wheel has turned again. Almost all the Rwandan refugees have left the DRC, save a rump from which the FDLR (Forces Démocratiques pour la Libération du Rwanda) is drawn, but now there are tens of thousands of Congolese refugees in Rwanda. At issue for Rwanda as the host state this time, for the international community and UN institutions in particular, is whether they have learned from the 1994 crisis the lessons they say they have, and, further, whether they are the right lessons for this crisis.

In late 2005 there were around 41,000 Congolese registered as refugees and living in camps in Rwanda, along with several thousand who were not registered, most of whom lived in the capital, Kigali.[1] Most of the Congolese refugees in Rwanda are Banyarwanda[2] Tutsis from North and South Kivu. Among the more recent arrivals, several hundred Congolese from North Kivu crossed during 2005 to escape an upsurge in fighting there, while in June 2004 several thousand mostly Banyamulenge[3] former residents of the city of Bukavu and surrounding areas in the South Kivu province of the DRC fled ethnic cleansing[4] there by members of the Congolese Armed Forces (FARDC).

This latter group of refugees initially went both to the small Rwandan border town of Cyangugu, just 3 kilometres from Bukavu, and a nearby camp called Nyagatare, originally intended as a transit centre for Rwandan refugees returning from the DRC, and another 4 kilometres inland along the main road east towards Kigali. In May 2005, most of these refugees were transferred to a new camp in Byumba called Nyabiheke, save for those who opted either to return home or stay with people in Cyangugu.

In addition to these civilian refugees, there has also been a group in south-western Rwanda of around three hundred Congolese soldiers under the command of Colonel Jules Mutebutsi, who fled the DRC in mid-2004 after clashing with the UN observer mission in Congo (Mission de l'Organisation des Nations Unies en République Démocratique du Congo, MONUC). Mutebutsi's troops were disarmed by the RDF on arrival in Rwanda, and were interned under RDF guard during the period of fieldwork for this study[5] in another camp called Ntendezi, a further 25 kilometres inland from Nyagatare. Mutebutsi and his followers were moved in late August 2004 by the Rwandan government to Coko camp in Gikongoro province, 20 kilometres from the Burundian border, also

TABLE 5.1 Origins of refugees in selected Congolese refugee camps, 2004

(a) Kiziba and Gihembe populations, 2004/05

	Jan '04	Oct '05
Kiziba	16,046	17,103
Gihembe	17,612	17,237

(b) Kiziba camp, area of origin (2004)

DRC province	Number	% of total
North Kivu	13,984	88
Katanga	1,099	7
South Kivu	681	4.2
Others	157	0.8

(c) Gihembe camp, area of origin (2004)

DRC province	Number	% of total
North Kivu	17,541	99.6
Katanga	12	0.1
South Kivu	54	0.3
Others	0	0

Source: UNHCR

under the guard of the RDF. UNHCR refused to consider Mutebutsi's men as refugees, the RDF progressively weakened its surveillance of them, and by late 2005 many had left Coko – armed – for the DRC.

There are two older and more established Congolese refugee camps in Rwanda where there appear to have been serious instances of refugee militarization. One is called Kiziba, in Kibuye province, and the other is Gihembe, in Byumba. Most of the residents of these camps are Banyarwanda Tutsis from North Kivu. In late 2005, they accommodated about 34,000 people.[6]

Also in late 2005, there were in addition 3,000 Burundian registered refugees, most of whom were in a camp in Gikongoro province, a few thousand more unregistered refugees living in Kigali, plus an estimated several hundred Ugandans recognized as refugees by the Rwandan government but not by UNHCR. At the end of 2002, meanwhile, UNHCR (2002) estimated that there were around 85,000 Rwandan refugees worldwide, including 29,000 assisted by the agency.

Mthembu-Salter | 5

Box 5.1 Summary of fighting forces in the Great Lakes Region

AFDL: Alliances des Forces Démocratiques pour la Libération du Zaire-Congo. A coalition of Banyamulenge and other Zairean/Congolese armed groups formed in 1996, with considerable help from regional states, to overthrow Zairean president Mobutu Sese Seko. Laurent Desiré Kabila, a veteran guerrilla and smuggler, emerged first as spokesman and later leader, and went on to succeed Mobutu as the president of the DRC.

Ex-FAR: Ex-Forces Armées Rwandaises. The armed forces of the former Rwandan government which, with a youth militia called the *interahamwe*, perpetrated genocide and subsequently fled Rwanda in 1994. Most ex-FAR and *interahamwe* went to Zaire, joining forces with Kabila after his split with Rwanda in 1997, and many later joined the FDLR (see below).

FAB: Forces Armées Burundaises. The predominantly Tutsi former Burundian armed forces, which were superseded in early 2005 by the Force de Défense Nationale (FDN), which is made up of FAB soldiers and former rebel militia fighters. Estimated size: 45,000.

FARDC: Forces Armées de la République Démocratique du Congo. The 'new' Congolese armed forces, inaugurated in mid-2003 but existing more in name than in reality. The FARDC is made up of the fighting forces that waged war against one another from 1998 to 2003, and in general these units remain loyal to their factions rather than the unified army high command. Estimated size: 82,000.

FDLR: Forces Démocratiques pour la Libération du Rwanda. DRC-based anti-Rwandan government militia, composed of ex-FAR and *interahamwe* and newer recruits. The FDLR leadership has said it will

---

Methodology The findings presented in this chapter are derived from a variety of sources. The author conducted fieldwork in Kigali, Cyangugu and Nyagatare and Ntendezi camps in Rwanda and Bukavu in South Kivu, DRC, during August 2004. The fieldwork consisted of semi-structured interviews with a wide range of informants, commissioned refugee surveys in Nyagatare and Cyangugu town and a commissioned survey of admission trends at the Cyangugu hospital most used by refugees. Details of interviewees may be found in the Appendix.

The 2004 fieldwork did not include visits to Kiziba, Gihembe or Nyabiheke, and analysis of the situation in these camps is drawn from published material and other secondary sources, and interviews with other researchers

184

go home if the Rwandan government allows it to become a political party, but the Rwandan government refuses to negotiate. The FARDC and MONUC are attempting to secure the demobilization and repatriation of the FDLR through persuasion and military force, but most of its fighters remain on the ground in eastern DRC. Estimates as to size vary widely, between 10,000 and 40,000.

FNL: Forces Nationales pour la Libération. Burundian Hutu militia committed to Hutu ethnic supremacy in Burundi, which refuses to accept the legitimacy of the government elected in September 2005. Estimated to number 2,000–3,000.

Mai Mai: Congolese ethnic militia who began fighting Banyarwanda militia in North and South Kivu in the early 1990s. During the 1997–2003 war, Mai Mai fought RDF troops in eastern DRC. The new DRC transitional government has officially integrated the Mai Mai into the FARDC, but in practice most Mai Mai retain loyalty to their immediate commanders only. No reliable estimates as to size exist, but likely to total tens of thousands.

MONUC: Mission de l'Organisation des Nations Unies en République du Congo. UN mission in the DRC, which began work in 2001, intended to help the warring parties implement their peace and political transition agreements. MONUC's military contingent numbers around 10,000.

RDF: Rwandan Defence Force. The armed forces of the current Rwandan government. Occupied much of eastern DRC during the 1997–2003 war, and is still alleged by many to retain a residual presence there and to be assisting dissident Congolese armed groups, especially in the Ituri region of North Kivu. Estimated to number around 60,000.

and representatives from the Rwandan government and international humanitarian agencies.

The bulk of the interviews were done in late 2004, but a fresh round of telephonic interviews was conducted in late 2005. There was, in addition, a desktop literature and media review of wider developments in the region and refugee militarization issues generally, drawing particularly on UNHCR's own resources.

Contemporary developments

Nyabiheke The Nyabiheke camp is in the central Byumba province, far from the Congolese border, was built by a US-based NGO called the

American Refugee Committee, and opened its doors in May 2005 (see map). In late 2005, the camp housed around 4,500 refugees from the DRC who were transferred from Nyagatare and other transit camps near the Congolese border, after crossing into Rwanda during 2004/05. UNHCR commented that the transfer of refugees away from Nyagatare to Nyabiheke was essential because the former camp was so close to the border, while the latter was an eight-hour drive away. The UNHCR country office also lauded the Rwandan government for establishing the camp, describing it as 'a sign of generosity and respect of international principles'.[7]

Six months after its establishment, Nyabiheke camp still lacked basic amenities but appeared calm, with no security incidents reported. Rumours have surfaced from time to time that the RDF has tried to recruit refugees from Nyabiheke, mainly on occasions when pupils from the camp failed to show up in school. UNHCR has not verified the recruitment allegations, which may mean they are untrue, or, as has been alleged, may show that UNHCR is not willing to endanger its relations with the Rwandan government.[8]

It is unclear whether any of Mutebutsi's soldiers have had access to Nyabiheke, though there have been no reports of any visits. Mutebutsi's soldiers had by late 2005 apparently dispersed, but most seem to have headed for the DRC rather than Byumba.

Nyabiheke camp was established after the fieldwork for this study was completed, but by all accounts Nyagatare's internal political structures and relationships with Rwandan state authorities, described below, have replicated themselves in Nyabiheke. Refugees did not travel to Nyabiheke with arms, and it is highly probable that, as in Nyagatare, the refugees are unarmed, not participating in military training and, as also in Nyagatare, neither attacking nor being attacked by the host population.

Nyagatare transit centre The Nyagatare transit centre in Cyangugu province was from June 2004 until their departure to Nyabiheke in May 2005 home to roughly three thousand Congolese refugees, most of whom fled from Bukavu in June 2004 following military operations against them directed by General Mbuza Mabe, the FARDC commander for South Kivu, the DRC's tenth military region. Mabe's June 2004 operation also prompted the return from Nyagatare to Bukavu of 563 Congolese non-Banyamulenge refugees who had earlier fled the predations of Mutebutsi and his ally, General Laurent Nkunda.[9] On 13 August 2004, there was a bloody massacre of 152 Banyamulenge refugees from the South Kivu town of Uvira who were living in the Gatumba refugee camp in Burundi. Many former Gatumba residents subsequently fled to Rwanda, and most ended up in Nyagatare.

Most of the Nyagatare refugees were Banyamulenge, but there were also a few members of South Kivu's other ethnic groups, such as Bashi and Bafulero, as well as a handful from other Congolese provinces. Many but not all of the Banyamulenge in Nyagatare had relations who were members of the former Rassemblement Congolais pour la Démocratie (RCD) administration in South Kivu, and it appears also that in many cases non-Banyamulenge refugees in Nyagatare also had family members associated with the previous RCD administration.[10] In addition, there were 283 Congolese Hutu Banyarwanda in Nyagatare from Kalehe, a rural area near Lake Kivu around 50 kilometres north of Bukavu, who arrived in July 2004 after what they alleged was ethnic cleansing by elements of the FARDC under Mabe's command:

> When the soldiers took us they made us write our names. They asked us our nationality. We said we were Congolese. They said there are no Congolese who speak Kinyarwanda.[11] They said that everyone who speaks Kinyarwanda is a Rwandan. We were maltreated. Many of us were killed. Our women and children were raped. The majority were raped. We were written down as being Rwandan refugees from 1994. But we said, no, we are Congolese. They said we are not because we speak Kinyarwanda. They were armed. We could say nothing.[12]

Nyagatare was administered by Rwanda's Ministry of Local Government (Minaloc), primarily through a member of the provincial government team based in the camp. Minaloc worked in partnership with UNHCR, which has an office in Cyangugu. External security around Nyagatare was supplied by the RDF, which deployed fifty soldiers there.[13] Officially, internal security was provided by the Rwandan police, but in practice this had only a light presence, and most of the work was done by a refugee security team. Movement into and out of Nyagatare camp was largely unregulated, but after the Gatumba massacre entry to the camp was restricted after 7 p.m.

Nyagatare was designed as a transit centre for Rwandan refugees returning from the DRC, and was generally acknowledged to be too close to the DRC border to function as a safe refugee camp. UNHCR and Minaloc initially intended to move camp residents to Kiziba, in Kibuye, but in the end the decision was taken to construct a new camp on a new site in Byumba, Nyabiheke.

Residents of Nyagatare were highly organized, with the main aspects of camp life governed by an elected committee. The committee consisted of a president and other members, whose tasks included dealing with the government, UNHCR and other agencies in the camp, including the World Food Programme and Médecins Sans Frontières (MSF), internal security, food distribution, hygiene sensitization and supervision, and children's education. Each committee member was in charge of one portfolio, and headed a subcommittee to carry out the tasks associated with it.[14] The committee had just two non-Banyamulenge, and its president, vice-president and security head were all Banyamulenge. Most of the Banyamulenge on the committee had leadership positions in the RCD administration in South Kivu. Banyamulenge control of camp structures was a cause of resentment and concern among camp residents from other ethnic groups.[15]

According to Semuhuza Butsiriko, the camp committee member in charge of internal security (who formerly worked under the RCD administration in the Ministry of Mines in South Kivu), his team had no powers of arrest, but did break up fights and intervene in disputes.[16]

There was a wide consensus that there were no firearms in Nyagatare.[17] The Cyangugu police had no record of any armed crimes involving Nyagatare residents, nor had any arms been seized from the camp. A commissioned study of admissions of Congolese refugees at Cyangugu's Gihundwe hospital showed that, while forty-seven had been admitted to the hospital with gunshot wounds since late May 2004, all these injuries were sustained in the DRC. According to Gihembe hospital staff, there were no admissions

TABLE 5.2 Congolese refugees admitted to Gihembe hospital in Cyangugu, 2004

Date of admission	Number of people	Reason for admission
27 May	14 (including 1 child)	All gunshot wounds*
28 May	2	All gunshot wounds
29 May	3 (including 2 children)	All gunshot wounds
30 May	8	All gunshot wounds
2 June	8 (including 1 child)	7 gunshot wounds, 1 hernia
3 June	1	Malaria
7 June	1 (child)	Malaria
8 June	2	1 gunshot wound, 1 malaria
10 June	4	All gunshot wounds
12 June	1	Malaria
13 June	6	3 malaria, 1 stomach, 1 pregnancy
16 June	2	Unknown
19 June	1	Unknown
20 June	8	All gunshot wounds

Note: * Gihembe nurses claimed that all Congolese refugee gunshot wounds were incurred in the DRC and not Rwanda

Source: Gihembe hospital

at the hospital for gunshot wounds among Congolese refugees sustained since they had been in Rwanda. There were also no admissions for knife wounds.

UNHCR, Rwandan government officials and all respondents in a random survey of camp residents maintained there was no military training in the Nyagatare camp. Even refugees hostile to the Banyamulenge and the internal camp authorities conceded as much in an interview, although there were allegations from some non-Banyamulenge refugees that, while they were still close by in Ntendezi camp, Mutebutsi's soldiers visited Nyagatare 'regularly' and held secret meetings with Banyamulenge refugees. Mutebutsi's soldiers were forbidden by the RDF to leave Ntendezi except to go to Gihembe hospital either for treatment or to visit the sick (see below), but it appears that some used these hospital trips to maintain contact with people in Nyagatare. In addition, Mutebutsi and many of his soldiers have mobile phones, as do many of the Nyagatare refugees, and it has therefore been easy for them to remain in contact.

TABLE 5.3 Nyagatare refugee random n-survey results

Number of respondents:	28
Number of men:	13
Number of women:	15
Number of respondents who say they have heard gunfire in the camp:	0
Number of respondents who say they have seen small arms in the camp:	0
Number of respondents who say there have been acts of violence involving small arms in the camp:	0
Number of respondents who say that other residents possess small arms:	0
Number of respondents who say there have been instances of armed conflict between camp residents and local people:	0
Number of respondents who said residents had been recruited by RDF:	0
Number of respondents who said residents had been recruited by RCD:	0
Number of respondents who reported the presence of soldiers in the camp:*	0
Principal reason for not going home:	
None	0
Insecurity at home	28
Intimidation in the camp	0
Waiting for orders to return	0

*Several respondents indicated that there were families of soldiers in the camp

Some refugees alleged that young men in Nyagatare had been offered USD100 plus Rwandan francs (Rwafr) 2,000 transport money by Mutebutsi's troops to join them, and claimed some had taken up the offer.[18] The allegation was denied by Mutebutsi and the RDF.[19] Still, young male residents of Nyagatare expressed their concerns to UNHCR about their possible recruitment into Mutebutsi's force, and it was striking during the fieldwork that few spent the night in Nyagatare, particularly after the Gatumba massacre.

According to a UN panel of experts investigating regional compliance with an arms embargo against the DRC, on 18 June 2004 the RDF entered Nyagatare, rounded up thirty young men and forced them into trucks. Some of those rounded up told the panel that they had been taken first to a police and then to an army compound, where they were asked to join Mutebutsi's forces. Some of the men told the UN panel that they were released only after intervention from UNHCR (Seudi et al. 2004). UNHCR has confirmed the incident, adding that all but two of the men came back to Nyagatare. The RDF insisted the incident was not a recruitment drive, but was rather the result of a screening exercise in Nyagatare, which discovered that a few of Mutebutsi's men were hiding among them; these were then moved to Ntendezi.[20]

According to UNHCR staff, the RDF's version might be correct. The panel was, however, adamant that the incident was an attempt to force civilian males in Nyagatare to join Mutebutsi's forces in Ntendezi. Whatever was really the case, UNHCR staff interviewed for this study said that after this incident they had no credible evidence that military recruitment took place inside Nyagatare. There was, for example, no continued disappearance of teenage boys from school in the camps as has happened in Kiziba, and to a lesser extent in Gihembe. UNHCR staff in Nyagatare also said they had no knowledge of any fund-raising activities for military or other purposes among the residents, although they did not absolutely rule out the possibility that it had happened secretly.

Cyangugu town During the fieldwork period, around eight hundred Congolese registered as refugees by UNHCR lived in Cyangugu town rather than Nyagatare. Most of them apparently had friends or family in Cyangugu.[21] There was no evidence during the fieldwork that the Cyangugu-based refugees possessed firearms or were involved in military training, although some refugees alleged that a few of the young men among them had been in contact with Mutebutsi's men. Many of the Congolese refugees living in Cyangugu opted to stay where they were when the Nyagatare refugees moved to Nyabiheke, and some Nyagatare refugees joined them in Cyangugu rather than make the move to the new camp. Having opted to stay outside the camp, Cyangugu-based refugees have received no assistance from UNHCR, and what they are doing and whether or not they are still in Rwanda is unclear.

TABLE 5.4 Cyangugu refugee random n-survey results

Number of respondents:	10
Number of men:	8
Number of women:	2
Number of respondents who say they have heard gunfire in town:	0
Number of respondents who say they have seen small arms in town:	0
Number of respondents who say there have been acts of violence involving small arms in town:	0
Number of respondents who say that other refugees possess small arms:	0
Number of respondents who say there have been instances of armed conflict between refugees and local people:	0
Number of respondents who said refugees had been recruited by RDF:	0
Number of respondents who said refugees had been recruited by RCD:	1*
Number of respondents who reported the presence of soldiers in the town:	0
Principal reason for not going home:	
None	0
Insecurity at home	10
Intimidation in the camp	0
Waiting for orders to return	1

Note: * Said it happened once.

There was no evidence that these refugees were distributing or trafficking small arms in or around Cyangugu. The provincial police commander conceded, however, that, with up to two thousand Congolese crossing into Rwanda each day at the two main border crossings between Cyangugu and Bukavu to trade, some may have been bringing concealed weapons with them. Crime statistics, however, did not reflect a significant increase in small-arms-associated crime since the refugees' arrival. There were no recorded instances of illegal firearms possession in the province during January–July 2004, but there was a record of eleven armed robberies. Eight

TABLE 5.5 Cyangugu province violent crime statistics, 2004

	Jan	Feb	Mar	April	May	June	July	Total
Armed robbery	3	1	0	0	2	3	2	11
Murder	1	2	0	0	2	1	1	7

Note: The only violent crime reported in Cyangugu province during the review period was armed robbery and murder. The totals were described by the provincial police commander as 'similar' to previous years.

Source: Superintendent Francis Nkwaya, provincial police commander, Cyangugu

cases of armed robbery went to court, and in each instance, according to the police commander, the perpetrators were Rwandan but the firearms came from the DRC. There were also seven murders during the same period but, according to the commander, none of the suspected perpetrators was Congolese. In fact, as of August 2004 no Congolese refugees had been arrested for any misdemeanour in Cyangugu since they arrived two months before, which was attributed by the commander to the fact that 'our army is very strict with them'.[22]

Mutebutsi and his soldiers The complex events that led to Mutebutsi and his men crossing into Rwanda are reviewed in the next section. Here we review the situation since Mutebutsi was interned.

Mutebutsi and his forces crossed into Rwanda on 21 June 2004, where they were disarmed by the RDF and taken to Ntendezi camp, 25 kilometres east of Cyangugu, and put under the guard of over one hundred RDF troops. During the fieldwork period, Mutebutsi and over three hundred other men were still in Ntendezi, but they were moved on 24/25 August 2004 to Coko camp, in a remote part of Gikongoro province. Coko is a considerable distance from Cyangugu and the journey is a difficult one, but the camp is only a few kilometres from the Burundian border. No formal complaint about this has been made, but many international observers have been privately unhappy about Coko's proximity to Burundi, particularly given the increasingly close cooperation in northern Burundi between the RDF and the Burundian armed forces.

The Rwandan government initially insisted that Mutebutsi and his men were refugees and should be assisted by UNHCR. Just prior to the move to Coko, the then RDF spokesman, Patrick Karegeya, commented, 'We are fed up with looking after them. We spend so much time answering questions like yours about them.'[23]

Moving Mutebutsi's soldiers from Ntendenzi to Coko, and thus farther from the DRC border, met an important UNHCR requirement, although their being close to another border was problematic. But there were still two more important requirements to be fulfilled before UNHCR could consider giving the men refugee status:

- each soldier must renounce combatant status and this must be verified; and
- checks must be carried out to ascertain whether any were suspected of crimes against humanity.[24]

These checks were never concluded and, to the immense irritation of the Rwandan government, UNHCR never recognized Mutebutsi or his followers as refugees. During 2005, the Rwandan government changed tack, arresting Mutebutsi and putting him under house arrest in Kigali (though he is widely rumoured to have de facto freedom of movement there) but loosening RDF surveillance over his soldiers in Coko considerably. According to one well-placed Rwandan government source (who spoke on condition of anonymity), 'Mutebutsi is in detention and anyone who wants to see him can do so. But since UNHCR won't treat Mutebutsi's soldiers as refugees, we are not going to look after them and be accountable.'[25]

In mid-September 2005, FDLR fighters in South Kivu were reported to have captured forty-seven of Mutebutsi's soldiers, including a senior commander called Colonel Eric Rurihombere, all armed, and said to have come from Coko camp, via Burundi.[26] Three were reported to have escaped. After that, depending on which source one believes, the FDLR either released the soldiers having first confiscated their weapons, or handed them over to a predominantly Banyamulenge FARDC unit comprised of Patrick Masunzu's fighters, which either released them or failed to prevent them escaping. Whatever really happened, by the time MONUC arrived to investigate Mutebutsi's soldiers had gone.[27]

Masunzu is a Banyamulenge loyal to Kabila, who fought the RCD and RDF in South Kivu's Haut Plateau from 2000 to 2002, with strong support from the Banyamulenge in the region. Masunzu said he fought to end the pernicious impact of Rwanda's military involvement in the DRC on the Banyamulenge, which was causing the rest of the Congolese people to regard them as 'fifth columnists' of Rwanda. The Rwandan government and the RCD dismissed Masunzu as a criminal. At one stage during the war, Mutebutsi was deployed by the RCD to arrest Masunzu, but failed to do so, and this was why Mutebutsi was unable to retreat to the Haut Plateau after his clash with MONUC in mid-2004.

The Rwandan government allowing those of Mutebutsi's soldiers it had interned in Coko to rearm and re-enter the DRC appears a clear violation of the ongoing UN arms embargo against the DRC, though neither the UN Security Council nor Rwanda's major donors have ever said so publicly. Just after Mutebutsi's troops crossed into Rwanda in mid-2004, a UN panel of experts investigating regional compliance with the embargo concluded that their internment in Ntendezi by the Rwandan authorities was a violation of the arms embargo, arguing that internment meant Rwanda had given Mutebutsi a 'rear retreat'. The panel warned that the men 'remain a latent threat to the DRC': 'The Group of Experts is concerned that the regroupment [of Mutebutsi's forces] within a Rwandan military camp where Rwandan officers, trainers and other troops are located affords immediate and unchecked access to military advice, training and logistical support on the part of Rwanda' (Seudi et al. 2004). When interviewed for this study during his detention in Ntendezi, Mutebutsi claimed he and his men had renounced combatant status and were genuine refugees, denouncing UNHCR for abandoning him while at the same time allegedly supporting genocidal Rwandan *interahamwe* 'refugees' in Congo-Brazzaville.[28] Perhaps because of the lack of material support from UNHCR, Mutebutsi and his troops lived in notably worse conditions in Ntendezi than those experienced in Nyagatare. While at Ntendezi, nearly all the men could be found in some form of uniform and observing at least some military discipline, leaping up and saluting when Mutebutsi walked past them.[29] The men did not appear to be in a state of military readiness, however, nor was there evidence of military training, although it was not possible to be certain that there has been no military training. The RDF was, however, adamant that no military training had been permitted in Ntendezi, nor would be in Coko, and this was affirmed by Mutebutsi.

After it created Ntendezi for Mutebutsi's soldiers in mid-2004, the Rwandan government argued that it had fully met its international obligations by separating military from civilian refugees, and expressed frustration that this had not been recognized by the international community. According to Karegeya, 'It's become a problem that we have done what we were supposed to do. We are being punished for doing the right thing.'[30]

Certainly, the Rwandan government had, as required by UNHCR, disarmed Mutebutsi and his men and separated them from civilian refugees, even if there was more contact between them during Mutebutsi's stay in Ntendezi than Mutebutsi or the Rwandan authorities admit.

The reported events of September 2005, however, require a reassessment of the situation, since even if the RDF did not itself rearm the Mutebutsi soldiers who crossed into South Kivu, it certainly and apparently deliberately did nothing to stop them. In other words, either through omission or commission, the RDF has assisted the outward militarization of Mutebutsi's followers.[31] There are also widespread allegations, vehemently denied by Rwanda and Mutebutsi, that some of Mutebutsi's men were present in the Gatumba camp in Burundi immediately prior to the attack of 13 August 2004, though the evidence for this is circumstantial and of uncertain quality.

Kiziba and Gihembe Kiziba and Gihembe were established in December 1996 following the closure of the Umubano refugee camp in Gisenyi owing to insecurity, and most of the residents in both are Tutsi Banyarwanda from North Kivu. In late 2002 the Rwandan government, in conjunction with the RCD, which controlled eastern DRC at that time, forced 9,500 refugees from Kiziba and Gihembe to return to North Kivu, and the operation was suspended only after strong protest from UNHCR. Many of the repatriated refugees subsequently returned to Kiziba and Gihembe, which in August 2004 had populations of approximately 16,000 and 17,600 respectively (UNHCR 2004a).

According to the UN Panel of Experts on the arms embargo against the DRC, Nkunda and General Obedi, another former Armée Nationale Congolais (ANC, the RCD's armed wing) commander, visited Kiziba and Gihembe several times between late 2003 and mid-2004, accompanied by senior Rwandan government and RDF officials, for what the panel alleges were 'recruitment drives'. The panel reported that:

> On both 2 March and 14 April [2004], in the presence of Rwandan officials, Nkunda personally requested that refugees enrol and conveyed to them that the time had come to continue warfare inside the Democratic Republic of the Congo against the Kinshasa Government. Highly credible reports and documentation indicate that the same activities were carried out in the Kiziba refugee camp in Kibuye which the Group of Experts did not have the time to independently verify.
>
> Rwandan officials, along with Nkunda and other Congolese officials, used intimidation tactics to further the recruitment aims. During the recruitment drives, refugees were threatened with the loss of their Congolese citizenship and were told that Rwandan hospitality had been exhausted. When certain members of the refugee population resisted Nkunda's solicitation, they were directly threatened by Rwandan officials.
>
> From its interviews with refugees in Gihembe camp, eyewitness sources and humanitarian organizations, the Group of Experts concluded that Rwanda's refusal to provide the refugees with appropriately documented refugee status or identity cards was a tool used to pressure the refugees into military service inside the Democratic Republic of the Congo on behalf of dissident forces. (Seudi et al. 2004)

When UNHCR raised concerns about Nkunda's visits to Gihembe and Kiziba with the Rwandan government at the time, it was told that these were 'family visits'. The Rwandan government has claimed that UNHCR never officially complained about Nkunda trying to recruit at Kiziba or Gihembe. According to Richard Sezibera, special envoy to Rwandan president Paul Kagame in the Great Lakes Region: 'Before we started having problems in May and June in South Kivu, we weren't stopping people coming in. But Nkunda hasn't been here since the clashes. We aren't allowing him into Rwanda any more. There is no wall around the camps, so it is possible for people to come in, but there is no need for us to facilitate recruitment.'[32]

Even if UNHCR did not lay a formal complaint, however, the UN panel reported that officials working in the camp were privately clear that Nkunda was trying to recruit during this period in Kiziba and Gihembe. In the view of the UN panel, Nkunda's recruitment drive met with some success, particularly in Kiziba, where throughout the rest of 2004, and apparently during 2005 too, children periodically left school in the camps.

> Departures increased drastically in August [2004]. According to testimony from fellow refugees and aid workers, those who accepted enlistment left the camp alone, at dusk, usually during study period, and assembled on a nearby hilltop where vehicles would be waiting for them.
>
> Refugees as well as aid workers, including human rights and religious organizations, informed the Group that some of the children had been sent for military training at either a military installation nearby in Kibuye or in the eastern part of Rwanda, while others went directly to the Democratic Republic of the Congo for military purposes.
>
> As from July, the constant decrease in school attendance was noted by the camp management and became a cause for concern. Indeed, most students who had left the camp had yet to complete their school year, which ended in September. The Group obtained a list containing the names and descriptive information of the 129 secondary school pupils who had left the camp. The Group documented at least 36 primary schoolchildren who did the same. Although difficult to ascertain, it is likely that children who did not attend school would also have exited the camp unnoticed. (Seudi et al. 2005)

This analysis has been strongly disputed by a former investigator with the UN panel, William Church. In March 2005, Church released a stinging critique of the July 2004 and January 2005 reports of the UN Panel of Experts about implementation of the UN arms embargo against the DRC, alleging that the panel had distorted the evidence, particularly as regards Rwanda, to paint a far more damning picture of the Rwandan government's actions then was warranted. According to Church,

- They [the researchers] misrepresent the exact number of students suspected as recruited.
- They omitted the material information that their grades support the reason why these students left the camp.
- They misrepresented the relationship of the time frame between the Nkunda visit and the first reported recruitment.
- They omitted the information that students left the camp in the same time frame and were not suspected of being recruited. (Church 2005)

Church's report was received enthusiastically in the Rwandan pro-government press, but was widely condemned within the UN, and there were allegations, denied by Church, that he was in the pay of the Rwandan government. Regarding the alleged Kiziba recruitments, UN panel member Kathi Lynn Austin has conceded that UN agencies have not gone on record with allegations and that no systematic checks have been made in the DRC about whether children said to have gone to their home towns and villages have indeed done so. Austin insisted, however, that informants consistently told her privately that most of the school disappearances are linked to recruitment into Nkunda's forces. Nkunda was said to be making payments for recruitment to family members of recruited children and to members of the refugee committee running the internal affairs of the camp. In contrast to Kiziba, it appears, at Gihembe refugees had resisted efforts by their refugee committee to facilitate recruitment from among the camp's children, and had replaced this committee with another not prepared to cooperate with Nkunda.[33]

The Rwandan government is adamant that no child soldiers are or have been recruited from Kiziba and Gihembe. If the allegations are true, why are international agencies keeping silent? While many people within international agencies appear privately convinced that recruitment is going on, they cannot prove it since no systematic effort has been made to track the children who have left Kiziba in the DRC. Without hard proof, international organizations do not dare make recruitment allegations publicly, as the Rwandan government's response would be ferocious, and would damage the organization's ability to operate in the country.

Box 5.2 William Church, a UN Panel of Experts, and an earlier draft of this chapter

Early in 2005, the author of this chapter was telephoned by Church, calling from Rwanda. Church said he had obtained an early draft of this chapter and wanted permission to quote from it for a piece he was writing in criticism of the recently released UN Panel of Experts' report on the arms embargo against the DRC. Church explained that he had once worked for the US Central Intelligence Agency (CIA), and had also recently worked for the panel, until quitting in protest at its alleged political bias. Church was informed he was free to quote whatever he liked from the unpublished draft, as long as he quoted accurately.

Church ended up citing the draft in several instances. With regard to alleged recruitment at Nyagatare, Church quoted from the draft to the effect that UNHCR staff had said the RDF may indeed have been, as it claimed, trying to root out any of Mutebutsi's men who may have been hiding. Inaccurately, though perhaps unintentionally, Church's paper gave the impression that fieldwork for the draft had been conducted in Kiziba and Gihembe, and quoted with approval the finding in the draft that UN agencies had not officially reported allegations of recruitment from Kiziba and Gihembe. Church's paper did not, however, cite additional comments in the draft that allegations had privately been made by international workers in Kiziba which, if true, would constitute refugee militarization by the Rwandan government.

After Church's report came out, the author of this chapter was criticized by some, particularly within MONUC, for apparently lending his name to it. The author's view is that a misleading quote is the responsibility of the one quoting and not the one quoted. That said, by quoting in the way he did, Church presented an inaccurate impression of the author's views. It is hoped this chapter affords readers an opportunity to make up their own minds.

The build-up to the present

It is beyond the scope of this study to provide a comprehensive account of the origins of the conflict in eastern DRC. Instead, and mindful of the significant role that accounts of conflict in the Great Lakes Region have played in the conflict itself (Pottier 2002), this section attempts merely a brief overview of the main events that have led to the current presence of Congolese refugees in Rwanda.

1996–2004 Banyarwanda Congolese refugees first came into Rwanda in 1996, fleeing a hostile alliance in the Kivus of ethnic Congolese militia and Rwandan ex-FAR and *interahamwe*, who had fled Rwanda after their defeat by the Rwandan Patriotic Front (RPF) in 1994. Rwandan troops, who included many recent Banyarwanda refugee recruits in their midst, proceeded to invade what was then Zaire in 1996, partly because of the Banyamulenge refugee influx but, more importantly, in order to break up the Rwandan refugee camps there, which had become deeply militarized. This militarization had happened because the ex-FAR and *interahamwe*, with the assistance of the Zairean armed forces, had been able to regroup militarily, acquiring new weapons and training regularly, and had also established considerable authority over civilian refugees, in part by their taking over the distribution of humanitarian resources within the camps.

This authority was used to intimidate international humanitarian workers in the camps and to prevent civilian refugees from returning to Rwanda. In addition, the ex-FAR and *interahamwe* conducted raids into Rwanda with increasing frequency, particularly targeting Hutus who were collaborating with the new regime (EIU 1996). As in 1994, however, the ex-FAR and *interahamwe* proved no match for the RDF, which had little difficulty breaking up the refugee camps in eastern Zaire, resulting in a huge return of refugees to Rwanda. Tens of thousands of refugees did not, however, return. Some of these fled deeper into Zaire and the rest, it appears, were slaughtered.

As well as breaking up the refugee camps, the RDF provided strong support to a new armed group inside Zaire called the Alliance des Forces Démocratiques pour la Libération du Congo-Zaire (AFDL), and within just one year the result was the fall of President Mobutu and the installation of the AFDL's Laurent Desiré Kabila in his place in Kinshasa.

The initial impact of Mobutu's fall was to improve the position of Banyarwanda in eastern Democratic Republic of Congo (as it was renamed by Kabila), and many of the Congolese Banyarwanda refugees still living in Rwanda went home. Before long, however, the relationship between Kabila and the Rwandan government deteriorated. Kabila expelled Rwandan forces from the DRC in July 1998 and instead cultivated relations with the ex-FAR and *interahamwe*. As a result, the persecution of Banyarwanda Tutsis in the Kivus resumed, and Banyarwanda refugees who had remained in Rwanda stopped returning to the DRC.

The Rwandan government quickly helped set up a new Tutsi Banyarwanda-dominated political and military organization in the DRC called the Rassemblement Congolais pour la Démocratie (RCD). Many Banyarwanda refugees in Rwanda joined the RCD, which launched a military rebellion in eastern DRC in August 1998, and together with the RDF subsequently quickly took control of eastern DRC. Most Banyamulenge refugees still living in Rwanda went home during this period.

The RCD's military campaign was initially also supported by Uganda, but was opposed by Angola, Zimbabwe and Namibia, which intervened militarily on the side of the Kinshasa government. The war quickly stalemated, and the RDF remained in the DRC until it withdrew in October 2002, following an agreement between the Rwandan and DRC governments brokered by Mbeki earlier in the year. Since then, and although it is strongly denied by the Rwandan government, the RDF has been widely alleged to have retained a covert residual presence in certain parts of eastern DRC (Mthembu-Salter 2005).

Marathon political negotiations in Sun City, South Africa, during 2002/03 resulted in broad-based agreement from all the main Congolese political factions on the terms for establishing a new transitional government. The new government, headed by Kabila's son Joseph (Kabila senior had been assassinated in January 2001), was formed in June 2003. Along with Kabila's faction, the Mouvement pour la Libération du Congo (MLC),[34] and a loosely constituted coalition of Kinshasa-based opposition political parties, as part of the government the RCD was awarded one of four vice-presidencies, ministerial positions, parliamentary seats, diplomatic postings and parastatal directorships.

The DRC transitional government gradually achieved a semblance of cohesion and began establishing its authority over the whole country. New governors and deputy governors were appointed to every province in May 2004, again with equal representation for all the government's component parts. The factions making up the new government also successfully negotiated the conditions for the highly difficult task of integrating the formerly warring armies of its constituent parts, agreeing to a DDR programme in early 2004. Implementation, however, proved very slow and was still far from complete by late 2005. Despite all the uncertainties in the east of the country, and the fact that actual disarmament had not yet started, the government launched preparations in mid-2004 for national elections, which were at first scheduled for 2005, and subsequently delayed, amid much popular protest, to mid-2006.

Mutebutsi and the Congolese refugees In early 2004, Colonel Jules Mutebutsi, who during the RCD's occupation of eastern DRC had been the commander of the Uvira Brigade of the ANC, was appointed by the DRC transitional government as the tenth military region's deputy commander, under General Prosper Nyabiolwa. Nyabiolwa was a Kabila loyalist, and tensions between the two men led to clashes between their forces in Bukavu in February 2004. Nyabiolwa was subsequently removed from his position by the transitional government and replaced by General Mbuza Mabe. This did not alter the underlying power struggle, and Mabe's and Mutebutsi's forces began fighting each other in Bukavu on 26 May. Nkunda's forces joined Mutebutsi's to combat Mabe, and together they captured Bukavu on 2 June. The Rwandan government at this point closed its border with the DRC, but was nevertheless widely accused of assisting both Nkunda's and Mutebutsi's forces. The charges were denied by the Rwandan government. Nkunda and Mutebutsi held Bukavu for a week, during which time hundreds of residents fled the city following extensive killing and looting by Mutebutsi's and Nkunda's troops, and, it is widely alleged, systematic rape. Many of those who fled crossed into Rwanda, ending up in Nyagatare.

The story of one woman, the wife of a wealthy Bukavu businessman, ran as follows:

It was on a Wednesday [2 June]. Two Tutsi soldiers came into my house. They asked for money. We gave them some. They wanted more. They took two phones. Then they asked for more money. They started shooting. We gave them more money and they left. At 2 p.m. other soldiers came looking for money. Those ones were Congolese. We told them the other soldiers had taken our money. They said they were looking for Mabe. We said, 'He's not here.' They again demanded money. We gave them a phone. They left. At 4 p.m. soldiers came again to our house.

We decided it would be impossible to sleep in the house that night. At 6 p.m. we headed for another district. There it was calm and things were going normally. A friend telephoned from Cyangugu and said that we must sleep outside because they were raping women ... I took the children to sleep with me in the garage. My husband stayed in town to protect the house.

On the Thursday I left with the children for Rwanda. Once the border was closed by Rwanda we registered with UNHCR ... We came back when Mabe retook the city.[35]

Nkunda and Mutebutsi withdrew from Bukavu following negotiations with MONUC, who insisted that Mabe, as the appointed commander of the tenth military region, be allowed to take back the city. This was bolstered by a threat from Louis Michel, the Belgian foreign minister, that a European-led intervention force might be deployed if he was not permitted to do so (International Crisis Group 2004).

Nkunda headed north to Kalehe while Mutebutsi went south to Kaman-yola. Following Nkunda's and Mutebutsi's withdrawal, Mabe's forces took full control of Uvira and Bukavu and went on their own looting and killing spree, driving Banyamulenge people and any non-Banyamulenge associated with the RCD out of the two towns. Banyamulenge refugees are adamant that MONUC forces in Bukavu did nothing to try to stop the ethnic cleansing, although they did intervene to save lives. Those fleeing Uvira went to Burundi, where they were registered as refugees by UNHCR in the Gatumba refugee camp, while those fleeing Bukavu crossed into Rwanda at a crossing called Ruzizi I, and were registered as refugees by UNHCR at Nyagatare.[36] It was widely reported in international media at the time that the refugees who fled Bukavu were fleeing *for fear of* persecution, but the refugees insist that the persecution was real, that they were attacked, and that many were killed. MONUC officials confirm this, and in addition many of the refugees arrived in Rwanda with bullet wounds. The arriving refugees were screened by UNHCR and many were taken to Nyagatare, although others headed straight for friends and family in Cyangugu. At the same time, most of the Congolese who had fled to Rwanda during Mutebutsi's and Nkunda's occupation of the city returned.

On 20 June MONUC and Mutebutsi's forces exchanged fire near Kamanyola, 40 kilometres south of Bukavu. Each side accuses the other of firing first.[37] Mutebutsi subsequently escaped into Rwanda, where he was quickly disarmed by the RDF and escorted with his men to Ntendezi.

Who is doing what, and why

The premise underlying research into refugee militarization is that refugees are not mere objects of humanitarian assistance but are instead primarily subjects as capable of agency as anyone else. Assessing the agency of refugees is thus critical to an evaluation of their militarization in each context. Yet the agency of the refugees is not expressed in circumstances of their own making, and the agency of other important actors is important too. This section considers the roles and intentions of Rwanda's Congolese refugees, Mutebutsi and his soldiers, Nkunda, the Rwandan government, UNHCR and the UN Security Council.

Banyamulenge refugees The predominantly Banyamulenge RCD controlled South Kivu and the rest of eastern DRC from 1998 to early 2004, but the advent of a new transitional government in Kinshasa in mid-2003 steadily brought this dominance to an end. Although Banyamulenge retained a few civilian political positions in South Kivu, the key change was the appointment in early 2004 of General Mbuza Mabe as military commander for the province. Within just a few months of Mabe's appointment as tenth military region commander, the wheel turned rapidly for urban Banyamulenge, and they were driven from their homes in Uvira and Bukavu in June 2004.

When interviewed in August 2004, most ordinary Banyamulenge refugees in Nyagatare said they wanted to return home but did not think it safe to do so. Every respondent in a small n-sample survey conducted in Nyagatare gave this as the reason for not returning, with many explaining that ethnic hatred against Banyamulenge in Uvira and Bukavu was at an all-time high. One refugee told the following story:

> I am a Banyamulenge woman. I have six children. I left Bukavu because there was so much war. Mabe's soldiers killed women, men, children, students. They looted everything. Even our clothes. I was left with just my shorts. But my family was safe. They killed my neighbour and her family.

202

We walked to the border during the night. They attacked us even there. The other tribes wanted to chase all the Banyamulenge away, but God protected us. Our problem was that we couldn't hide, because we look different to other people.[38] We are OK here. We have soldiers to protect us. But since the Gatumba massacre I don't think we are safe to return.[39]

Benoit Kadege, one of the political leaders of the Banyamulenge refugees in Rwanda, and a hardliner, stated in an interview that the Banyamulenge would return only if their security is guaranteed, their properties are returned and repaired, and that in addition 'The Kinshasa government must recognize that we are under a genocide. People have been killed because they are Banyamulenge.'[40]

Kadege did not expect much assistance from Rwanda, and instead demanded safe passage for the refugees in the country to the predominantly Banyamulenge area of Minembwe, in South Kivu's Haut Plateau. A number of refugees agreed that they would rather be in Minembwe than Rwanda.[41] The main problem with this scheme, however, has been the strong influence in Minembwe and the rest of the Haut Plateau of Masunzu. Most of the former public officials in Nyagatare owed their positions to the RCD, and would also probably not be able to coexist peacefully with Masunzu's forces in Minembwe. Ordinary Banyamulenge refugees, however, would be unlikely to have any such difficulties, and many secretly support Masunzu anyway.[42]

Political leaders among the Banyamulenge refugees in Rwanda were reluctant to discuss whether they wanted to attempt the recapture of South Kivu by force, preferring to emphasize, prior to the Gatumba massacre at least, that they still supported the DRC transitional government.[43] After Gatumba, however, Banyamulenge refugee leaders demanded that the RCD suspend its participation in the transitional government. Kadege called for retaliation. The RCD was split on the issue of suspending participation in the transitional government, with Azarias Ruberwa, one of the DRC's four vice-presidents, the most prominent member of the party opting to do so until Thabo Mbeki, president of South Africa, prevailed upon him to return during a visit to Kinshasa on 29–30 August 2004.

Repeated concerns expressed to UNHCR by young Banyamulenge men in Nyagatare about possible recruitment did not indicate great desire on their part to go back to the DRC and fight. The question for Banyamulenge refugees in Rwanda who are not former members of the RCD administration appeared to be whether Masunzu's policy of strategic engagement with Kabila, or indeed anything at all, could deliver security to them, enabling them to return peacefully to Bukavu and Uvira. If nothing delivers the security they are looking for, more of the Rwanda- and Burundi-based Banyamulenge refugees could be expected to endorse the military option.

Mutebutsi and his soldiers

Kabila wants a genocide. The question is: how can we stop him?[44]

Mutebutsi insisted when interviewed in August 2004 that he had renounced his military status, but claimed at the same time to be a soldier. He refused to be drawn on whether he wanted to return to South Kivu by force of arms, saying that his movements were restricted by the RDF and he could not contemplate such a course of action. Mutebutsi added that his and his men's weapons had been taken from them and they did not have the power to get them back. This was confirmed at the time by the RDF.[45] Furthermore, the International Committee of the Red Cross (ICRC) had visited Ntendezi for an assessment on the grounds that the residents were 'interned' and could thus be considered prisoners.[46]

While not openly advocating a return to the armed struggle, in August 2004 Mutebutsi displayed little faith in a negotiated solution either. Asked whether he supported Nkunda's armed resistance against elements of the FARDC loyal to Kabila, Mutebutsi replied, 'We support anyone who protects the people.'[47] As Mutebutsi has said he considers there to be a policy of genocide in operation against the Banyamulenge, it seems likely that, if given the opportunity by the Rwandan government to rearm and return to South Kivu in force, he would take it. Mutebutsi's appeals to UNHCR during 2004 for refugee status, however, showed that he did not think it likely the Rwandan government would provide such an opportunity.

Mutebutsi was moved from Coko and placed under house arrest in Kigali in 2005. Although he is alleged to enjoy some freedom of movement nevertheless,[48] the Rwandan government has prevented him from returning to the DRC and continuing his armed struggle there. By contrast, the government has allowed Mutebutsi's soldiers to leave Coko, rearm and return to the DRC. An unknown number of Mutebutsi's soldiers have taken up the opportunity and have headed for South Kivu, where they could play a disruptive role in the build-up to the DRC's scheduled 2006 general elections.

North Kivu Banyarwanda refugees No fieldwork among the North Kivu Banyarwanda refugees in Kiziba and Gihembe was undertaken for this study. According to UNHCR, Kiziba and Gihembe are civilian in character. Yet credible findings by researchers from the UN panel investigating the arms embargo against the DRC, and other UN researchers investigating child soldiers, have indicated that a combination of financial incentives, pressure from the Rwandan authorities and, for some, a commitment to Nkunda's armed struggle has led to a positive response within the Kiziba refugee population to recruitment into Nkunda's forces. By contrast, there has apparently been an almost universally negative reaction among Gihembe camp residents.

It is probable, nevertheless, that most North Kivu Banyarwanda who want to fight are not in Rwanda but have already returned to the DRC, since Nkunda and his forces, who are predominantly North Kivu Banyarwanda in composition, are still operational in North Kivu, and the province remains, for the moment, under the control of the RCD.

Nkunda Nkunda was forced to flee his military positions following a FARDC offensive in late 2004 but by late 2005 appeared to have re-established himself militarily in North Kivu, and was reported as attracting 'hundreds' of FARDC deserters to his side. After issuing a tract hostile to the government, in September 2005 Nkunda was officially dismissed from the FARDC and an international warrant of arrest was issued against him.[49] Nkunda nevertheless appeared to retain relations with North Kivu governor Eugene Serufuli, and with former ANC general Obedi, and it is feared he is being groomed to play a spoiling role in the province during the 2006 elections.[50]

Nkunda, it appears, tried to recruit refugees from Kiziba and Gihembe in early 2004, and as has been discussed above Nkunda's efforts seemed to have met with some success in Kiziba but less so in Gihembe. Assuming UN panel researchers are right to claim that recruitment into Nkunda's forces from Kiziba has persisted during 2005, the silence of the international community on the issue may have been interpreted by Nkunda and the Rwandan government as implying tacit condonement, in which case the expectation should be that recruitment from Kiziba will carry on.

The Rwandan government In 1996/97 and again in 1998 the Rwandan government provided highly effective military support to Banyamulenge political aspirations in the DRC. The first Rwandan intervention eventually led to the toppling of Mobutu and the accession of Laurent Desiré Kabila to the Congolese presidency. The second Rwandan intervention, which followed attacks on Banyamulenge in South Kivu by other ethnic militia, nearly resulted in the toppling of Kabila, but actually instead brought about a bloody regional war in the DRC that lasted until 2002. It is therefore not surprising that many suspect something similar could happen in the near future, and that Rwanda could once again intervene in the DRC, citing the Banyamulenge plight as its justification.

A profound worsening in the Rwandan government's relationship with the Banyamulenge, however, made future military–political collaborations less likely. The RDF spent the last two years of its occupation of eastern DRC engaged in a vicious counter-insurgency campaign against Masunzu and his Banyamulenge supporters deep in the Haut Plateau, allegedly devoting more attention to this than to its stated objective of combating Rwandan militia implicated in the 1994 Rwandan genocide.[51] Masunzu survived the onslaught in large part because of the support he enjoyed from Banyamulenge, transforming the former confidence of the Rwandan government in the community into hostility and distrust.

Moving the civilian Banyamulenge refugees away from the Congolese border, from Nyagatare to Nyabahike, strongly suggested that the Rwandan government would not support their external militarization. Concerning Mutebutsi personally, one RDF commander interviewed in August 2004 described him as 'finished',[52] and putting him under house arrest in Kigali in mid-2005 suggested that the Rwandan government had taken much the same view. The government has, however, as we have seen, been prepared either to permit or assist the external militarization of Mutebutsi's soldiers.

Unlike with the Banyamulenge, relations between the Rwandan government and North Kivu Banyarwanda Tutsi have never ruptured. Because of this, the Rwandan government is more inclined to assist the military efforts of North Kivu Banyarwanda, which may explain its stance regarding refugee militarization in Kiziba. On the other hand, the Rwandan government has repeatedly insisted that it will not back Nkunda militarily, and its deportation of some Nkunda supporters from Rwanda in September 2005 seemed to suggest it meant it.[53] It has, however, been claimed that the expulsions were just a cynical ploy by the government to conceal continuing close links between the Rwandan government and Nkunda.[54]

UNHCR An important aspect of UNHCR's mission is to preserve the civilian character of refugee camps. To help it do this in the complex circumstances in which the agency invariably finds itself, and in large part inspired by its disastrous experience with Rwandan refugees in eastern DRC (then Zaire) in 1994, UNHCR has devised a 'ladder of options'. The first 'rung' of the ladder is 'preventive and corrective measures', which include excluding 'ineligible elements' from refugee status (Bui 1998). The refusal of UNHCR to accede to Rwandan government demands to recognize Mutebutsi's troops as refugees was inspired by this, as was its pushing for the move of Congolese refugees in Nyagatare and Cyangugu to Nyabiheke, much farther from the DRC–Rwanda border.

If the UN Panel of Experts is right and UNHCR officials in Kiziba have private suspicions that recruitment is going on, the silence of UNHCR on the matter is highly problematic. It may be that the reason UNHCR in Rwanda is keeping silent is that it lacks the proof to substantiate the suspicions of its staff. In that case, there is surely a strong case for UNHCR in the DRC, assisted by MONUC, properly to check to determine where students who have left Kiziba moved to, make the results public and then act on them, even if the consequence is a negative response from the Rwandan government. If this does not happen, the Rwandan government's contention that there is no recruitment will obviously appear much stronger.

UN Security Council Refugee militarization is at heart a political and security issue. As persuasively argued by refugee militarization expert Margaret McGuinness (2003: 161), 'To address the problem of politicization and militarization, states need to address the underlying conflict; to ensure the rights of refugees, they must try to prevent the persecution that created refugees in the first place.' The UN Security Council has many times been accused of ignoring this, but in the case of the DRC, has genuinely tried to address the underlying conflict. MONUC's deployment and consistent diplomatic work have been complemented by the substantial reconstruction work and economic reform process funded by the World Bank and the International Monetary Fund. Whether or not these efforts prove sufficient to address the underlying conflict, clearly the Security Council has understood the need to try.

The UN Security Council and MONUC faced an extremely difficult and delicate task as the DRC's 2006 elections approached, having to facilitate voter registration, cajole political parties into agreeing on a draft constitution and electoral law and push forward the integration of the country's many armed forces. The apparent reluctance in this context of the UN Security Council to take up the contention of the UN Panel of Experts that the Rwandan government is facilitating the ongoing external militarization of Congolese refugees from Rwanda has thus perhaps been understandable. Yet while understandable, the position is mistaken, since if the panel is right, Rwanda is playing a destabilizing role in North Kivu which it is in the interests of MONUC and the UN Security Council to prevent. But if the panel is wrong, Rwanda's allegations of its political bias will demand serious consideration. Either way, the UN Security Council needs to know.

The surest way, meanwhile, for the Security Council to prevent militarization among Congolese refugees in Rwanda is to facilitate their peaceful return to the DRC. By late 2005, however, there was little prospect of this, and instead it seemed increasingly certain that elections would come and go in the DRC with Congolese refugees still in Rwanda.

Conclusions and recommendations

How militarized are Rwanda's Congolese refugees? One of the main findings of this study is that there is a considerable difference in the level of militarization of Banyamulenge refugees from South Kivu and Banyarwanda refugees from North Kivu.

Civilian Banyamulenge refugees in Rwanda have not become militarized. The main location of these refugees since May 2005 has been Nyabiheke, a long way from the Congolese border, and the camp appears free of small arms and military training. The evidence suggests that Nyabiheke, like Nyagatare before it, is civilian in character, although Banyamulenge who were formerly prominent in the RCD administration in South Kivu, which was closely linked to the military, dominate camp political structures. Civilian Banyamulenge refugees have at no time preyed on Rwandans in their vicinity, and have not attacked the DRC.

When Mutebutsi and his troops were camped near Nyagatare, there was clandestine contact between them and civilian Banyamulenge refugee leaders, but contact became much more difficult after Mutebutsi's troops moved to Coko, and the refugees to Nyabiheke. In contrast to civilian Banyamulenge refugees, Mutebutsi's soldiers, although initially disarmed and interned, have apparently since been allowed by the Rwandan government to rearm and return to fight in the DRC – a classic instance of outward militarization.

As has been discussed, the evidence suggests a worrying degree of outward militarization among North Kivu Banyarwanda refugees in Kiziba, and to a lesser extent in Gihembe. Although this is strongly denied by the Rwandan government, the refugees' militarization appears to have taken place because of recruitment efforts by Nkunda, the facilitation of these efforts by the Rwandan authorities, the cooperation of the refugee committee in Kiziba, and the willingness of at least some of the Kiziba refugees to be recruited.

Have the lessons of 1994 been learned, and are they the right lessons? In the introduction to this chapter, the question was posed as to whether Rwanda as the host state, the international community and the UN in particular had learned the lessons from the militarization of the Rwandan refugee camps in eastern DRC ten years ago, and second, whether, if so, the lessons were the right ones for the current refugee crisis. We are now in a position to attempt answers to these questions.

HOST STATE An important lesson supposedly to be learned from the Rwandan refugee camps in eastern Zaire was that the host state must take the lead in separating combatants from civilians, neutralizing the threat posed by combatants, preserving the civilian nature of refugee camps, and moving the camps away from borders.

The Rwandan government's performance on this count is mixed. It took the initiative after the mid-2004 Congolese refugee influx of separating combatants from civilians, and then kept them separated. The Rwandan government also largely preserved the civilian nature of its refugee camps and, despite a severe land shortage, established a new refugee camp for Congolese in Byumba, suitably far away from the Congolese border.

The Rwandan government permitted the resurgence of the military threat posed by Mutebutsi's soldiers, however, and may have assisted their rearming and returning to their country. In addition, the Rwandan government appears to have facilitated the external militarization of refugees from Kiziba camp. Thus the Rwandan government seems not to have learned the lesson from the Rwandan refugee camps in eastern Zaire, but appears instead, albeit on a far lesser scale, to have adopted a similar strategy to Mobutu's, using refugees to advance its strategic interests in the region.

UNHCR UNHCR has tried to implement its 'ladder of options' with Rwanda's Congolese refugees to preserve the civilian character of refugee-populated areas. First, the move from Nyagatare to Nyabiheke in mid-2005, which was advocated and assisted by UNHCR, made the militarization of these refugees much harder. Second, UNHCR's withholding of refugee status from Mutebutsi and his men made contact between them and civilian refugees harder than it would otherwise have been, retarding potential refugee militarization. UNHCR's stance, however, also encouraged the Rwandan government to abandon its commitment to interning Mutebutsi's soldiers, which contributed to their remilitarization.

Many people working for international agencies in the Rwandan refugee camps of eastern Zaire knew early on that the camps were being militarized, but the agencies themselves took a very long time to speak out. This failure to speak out assisted the process of militarization. Now the wheel has turned again, and those working for international agencies in Kiziba believe that refugees are being recruited from there to fight for Nkunda. Yet again agencies are not speaking out, this time, perhaps, because there is no firm proof it is happening. There can be no firm proof, however, without investigation. To avoid unwittingly assisting refugee militarization once again, the investigation should happen as soon as possible, and should ideally be conducted by UNHCR and MONUC. If the investigation confirms that refugees are being recruited, UNHCR must speak out against it.

It seems unlikely that if refugee militarization were confirmed, the more extreme steps in the ladder of options, such as UN troop deployment with a Chapter VI or VII mandate, would ever be pursued by the UN system fast enough to make a difference. Furthermore, as Stedman and Tanner (2003: 15) have astutely observed, when UNHCR discovers that refugee militarization is happening and that it cannot prevent it, the vital last rung of its options ladder – disengagement – is missing.

THE UN SECURITY COUNCIL AND MONUC The main lesson for the UN Security Council from the disastrous experience of the Rwandan refugee camps in Zaire was that it must not replace a political response to such crises with a purely humanitarian response. Mercifully, the Security Council appears so far to have learned this lesson with the DRC, as shown by the Council's deployment of MONUC and its sustained, multi-faceted, diplomatic pressure on the potential belligerents there.

MONUC has not, however, done enough to stop ethnic cleansing in the region. MONUC officials in eastern DRC have tended to gloss over the fact that Banyamulenge were ethnically cleansed from Bukavu in June 2004, arguing that Banyamulenge flight was inevitable because of the terrible abuses committed prior to this by Nkunda and Mutebutsi's predominantly Banyarwanda Tutsi forces in the city. The suggestion appears to be that there was nothing MONUC could have done to restrain Mabe's forces, but this is surely untrue. Given the history of genocide in the Great Lakes Region, ethnic cleansing is a dangerous development that requires the UN Security Council specifically to instruct MONUC to do its best to stop it.

The UN Security Council failed to appreciate and take steps against militarization in the Rwandan camps of eastern Zaire for a complex variety of reasons. One – perhaps – was a failure of intelligence. Another – almost certainly – was the continued close bond between the ex-FAR and the French government, a permanent member of the Council. A further factor, without doubt, was the fear that strong action against the *interahamwe* in the camps would conflict with the humanitarian ethic of care for refugees. In addition, it was by no means clear what should be done to contain the ongoing refugee militarization.

The results of the Security Council's failure to act against refugee militarization in eastern Zaire, however understandable, were disastrous. The subsequent military campaign by the RDF and its allies of the time to end militarization in the Zairean camps, essentially by destroying them, cost thousands of lives and launched a war that has still completely to finish.

An obvious lesson for the Security Council, then, is that it must act decisively against refugee militarization in the region. This implies that the Security Council should order further investigation into two apparent instances of militarization of Congolese refugees in Rwanda, namely the presence of former Coko resident soldiers of Mutebutsi's in South Kivu, and the alleged recruitment of refugees from Kiziba to fight for Nkunda. Thus far, the UN Security Council has shown no desire to do either. Its continued failure to do so, however, could prove costly.

Recommendations The *Rwandan government* should prevent Mutebutsi's soldiers from leaving Rwanda armed and of their own volition, and instead should negotiate their formal and transparent hand-over to the FARDC. The government should also take strong and transparent measures to prevent any recruitment of Congolese refugees into Nkunda's forces, and should cooperate with any investigation into the whereabouts of ex-students from camps who are said already to have been recruited. More generally, the Rwandan government should adhere in practice to its stated commitment to negotiated, political solutions to the DRC's profound governance problems, and desist from any form of military intervention in the country.

UNHCR's implementation of its 'ladder of options' has facilitated the move from Nyagatare to Nyabiheke of Banyamulenge refugees and made contact difficult between these refugees and Mutebutsi's soldiers. UNHCR should have screened Mutebutsi's soldiers soon after they arrived, however, to determine early on their refugee status. If UNHCR had concluded they were not refugees, the Rwandan government should have been asked to repatriate them under international supervision. UNHCR should investigate the UN panel on the DRC arms embargo's claim that refugees from Kiziba have been recruited, and if this is found to be true, it must act swiftly and firmly on the findings.

The *UN Security Council* needs to take steps against refugee militarization and against the forces that drive people in the region to become refugees in the first place. To these ends, the Security Council should demand that the Rwandan government control effectively the movements of Mutebutsi and his soldiers, and also discuss with the DRC authorities the modalities of handing them over. The Council should also order an investigation of claims that Kiziba refugees are being recruited to fight for Nkunda, and take strong action if the claims are found to be true. At the same time, the Council needs to take ethnic cleansing in eastern DRC more seriously. The Council must make very public its strong opposition to ethnic cleansing and deploy MONUC to prevent it, even if this entails MONUC taking on FARDC units. MONUC must not shy away from such a confrontation on the grounds that this might undermine the political transition in the DRC, since ethnic cleansing itself undermines the transition and makes war more likely. For everyone's sakes, ethnic cleansing in the Kivus must be stopped, and in Uvira and Bukavu it must be reversed, before the 2006 elections if possible, by enabling the Banyamulenge refugees in Rwanda to go home.

Appendix: Key informants interviewed for the study

UNHCR	Kalunga Lutato, Rwanda resident representative Field workers in Cyangugu Jaya Murthy, Bukavu
UN Panel of Experts investigating DRC arms embargo	Kathi Lynn Austin
Rwandan governmen	Joseph Mutaboba, Ministry of Internal Securityt Richard Sezibera, presidential envoy to the Great Lakes Region Patrick Karegeya, RDF spokesman Vincent Muragwa, executive secretary, province of Cyangugu Lt Col. George Rurigamba, RDF commander, Cyangugu Superintendent Francis Nkwaya, provincial police commander, Cyangugu James Kimonyo, Rwandan ambassador, South Africa
Refugees	Jonas Jondwe, president of refugee camp committee, Nyagatare Semuhuza Butsiriko, security liaison, refugee camp committee, Nyagatare 20–25 Nyagatare refugees who spoke on condition of anonymity Returned refugees in Bukavu, who spoke on condition of anonymity
MONUC	Tim Reid, Political Affairs Officer for disarmament, demobilization, repatriation and reintegration, Bukavu Kinshasa-based investigators and political officers who wished to remain anonymous
Others	Colonel Jules Mutebutsi Benoit Kadege, president of the Banyamulenge *mutuelle* Esperance Nyirahabimana, head of nursing, Gihundwe hospital, Kamembe Hans Romenka, Life and Peace Institute, Bukavu Helen Vesperini, Agence France Presse correspondent, Kigali

Notes

1 UNHCR. Correct as of October 2005.

2 That is, of Rwandan origin.

3 Congolese Tutsis from South Kivu who claim the Haut Plateau, west of Uvira, are known as Banyamulenge.

4 By this is meant that the refugees were driven out of their home area on the basis of their ethnicity.

5 August 2004.

6 World Food Programme Emergency Report no. 44, October 2005, <www.wfp.org/english/?ModuleID=78&Key=660#646>.

7 IRIN (2005a).

8 Telephone interviews with UN-affiliated researchers who requested anonymity, November 2005.

9 Interview with Jaya Murthy, UNHCR Bukavu, 19 August 2004.

10 Interview with Jonas Jondwe, president of the Nyagatare camp committee, 12 August 2004. Jondwe himself used to be an *inspecteur du territoire* in the cabinet of the governor of South Kivu.

11 Rwanda's national language, also spoken by Banyarwanda from the DRC.

12 Focus group of six refugees from Kalehe in Nyagatare camp, August 2004.

13 Interview with Lt Col. George Rurigamba, RDF commander, Cyangugu, 16 August 2004.

14 Interview with Jonas Jondwe, president of the Nyagatare camp committee, 12 August 2004.

15 Interviews with refugees, Nyagatare, August 2004.

16 Interview with Semuhuza Butsiriko, camp committee member in charge of internal security, Nyagatare camp, 14 August 2004.

17 Interviews with UNHCR, MSF, Rwandan government, RDF, Rwanda police, Nyagatare camp committee, plus the results of a random n-survey of refugees in Nyagatare.

18 Interview with refugees, Cyangugu, August 2004.

19 Interviews with Col. Jules Mutebutsi, 14 August 2004, and Lt Col. George Rurigamba, 16 August 2004.

20 Interview with Lt Col. George Rurigamba, 16 August 2004.

21 Interview with UNHCR staff, Cyangugu, 12 August 2004.

22 Interview with Superintendent Francis Nkwaya, provincial police commander, Cyangugu, 17 August 2004.

23 Interview with Patrick Karegeya, RDF spokesman, Kigali, 22 August 2004.

24 Interview with Kalunga Lutato, UNHCR country representative, Kigali, 5 August 2004. The reference to possible crimes against humanity relates to the conduct of Mutebutsi and some of his men in Kisangani during 2000/01.

25 Telephone interview, 3 November 2005.

26 Internal MONUC document, September 2005; also news reports, e.g. 'DRC troops nab 47 rebels', News24.com, 16 September 2005.

27 Interview with MONUC investigator, Kinshasa, 19 September 2005.

28 Interview with Col. Jules Mutebutsi, Ntendezi, 13 August 2004.

29 Observations from visit to Ntendezi, 13 August 2004.

30 Interview with Patrick Karegeya, 22 August 2004.

31 'External militarization' refers to attacks on the refugees' home country; 'internal militarization' refers to internal organization of refugees and their role in the host country (see Muggah 2004).

32 Interview with Richard Sezibera, Kigali, 9 August 2004.

33 Telephone interview with Kathi Lynn Austin, 7 November 2005.

34 An armed group, led by Jean-Pierre Bemba, and backed by Uganda, that had been fighting against the Kinshasa government from bases in northern DRC since the late 1990s.

35 Interview with returned refugee, Bukavu, 20 August 2004.

36 Interviews with refugees, Nyagatare, August 2004.

37 IRIN (2004a) and interview with Col. Jules Mutebutsi, 13 August 2004.

38 A reference to the allegedly thin noses of Banyamulenge and other Tutsi.

39 Interview with female Banyamulenge refugee, Nyagatare, 17 August 2004.

40 Interview with Benoit Kadege, 13 August 2004.

41 Interviews with Banyamulenge refugees, Cyangugu, August 2004.

42 Interview with Banyamulenge intellectual, Cyangugu, August 2004.

43 For example, interview with Jonas Jondwe, 12 August 2004.

44 Interview with Col. Jules Mutebutsi, 13 August 2004.

45 Interview with Lt Col. George Rurigamba, 16 August 2004.

46 Interview with François Wuarin, Chief of Delegation, ICRC, Kigali, 6 August 2004.

47 Interview with Col. Jules Mutebutsi, 13 August 2004.

48 Telephone interview with UN researcher requesting anonymity, 10 November 2005.

49 IRIN (2005b).

50 Interview with MONUC investigator, Kinshasa, 19 September 2005.

51 Interview with MONUC officer, Bukavu, 19 August 2004.

52 Interview with senior RDF commander, Cyangugu, August 2004.

53 Interview with MONUC investigator, Kinshasa, 19 September 2005.

54 Telephone interview with UN researcher requesting anonymity, 10 November 2005.

References

Bui, Q. (1998) *Ensuring the Civilian and Neutral Character of Refugee-populated Areas: A Ladder of Options*, Geneva: Centre for Documentation and Research, UNHCR.

Church, W. (2005) 'United Nations Panel of Experts report on Democratic Republic of Congo', Mimeo, accessed 24 January, <www.geopoliticalreview.com/archives/000891.PLP>.

Crisp, J. (2000) *Africa's Refugees: Patterns, Problems and Policy Challenges*, New Issues in Refugee Research Working Paper no. 28, Geneva: Evaluation and Policy Analysis Unit, UNHCR.

EIU (Economist Intelligence Unit) (1994–2005) *Country Reports – Rwanda*, London: EIU.

— (1998–2005) *Country Reports – Democratic Republic of Congo*, London: EIU.

International Crisis Group (2004) *Pulling Back from the Brink in Congo*, Brussels: International Crisis Group.

IRIN (Integrated Regional Information Network) (2004a) 'DRC: UN troops return fire on dissident soldiers', accessed 21 June 2005, <www.plusnews.org/report.asp?ReportID=41800&SelectRegion=Great_Lakes>.

— (2004b) 'DRC: government troops seize rebel stronghold, general says', 15 September, <www.irinnews.org/report.asp?ReportID=43167&SelectRegion=Great_Lakes&SelectCountry=DRC>.

— (2005a) 'DRC–Rwanda: UN agency transfers Congolese refugees to new sites away from congested Rwanda–DR of Congo border', 29 April, <www.un.org/apps/news/story.asp?NewsID=14151&Cr=democratic&Cr1=congo>.

— (2005b) 'DRC: troops from the 124th Battalion desert to join dissident general', 12 September, <www.irinnews.org/report.asp?ReportID=49012>.

Jacobsen, K. and L. Landau (2003) *Researching Refugees: Some Methodological and Ethical Considerations in Social Science and Forced Migration*, New Issues in Refugee Research Working Paper no. 90, Geneva: Evaluation and Policy Analysis Unit, UNHCR.

Jaquemet, S. (2004) *Under What Circumstances Can a Person Who Has Taken an Active Part in the Hostilities of an International or Non-international Armed Conflict Become an Asylum Seeker?*, Legal and Protection Policy Research Series, Geneva: UNHCR

McGuinness, M. (2003) 'Legal and normative dimensions of the manipulation of refugees', in S. Stedman and F. Tanner (eds), *Refugee Manipulation: War, Politics and the Abuse of Human Suffering*, Washington, DC: Brookings Institution Press.

Mthembu-Salter, G. (2004) 'Rwanda', in A. Reid (ed.), *Lion Cubs? Lessons from Africa's Success Stories*, London: Policy Exchange.

— (2005) 'Democratic Republic of Congo – recent history', in I. Frame and K. Murison (eds), *Africa South of the Sahara 2006*, London: Europa.

Muggah, R. (2004) *Protection Failures: 'Outward' and 'Inward' Militarization of Refugee Settlements and IDP Camps in Uganda*, Geneva: Small Arms Survey.

Pottier, J. (2002) *Re-imagining Rwanda: Conflict, Survival and Disinformation in the Late Twentieth Century*, Cambridge: Cambridge University Press.

Reid, A. (ed.) (2004) *Lion Cubs? Lessons from Africa's Success Stories*, London: Policy Exchange.

Seudi, L.-P. et al. (2004) Letter dated 9 July 2004 from the Coordinator of the Group of Experts on the Democratic Republic of the Congo addressed to the Chairman of the Security Council Committee established pursuant to resolution 1533 (2004), New York: UN.

— (2005) Letter dated 4 January 2005 from the Group of Experts on the Democratic Republic of the Congo addressed to the Chairman of the Security Council Committee established pursuant to resolution 1533 (2004), New York: UN.

Stedman, S. and F. Tanner (eds) (2003) *Refugee Manipulation: War, Politics and the Abuse of Human Suffering*, Washington, DC: Brookings Institution Press.

UNHCR (United Nations High Commissioner for Refugees) (2002) *Annual Statistical Report*, Geneva: UNHCR.

— (2004a) *Country Information Brief for Rwanda*, Kigali: UNHCR.

— (2004b) *Ensuring the Civilian and Neutral Character of Refugee-populated Areas*, Geneva: UNHCR.

— (2004c) *A Comparative Review of Refugee Security Mechanisms*, Geneva: UNHCR.

Yu, L. (2002) *Separating Ex-combatants and Refugees in Zongo, DRC: Peace-keepers and UNHCR's 'Ladder of Options'*, New Issues in Refugee Research, Working Paper no. 60, Geneva: Evaluation and Policy Analysis Unit, UNHCR.

6 | From bad to better: reflections on refugee and IDP militarization in Africa

SUE J. NAHM

Dramatic geopolitical changes have transpired since the establishment of the UN Convention Relating to the Status of Refugees in 1951. Transformations in both the nature and scale of refugee and internal displacement flows have provoked an urgent re-examination of normative and bureaucratic responses to refugee and IDP protection among a wide range of scholars and policy-makers.[1] While violence against refugees and militarization are not new phenomena, the manipulation of refugees and IDPs and the role of aid in prolonging and exacerbating conflicts have been the subject of increasing study and debate.[2] Owing in part to the increasing transparency generated by global media, and their focus on the effects of civil wars in the post-cold-war era,[3] the visible links between refugee flows, conflict and the response of state and non-state actors have forced scholars and specialists to re-examine traditional assumptions about the nature and root causes of conflict.[4] Particularly in the aftermath of the Rwandan genocide of 1994, refugee and disarmament specialists have grown increasingly aware of the dynamics of arms flows and protracted refugee and IDP situations (Loescher and Milner 2005; Lischer 2005; Terry 2002; Goose and Smythe 1994).[5]

Studies in this volume indicate that refugee scholars and disarmament experts could and should search for closer collaboration. Refugee studies, traditionally the domain of aid workers and humanitarian specialists, is increasingly being recognized by those concerned with international and regional security issues. As the relationships between refugee flows, arms transfers and national and international security are increasingly acknowledged, so too is the importance of learning across disciplines. The case study chapters presented in this volume thus fill a vital gap in the literature on conflict and armed violence and refugee/IDP camp militarization. By drawing on a combination of methodologies, including existing surveillance data, small-scale household surveys, focus groups and key informant interviews with a number of officials and refugees in Guinea, Rwanda, Tanzania and Uganda, they offer an evidence base from which to build proactive responses. Taken together, they provide a conceptual framework and a preliminary road map to address the prevalence of arms-related violence and weapons trafficking among refugees and IDPs.[6]

This volume is targeted primarily at donors, policy-makers, practitioners and academics concerned with improving the quality and quantity of refugee and IDP protection. By clarifying the historical and political economy dynamics of militarization and examining linkages with arms trafficking and armed violence, it seeks to identify areas where refugee and arms control specialists can benefit from shared research and collaboration. Together with the UNHCR, the Small Arms Survey and the Bonn International Center for Conversion have advanced five core thematic priorities for those seeking to mitigate refugee and IDP militarization. Discussed in detail in Chapter 1, these relate to: ascertaining the nature and extent of refugee militarization; recognizing the pre-conditions under which this can occur; documenting the scale, distribution and impacts of arms availability in and around camps; and learning from past UNHCR, host state and regional responses. Each of the chapters presented in this volume has presented baseline indicators for measuring progress in stemming refugee and IDP militarization. They represent only the first step, and despite their robustness, offer only a preliminary overview of what are complex social phenomena.

This concluding chapter provides an overview of the findings from the preceding chapters. It also draws on a rapidly expanding literature on protracted refugee situations and disarmament to inject a critical perspective on the gaps in our present knowledge. As such, it introduces a preliminary research agenda for future empirical work on refugee and IDP militarization, and its relationship to the diffusion, trade and trafficking of small arms and light weapons.

Defining and measuring militarization

The concept of militarization has been employed in this volume to describe the non-civilian attributes of refugee/IDP camps and settlements and the incursion of military elements into these areas.[7] To be sure, militarization encompasses a broad range of activities – activities that serve to undermine the security and 'neutrality' of refugee and IDP settlements and camps through the use of humanitarian assistance for non-humanitarian purposes. In most cases of militarization, refugees, IDPs or armed elements appropriate humanitarian resources for the furthering of their own political or military goals.[8] Thus, the concept of militarization extends beyond activities that are ostensibly violent. According to one scholar, humanitarian aid has been acquired at times to feed militants, sustain or protect their dependants, support the war economy or provide legitimacy to combatants (Lischer 2005). Militarization therefore refers specifically to the involvement of refugees and/or exiles in 'militaristic activities' such as politically inspired violence, military training, support for combatants and armed resistance. Muggah and Mogire found that the refugee militarization concept is more expansive than refugee camp militarization – including 'military-oriented activities undertaken by armed elements within and outside camps'.[9]

Refugee and IDP militarization is thus a multi-faceted concept and must be understood as such. Contributors to this volume have distinguished between different spatial dimensions of militarization. For example, Muggah has described 'outward' militarization as occurring when refugees and IDPs 'voluntarily or involuntarily participate in and support cross-border and internal wars – often in collusion with external interests'.[10] Outward militarization connotes the 'active' agency of refugees and IDPs in contributing to cross-border and domestic armed violence, or the manipulation of humanitarian assistance. By way of contrast, 'inward' militarization refers to the military targeting of refugees and refugee settlements, as well as 'coercion, intimidation, forced conscription into formal and militia forces, informal taxations, abductions, arbitrary arrest, and various forms of internationally and locally motivated punishment'.[11] In the case of inward militarization, refugees and IDPs, as well as the resources devoted to assisting them, are targeted or victimized by predatory rebel or military groups, thus undermining the humanitarian character of refugee camps and settlements.[12]

Ultimately, outward militarization, where it occurs, is heavily influenced by geopolitical and regional context. It does not occur in a vacuum. For example, Muggah finds that 'outward' militarization among Rwandan, Congolese and Sudanese refugees in Uganda has been on the wane since the late 1990s owing in part to the establishment of ceasefires, bilateral agreements and peace accords signed by warring factions in Sudan, Rwanda and the Democratic Republic of Congo (DRC). Put another way, the incentive for refugees within Uganda to participate in cross-border conflicts to support the cause of the various rebel factions in their countries of origin – be they the Rwandan Patriotic Front, the Forces Armées Congolaises or the Sudanese People's Liberation Army (SPLA) – has declined as a result of the cessation or reduction of ongoing conflicts or the higher penalties accorded to militarization itself. Relatedly, 'inward' militarization is more a function of domestic political context. Indeed, militarization among Ugandan IDPs in the northern region has actually increased over the same period as both the Ugandan People's Defence Force (UPDF) and the Lord's Resistance Army (LRA) have recruited large numbers of civilians into self-defence units or forcibly recruited and armed child soldiers, particularly in Gulu, Kitgum, Pader and other districts, in recent years.

Distinguishing between these two categories provides a tentative basis for understanding how and under what political and structural conditions refugee and IDP militarization takes place. Though at times crude, the distinction nevertheless provides a basis for appreciating the agency of refugees and IDPs, and determining cases in which displaced populations are otherwise manipulated or 'proactive' participants in military campaigns. Where refugees and IDPs are otherwise manipulated, they are often reluctantly caught up in a larger political struggle for recognition, land and resources.[13] The recognition of these dynamics has direct implications for international organizations and donors. Many of these factors are by now well known. Indeed, humanitarian agencies have become increasingly conscious of how aid can be politically manipulated (Anderson 1999). All but the most orthodox now acknowledge that aid is neither neutral nor impartial. Moreover, there is a growing recognition within UNHCR itself that refugee militarization is a layered and complex issue and that an appraisal of its root causes and persistence requires a clear and evidence-based appraisal of the interests of various actors, including relief agencies, rebels and refugees.

Prevalence of militarization

Is militarization as pernicious today as it was in the mid-1990s in western, central and eastern Africa? Does the persistence of refugee and IDP militarization continue to be influenced by ongoing wars in these regions, and the unregulated movement of small arms and light weapons across international borders? Though media and anecdotal reports of gross militarization abound, each of the chapters actually refutes these claims. Rather, they all observe a relative reduction in the severity and distribution of refugee and IDP militarization over the past five years. This is not to suggest that militarization no longer exists, but rather that it has experienced a dramatic and profound decline in the four countries reviewed in this volume.

There are many reasons for this dramatic de-escalation in refugee militarization. Chief among them are the diagnosis, attitude and response of host governments and international agencies such as UNHCR, and the introduction of interventions and proactive disarmament efforts in and around settlements and camps to precipitate demilitarization. Of equal importance are regional political factors – ranging from multilateral peace agreements and arms sanctions to strengthened border controls and joint efforts to police and monitor them. The chapters also indicate that the prevalence and dynamics of refugee militarization ebb and flow according to underlying historical factors. While international and national peace agreements obviously can contribute to the mitigation of militarization, there is also a historical dialectic at play that should be acknowledged and observed. Despite these important gains, the chapters also caution against an overly optimistic appraisal of the situation in Africa. Indeed, while the available evidence suggests a decline in outward militarization and modest improvements in the physical security of certain refugee and IDP populations, persistent armed violence and arms trafficking in all three regions indicate the ease with which the problem could re-emerge in the future (Florquin and Berman 2005). It is worth briefly revisiting each of the cases considered in this volume and teasing out some of the core lessons.

Guinea In the case of Guinea, refugee and IDP militarization has diminished considerably over the past few years. In the 1990s, however, militarization consisted of a combination of government conscription of refugees into military service and tacit support for armed elements of the United Liberation Movement of Liberia for Democracy (ULIMO) and Liberians United for Reconciliation and Democracy (LURD) in refugee camps. Between 1998 and 2003, these same refugee camps were attacked by members of the Revolutionary United Front (RUF) militias from Sierra Leone and infiltrated by Sierra Leonean Kamajors militias, owing in part to the perception that they constituted a military threat. For example, the 'Tomandou' and 'Massacoundou' camps were located fewer than 20 kilometres from the border of Sierra Leone and were reportedly 'the first camps in Guinea to have accommodated armed elements with the knowledge of Guinean authorities'.[14] Refugee camps became a magnet for armed violence by all sides. Rather than dismantling military elements in these camps, the government undertook a concerted counter-insurgency campaign and relocated refugees from the border and urban areas to more remote settlements. Throughout this period, refugees experienced direct attacks and intimidation from the government rebels and various militia groups.

As in other countries where refugee militarization occurs, the host state also played a role in aggravating the phenomena. In Guinea, the public security forces were responsible for the widespread violation of the rights of refugees. In September 2000, for example, RUF elements attacked the border towns of Massadou, Madina Woula and Pamalap, resulting in the relocation of urban refugees to detention centres and remote settlements away from the capital. Paradoxically, the perception that refugees constituted a threat to the internal security of Guinea resulted in the increased militarization of refugee settlements, as the Guinean Army,

'Young Volunteers', ULIMO and later LURD were encouraged to arm and defend the country against attack. Weapons explicitly provided to these elements and the conscription of refugees into military service contributed to the overall militarization of refugee settlements, particularly in the Forest Region of Guinea. Thus, refugees were subjected to inward and outward militarization by rebels hostile to the central government, as well as by Guinean authorities. The government's actions, intended as a defensive measure against armed incursions by RUF and militias supportive of Charles Taylor, ultimately precipitated massive internal displacement and increased the levels of militarization among refugees in Guinea. Milner and Christofferson-Deb find that President Conté's support for anti-Taylor groups, including ULIMO and LURD, played a significant role in the militarization of refugee camps within Guinea. Paradoxically, government complicity in support of refugee militarization occurred in part as a response to the perceived threat posed by militias engaging in cross-border attacks from neighbouring countries.

Importantly, the subsequent decline in refugee militarization in Guinea offers a number of important lessons for the international refugee community. The deployment in camps of a 'Mixed Brigade', made up of Guinean police and gendarmerie and formalized in an agreement with UNHCR in 2001, seems to have contributed to a significant reduction in armed criminality and military activity in camps located within the Forest Region and along the border with Liberia and Sierra Leone since then. Milner and Christofferson-Deb found that while refugee camps were no longer militarized in 2004, refugee-populated areas in southern Guinea may still harbour armed civilians and former combatants capable of reigniting violence.[15] To the extent that the boundaries between refugee camps and surrounding villages are not enforced, their study indicates that consideration of refugee militarization should be expanded conceptually to include areas beyond camp settlements – such as host communities and areas where refugees have spontaneously self-settled.

Rwanda Rwanda was the site of notorious refugee militarization in the 1990s. Much of this can be attributed to the systemic and regional armed conflicts in the region. Indeed, the Rwandan government has provided military and political support to rebels operating in neighbouring DRC throughout the past decade and has been repeatedly accused of supporting rebel movements in the Kivu region. Though various UN Panels of Experts seem to implicate Rwanda in a combination of support and arms deals, the government has issued explicit denials of any such complicity.

The chapter on Rwanda by Mthembu-Salter considers the dynamics of refugee militarization some ten years after the genocide. It finds that the majority of the estimated 27,000 Congolese refugees residing in camps along the western border of Rwanda fled ethnic cleansing by the Congolese Armed Forces (FARDC) in June 2004; but also detects a historical legacy of government involvement in their militarization.[16] Even today, the Rwandan Defence Force (RDF) is believed to maintain a presence in the eastern DRC, contributing to ongoing tensions between the two countries, as both governments accuse the other of supporting hostile rebel forces. As recently as February 2005, the Rwandan government threatened to attack the DRC in response to that country's perceived support for ex-soldiers of the Armed Forces of Rwanda (ex-FAR) and *interahamwe* in the Kivu provinces.[17] The evidence presented by the author suggests, however, that the level of militarization among refugees in Rwanda has nevertheless declined in recent times, despite ongoing mistrust between the DRC and Rwanda over the potential for refugee-related violence spilling over their respective borders.

Gregory Mthembu-Salter highlights the importance of agency among Congolese refugees in Rwanda in influencing the ebb and flow of militarization. They were not all just passive victims or subjected to coercive manipulation. Specifically, he focuses on the ascribed roles and intentions of refugees themselves in determining the likelihood of future militarization. For example, a small-scale survey administered in Nyagatare and Cynagagu finds that almost all of the Congolese refugees identified insecurity in their country of origin as the primary reason for not voluntarily returning.[18] More optimistically, an overwhelming majority indicated a desire to go home once the security situation improved. Thus, according to the author, the willingness of these refugees to take up arms in South Kivu is largely dependent on the prospects for future peace in the region and the success of the DRC transitional government.[19]

As in Guinea, the likelihood of renewed refugee militarization has declined in recent years. While the potential for renewed armed conflict between Rwanda and the DRC is very real, it seems unlikely that Rwanda will support Banyamulenge refugees politically or militarily, particularly given the RDF's counter-insurgency campaign against Masunzu and his Banyamulenge supporters.[20] Nevertheless, the potential for militarization exists to the extent that the concerns for security and the grievances of the Banyamulenge community in Rwanda continue to fester. Also, there is lingering concern that specific 'spoilers' could derail the nominal gains made in recent times: Mutebutsi and Nkunda, two military officers from eastern DRC, have allegedly visited and recruited soldiers from several refugee camps along Rwanda's eastern border – though these reports are hotly disputed. Similar reports also emerged in 2004 of a secret military training camp run by the RDF for refugees abducted from Kiziba and Gihembe camps, though the existence of these camps remains unsubstantiated.

Tanzania In spite of a long legacy of refugee militarization, the case of Tanzania represents something of a 'success story' in terms of redressing the problem. Even so, challenges remain. Despite the high level of organization within refugee camps and the implementation of a UNHCR-supported 'security package' for policing at the local and national levels, a significant number of Burundian refugees remain militarized, though fewer than in previous years. According to Mogire, the phenomenon is inextricably linked to Tanzania's long legacy as a refugee-hosting country. As in Guinea and Rwanda, public authorities are alleged to have supported armed elements (for example, Hutu rebels) in Tanzania throughout the 1990s. Reports issued by the UN (1995), the International Crisis Group (1999), Human Rights Watch (1999) and others reveal that Tanzania did in fact provide both explicit and tacit support for military activity by allowing military mobilization, recruitment, training, fund-raising, arms trafficking and cross-border attacks in the western region of the country.

As in other countries, the controversy over supposed refugee militarization has contributed to an overall intensification of regional insecurity. Though the Tanzanian government has consistently denied supporting the Burundian and Rwandan 'refugees' in their military activities, it is perhaps unsurprising that the country's support for rebel activity in neighbouring Burundi has contributed to ongoing tension between the two neighbours. Even so, Tanzania has actively sought ways to reduce refugee militarization in recent years. This is due in part to a combination of international scrutiny and domestic pressures applied to provide durable solutions to protracted refugee populations in the face of (rapidly) diminishing resources. Moreover, Tanzania's support for the integration of refugees into local communities has gradually eroded over the past decade as the country has become increasingly resistant to the long-term integration and local settlement of Burundian and Rwandan refugees.[21]

Uganda Though outward militarization has also decreased in Uganda, inward militarization – particularly of IDPs – has actually increased. The reasons for these trends are varied, though due in large part to a combination of bilateral agreements with the government of Sudan and the ongoing armed conflict prosecuted by the Museveni-led government ostensibly to protect and arm civilians against the Lord's Resistance Army (LRA) attacks and Karamoja pastoral fighters. Ongoing civil war in the country between the Ugandan People's Defence Force (UPDF) and the LRA has generated acute vulnerabilities among IDPs – particularly owing to the arming of local defence units and civilians and the lack of adequate humanitarian access to and support for IDPs in comparison to refugees. IDP and refugee settlements thus remain inwardly militarized. Human rights groups have repeatedly accused the UPDF of employing IDP and refugee settlements as 'buffers' against rebel forces and as part of its strategy to counter LRA rebels. While the majority of Uganda's refugee settlements are located more than 20 kilometres from international borders, and are thus considered by UNHCR to be less vulnerable to militarization, the current policy of heavy deployment of the UPDF in settlements and camps to fend off the LRA has perversely increased refugee and IDP insecurity.

Inward militarization has increased because of the government and the LRA's stated 'policy' of arming civilian militia groups, refugees and IDPs. Muggah has found that the Ugandan government has increased its recruitment and deployment of local defence units (LDUs) throughout the northern and eastern regions of the country over the past decade. The LRA are also notorious for their forced recruitment of children from among the Acholi populations. IDP camps have thus been militarized by both the UPDF and the LRA. While there have been few reports of outward militarization or active participation in cross-border or internal wars in the past year in refugee camps, inward militarization – or attacks, coercion, conscription into military service abductions, arrest and other forms of harassment – against IDPs in particular has been widespread. In August 2004, Uganda was estimated to have between 1.6 and 2 million displaced people owing to ongoing civil war, one of the largest internally displaced populations in the world at that time, with the highest rates of displacement in the northern and eastern regions. Many of these settlements continue to be subject to repeated violence, military attacks and abductions.[22]

As long as civil war remains an issue for refugee and IDP hosting countries (and their neighbours), militarization also remains a real threat. Indeed, common to both refugee-hosting and refugee-sending states is the prevalence of armed violence and war as both a cause and effect of displacement. Massive refugee influxes in Tanzania, Uganda, Rwanda and Guinea in recent years have been the result of internal conflict in these so-called 'bad neighbourhoods' and have contributed to chronic domestic insecurity and instability. With the exception of Tanzania, civil war and massive internal displacement have at some time compromised the host state's capacity to provide refugee protection and assistance. Moreover, common to all Africa's conflicts are the ubiquity and diffusion of small arms – particularly assault rifles, grenade launchers and semi-automatic weaponry.

Small arms and militarization

On a more positive note, over the past decade the UN and its member states have undertaken a number of international and regional initiatives to address the availability of and trade in illegal arms. High-profile initiatives, such as the UN *Report of the Secretary-General's High Level Panel on Threats, Challenges and Change* (UNGA 2004), have highlighted the importance of a comprehensive approach to 'preventing' and 'eradicating' the illicit manufacture, transfer and circulation of firearms. An important practical initiative is the UN Programme of Action to Prevent, Combat and Eradicate the Illicit Trade in Small Arms and Light Weapons in All Its Aspects, which began in 2001 and is under review in 2006.[23] The programme has emphasized the importance of promoting greater transparency regarding member states' conventional weapons holdings, and supporting the implementation and enforcement of regional African initiatives such as the *Nairobi Protocol for the Prevention, Control, and Reduction of Small Arms and Light Weapons in the Great Lakes Region and the Horn of Africa* (SAS 2005). Despite these and other efforts to reduce the flow of weapons to zones of conflict, the policy and research communities still lack compelling evidence of the origins, flows and procurement networks for arms in many of Africa's protracted conflicts. Clarifying the conceptual and empirical linkages between armed violence, small arms and refugee militarization is of pivotal importance if proactive and pragmatic solutions are to be found.

While highlighting important similarities, the chapters in this volume have revealed the complexity and heterogeneity of refugee militarization in Africa. Each of these cases has revealed the central role and complicity of host states in facilitating the trade and distribution of arms to 'armed elements' within and around camps and settlements. In certain cases, governments provided logistical, military and even political support to 'rebels' taking cover in refugee settlements or refugee and IDP camps. It should also be noted, however, that the simple presence of weapons in these settlements and camps did not always lead to concomitant rises in armed violence and criminal activity: it is still relatively unclear how and under what conditions the existence of weapons fuels militarization.[24] It is useful to recall that in certain cases refugee camps and settlements have served as trans-shipment points where weapons are collected and stored and then sent to urban centres for delivery to government or rebel groups in outlying areas, as in the case of Rwanda and Guinea. In others, the presence of illegal firearms may be linked to the presence of rebels and soldiers who use them to intimidate, coerce and pursue predatory activities within and outside such settlements and camps. Refugees themselves have often acquired illegal weapons and stored them for (future) use in neighbouring conflicts, as was the case among Burundian refugees in Tanzania.

Ultimately, refugee and IDP militarization must be situated in not just the overall regional security context, but also in relation to that of the host country. In each of the cases presented in this volume, refugee and IDP militarization was an iterative process and emerged as a result of progressive and deliberate military deployment and civilian armament. Relatedly, when overt cross-border support, deployment and internal militarization declined, so too did the outward and inward militarization of displaced populations. In Uganda, for example, covert Ugandan support for the SPLA has contributed to illicit arms trafficking between Sudan and Uganda. The Sudanese government has, in turn, armed and provided military support to the LRA in retaliation for Uganda's support for the SPLA. What is more, the arming of IDPs and refugees and the dispatch of self-defence units to refugee and IDP settlements to provide protection against attacks by the LRA and Karamoja have arguably increased the levels of weapons possession among the civilian population. In the case of Tanzania, refugee militarization lingers, though this is more a function of generalized insecurity and the involvement of a small number of refugees in local informal and criminal economies than anything else.[25] There appears to be a robust relationship, then, between the cross-border support for neighbouring insurgents, civilian possession and refugee/IDP militarization.

Lessons learned: the role of states, international organizations and donors

An underlying question that animates these studies is whether the lessons of the 1994 Rwandan tragedy have been learned and whether these lessons are applicable to the cases under investigation. In the case of Rwanda, the answer to both questions seems to be 'yes'. Mthembu-Salter argues that the lessons learned from the aftermath of the Rwandan genocide and the subsequent militarization of refugees in eastern DRC consisted, for host states, of separating combatants from civilians, moving refugee camps away from the borders of neighbouring countries, and taking action to preserve the civilian nature of refugee camps, while neutralizing the threat posed by combatants who take refuge in Rwanda. For the most part, Rwanda has implemented the necessary technical measures to preserve the civilian nature of refugee camps. The region remains, however, vulnerable to renewed outbreaks of regional refugee-related violence and conflict.[26]

Each of the chapters demonstrates convincingly that refugee and IDP militarization arises where there is ongoing regional conflict, systemic internal armed violence and host or foreign government complicity. As

Muggah has noted, '[refugee] militarization will be reduced only if the causes of conflicts are addressed'.[27] But addressing underlying political conflicts through regional and national peace agreements, while necessary, is a potentially insufficient entry point to reducing refugee/IDP militarization. It is vital that the incentives driving government complicity in militarization are also recognized and retailored if long-term solutions are to be realized (Loescher and Milner 2005). For example, despite the signing of various peace agreements and repeated assurances to the contrary, the existence of residual Hutu ex-FAR forces and *interahamwe* from the 1994 genocide continues to fuel tensions between the Rwandan and DRC governments. Indeed, Rwanda is widely perceived as having aided RCD soldiers who have fled across the Congolese border into Rwanda in recent years – and it is likely that tensions will continue to remain high.

Identifying and tailoring responses to the diverse and heterogeneous motives and constraints facing refugee-hosting states, including those that have provided logistical, political and military support for refugee militarization in the past, is a practical first step in devising mitigating strategies. In some cases, refugee and IDP militarization have occurred as part of a deliberate strategy to defend a comparatively weak government against rebel incursions or attacks. In Uganda, both the government and LRA rebels are reported to have armed and recruited refugees and IDPs in response to constraints on military expenditures. Even UPDF strategies to protect civilians and refugees, such as cantoning refugees and IDPs into camps, establishing local defence units and dispatching soldiers to protect these camps, may have contributed indirectly to militarization by making refugees and civilians more susceptible to attack and military recruitment. In other cases, refugee militarization is less explicit or even unintentional, and more a function of foreign government intervention with its own cluster of interests.[28] As many practitioners on the ground know only too well, regardless of how effective and well funded the externally driven political and humanitarian response, active host government support is a pre-condition for promoting demilitarization efforts. As Mthembu-Salter makes clear with regard to Congolese refugees in Rwanda, much hinges on how the Rwandan government envisages the refugee.[29]

In thinking about pathways to reducing militarization, it is also important to gauge the relative 'agency' of refugees and IDPs, and the political and structural factors that influence their motivations and behaviour. As these studies suggest, the existence of 'protracted' refugee and IDP situations has at times exacerbated militarization, since refugees engage in military and predatory activities in the context of extreme political and economic inequality, deprivation, dwindling opportunities and resource scarcity. Where the opportunities for medium- and long-term solutions are not present, and host state capacities and entitlements are lacking, pathologies are likely to emerge rapidly. As Mogire noted with regard to refugees in Tanzania: '[the] lack of opportunities – economic, social and educational – for refugees, especially young men and women, has provided a ready pool for recruitment'.[30]

Another pathway relates to inter-state trust and cooperation. Where relationships between neighbouring countries are characterized by mutual mistrust, itself proxied by allegations of refugee and IDP militarization, outward and inward militarization are, paradoxically, likely to occur. Regional coordination and peace efforts seem to provide one avenue for addressing the security threats posed by mutual mistrust between neighbouring countries.[31] Moreover, while the perceptions and attitudes of host states towards refugees and IDPs need to be carefully considered, it is equally important that the concerns and needs of refugees and IDPs themselves are taken into account when devising policies to mitigate the problem of militarization, particularly as forced repatriation efforts in recent years have met with increasing resistance on the part of refugees.[32]

Where even the basic pre-conditions for averting refugee/IDP militarization do not exist, the international community must carefully consider its options. The UNHCR's ladder of options has already been put to the test. And while the agency can potentially undertake a hard option in extreme cases (with DPKO in mitigating security threats and refugee militarization under a Chapter VI or VII mandate), the agency should also consider disengagement as a possible option when efforts at intervention and prevention fail. In some cases there are no 'good' options. Rather, the choice often consists of selecting the 'least bad' of many unsatisfactory possibilities. But while international responses may yield some modicum of success, it is ultimately host government complicity in facilitating (or not restraining) militarization of refugees and the internally displaced which may be the key factor in explaining its onset. Conversely, as the preceding chapters have amply shown, active government support in demilitarization is a 'necessary' condition for ensuring effective refugee and IDP demilitarization.

Effectiveness of camp settlement and technical measures

There is a tendency in the mainstream refugee studies literature to privilege political and normative solutions over technical and pragmatic responses. While the section above has stressed the acutely politicized dynamics influencing refugee and IDP militarization, the case studies have revealed some of the dividends of ostensibly 'technical' measures in so far as they improved the quality of life in camps and diminished their susceptibility to renewed militarization. As with the more 'political' solutions proposed above, technical responses are a 'necessary' but insufficient response to refugee/IDP militarization.

Technical solutions often focus on shaping the size and location of camps and settlements and screening them for armed elements. In each of the cases discussed in this volume, overcrowded, sprawling camps and settlements, as well as those within walking distance of international borders, are more susceptible to the onset of armed violence than those camps and settlements that are more sparsely populated and established farther from such frontiers. Concern regarding the size and density of camps relates in large part to problems of surveillance and enforcement. In large camps the activities of 'armed elements' and criminals are simply more difficult to monitor and control. In Tanzania, for example, overcrowding of refugee settlements remains a particular concern, as the average refugee population within camps is currently over 51,000.[33] Muggah has also argued against warehousing large populations of refugees in camps since 'it is the large-scale and protracted settlements and camps which appear to be in the greatest danger of internal militarization'.[34]

Proximity to an international border also increases the susceptibility of refugee settlements to cross-border attack, or their use as a staging ground for military activity. Host states and refugees themselves may, however, be resistant to locating camps and settlements farther from international borders. States, for their part, have an incentive to advance 'temporary' solutions, to prevent refugees from integrating with the local (and urban) populations, and often prefer to settle them on more marginal and inexpensive land. In Tanzania, large refugee populations are intentionally placed close to the border of the sending state in an effort to discourage long-term stays and facilitate their eventual repatriation. As Mogire points out with regard to Burundian refugees in Tanzania, many camps have been intentionally situated within walking distance – or 20–30 kilometres – of the Burundian border, making them vulnerable to attack and militarization.[35] At the same time, predominant ethnic, political, cultural and socioeconomic affinities often encourage refugees to linger closer to borders in the hope of eventually returning to their homeland.

Other technical approaches include the deployment of public security in and around settlements and camps. In Tanzania, Uganda and Guinea, the deployment of police and security officers in settlements and camps has proved relatively effective in countering the militarization of refugees – though less so in the case of IDPs in Uganda. According to Mogire, Rwandan Hutu refugees in Tanzania have become less inclined to militarize than those refugees located in eastern DRC largely because of the deterrent effects of police and their placement in camps by the host government.[36] Likewise, in Guinea, the deployment of the 'Mixed Brigade' in 2001, itself composed of Guinean military and police, is alleged to have significantly reduced levels of militarization in the six refugee camps.[37] While controversial, massive relocation efforts have also been relatively successful in mitigating the problem of militarized refugees along the border of Guinea, though the Forest Region remains highly militarized.

Screening exercises undertaken in Rwanda, Guinea and Tanzania have also been effective in addressing one aspect of militarization by preventing the intermingling of so-called 'armed elements' with refugees. But undertaking screening measures is not without challenges, and is again dependent on host government support, adequately provisioned and trained officials, and a capacity to deal with mass influxes (Da Costa 2004). For example, in Rwanda controversy surrounds the withholding of refugee status from Colonel Jules Mutebutsi, who fled to the country from the DRC in June 2004. The Rwandan government has been careful to separate Mutebutsi and the soldiers accompanying him from the other Congolese refugees, thereby complying with UNHCR policy. There are concerns on the part of the UN, however, that Mutebutsi and the soldiers accompanying him may be guilty of having committed crimes against humanity and may not have fully renounced combatant status.[38] Ultimately, where screening exercises are conducted, it is important that they are carried out with independent verification mechanisms in place in order to ensure agreement on the status of those seeking assistance as refugees in the host country. In Guinea, for example, screening efforts undertaken by the Guinean military have been conducted under the supervision of the Bureau National pour la Coordination des Réfugiés. A joint mission by the Commission for Human Security and the Emergency and Security Section of UNHCR, visiting the camps in February 2002, confirmed that there had been considerable improvement in the security of the six camps in Guinea.[39] While there have been isolated incidents indicating that rebels may be residing in refugee camps, as reported by Human Rights Watch and USCR regarding Kounkan camp in 2002,[40] the overall screening and relocation efforts undertaken by the Guinean government have been characterized by a degree of trust and cooperation between the government and UNHCR that is lacking in the Rwandan context.

International protection efforts

The phenomenon of refugee and IDP militarization presents an array of formidable challenges for those concerned with the promotion of regional security and peace, with the practicalities of aid delivery and protection.

Ongoing responses have combined proactive interventions focusing on 'armed elements' on the ground (with support from host governments and DPKO) as well as the elaboration of guidelines to improve practice at the field level. The formulation of guidelines to ensure refugee and IDP protection and demilitarization[41] coincides with a parallel increase in spending by donors and international agencies on the promotion of humanitarian standards in assistance. As well as complying with the oft-quoted objective of 'doing no harm', aid agencies, including UNHCR and its implementing partners, are implored to design strategies and deliver aid in such a way that it is principled, not overtly political, effective and professional. These norms and standards are embodied in, among others, the SPHERE project.[42]

A growing number of humanitarian and development agencies are, however, becoming involved in preventing and responding to refugee/IDP militarization. Non-governmental agencies working in conflict-affected areas in the context of diminishing resources are increasingly expanding their mandates from comparatively narrow focuses on relief assistance to more ambitious and broad-scoped activities that include conflict management, peace-building and development. Some aid agencies have also become increasingly involved in the DDR[43] of erstwhile combatants, the establishment of educational facilities and public health clinics, and other similar longer-term development efforts.[44] The DDR of 'foreign ex-combatants', themselves often entrenched in refugee camps, is now being advanced as part of the World Bank's nine-country Multi-country Demobilization and Reintegration Programme (MDRP), as well as in Liberia, Sierra Leone and ultimately Côte d'Ivoire.

The international community is only now beginning to engage with the issue of refugee/IDP militarization in a concrete fashion. Debates about how to allocate humanitarian aid in 'transition' situations and how to bridge the 'relief–development' gap have also expanded significantly in the past decade, as policy-makers and scholars continue to wrestle with the ethical and practical implications of aid, negotiating access, balancing neutrality and principled engagement, and providing for the security of their personnel.[45] The time is thus ripe for a robust and evidence-based assessment of efforts to demilitarize and constrain armed violence in camps and settlements.

UNHCR This volume has highlighted UNHCR's long-standing engagement with the practicalities of refugee/IDP militarization. Though the agency has only recently begun to develop a robust and normatively coherent response to the problem, as early as 1979 refugee camp militarization came to the attention of the Executive Committee of UNHCR in the context of armed conflict under way in southern Africa. By 1981, the former high commissioner of UNHCR, Felix Schnyder, had commissioned a comprehensive study of the issue and concluded in his report in 1983:

> [in] the case of military attacks on refugee camps and settlements the political and non-political – i.e. humanitarian – elements are always closely interrelated. It may not therefore be possible for the High Commissioner to undertake effective action – even to achieve his purely humanitarian objectives – otherwise than in close cooperation with the political organs of the United Nations, and in close consultation with the United Nations Secretary-General which should be established in every case. (cited in UNHCR 1999)

Though the agency has long been engaged with the issue, UNHCR has recognized that its political dimensions extend well beyond its existing mandate. Indeed, this volume finds that international donors and host governments must be, certainly in principle, the 'first responders'. That is to say, refugee/IDP militarization is ultimately a political problem requiring political solutions: technical interventions will achieve only so much.

Nevertheless, UNHCR is adopting an increasingly proactive definition of 'refugee protection' within the provisions contained in the 1951 Convention and accompanying Protocol of 1967. Over the past two decades it has also introduced a range of innovative institutional mechanisms to address protection regionally and locally. While UNHCR continues to affirm the primacy of host states' responsibility for ensuring the security and civilian and humanitarian character of refugee camps and settlements, the UN Security Council and the UN secretary-general have worked to strengthen international and regional responses, particularly where host states are too weak, unwilling or incapable of providing security themselves. In 1998, UNHCR and the then Organization of African Unity (OAU) issued a joint statement that recognized the 'need, in extreme cases, for international intervention in refugee situations to ensure that the civilian character of camps is maintained' (ibid.). By the beginning of the twenty-first century, the central pillar of UNHCR's response to refugee and IDP militarization was the 'ladder of options'. As part of its overall drive to apply the 'ladder', the agency has also leveraged increased resources for the deployment of international and national security personnel in camps and settlements of refugee-hosting countries. Though practical strategies included in the ladder have existed and been applied for years, the UNHCR's proposal of advancing UN and multinational military interventions in the case of extreme situations is novel, if ambitious.[46] Indeed, its effectiveness has yet to be adequately assessed.

In addition to the 'ladder', the UNHCR has issued a series of guidelines through its *Handbook on Emergencies* to support protection and programme officers in their efforts to promote the safety and security of refugees.[47] Thus, at the camp and settlement level, UNHCR has advocated the relocation of refugees and IDPs away from the borders of neighbouring countries; a reduction in the size of camps; the screening of refugees, so as to separate combatants from civilians; and the provision of logistical support for security and policing of camps and settlements. These efforts have yielded modest gains. For example, in Tanzania Mogire has found that increased personnel and coordination of policing efforts within camps seem to have alleviated insecurity and dissuaded some refugees from engaging in military activity. Milner and Christoffersen-Deb observed that, in Guinea, a joint agreement or *protocol d'accord* between the government and UNHCR in November 2001 contributed to a marked decrease in military activity in refugee camps – as measured by reported intentional injury rates and anecdotal evidence.

UNHCR efforts to promote refugee protection and ensure the civilian character of asylum have been most effective when coupled with active support and cooperation from host governments. For example, in Tanzania UNHCR and the Ministry of Home Affairs currently co-manage the settlement and protection needs of all refugees. UNHCR and the Tanzanian government have both placed protection officers and representatives in each camp. Within each refugee camp, 'security promotion' committees, known colloquially as *sungu-sungu*, are also organized to patrol the camps.[48] As noted above, UNHCR has also worked closely with the Guinean and Canadian governments to reinforce security personnel with federal police officers who are responsible for training police on basic policing and human rights principles. According to Milner and Christoffersen-Deb, 'the contribution of the Canadian deployment has raised the standards of camp security in Guinea to a level unrecognizable from 2001'.[49] But Uganda presents a counter-factual. Indeed, the mere presence of security personnel does not necessarily ensure refugee and IDP protection and may contribute to overall militarization, particularly where the distinction between ostensibly civilian and military units is unclear.

It is also important to reflect on instances where UNHCR's interventions have not necessarily yielded positive returns. For example, in contrast to its success in Guinea, UNHCR's operations in Rwanda have been criticized by Mthembu-Salter. He notes that the agency's approach to containing militarization through the 'ladder of options' does not include a potential disengagement or 'exit strategy' should efforts to prevent militarization fail. He warns further that even under the Chapter VI or VII mandate, troop deployment may not be implemented fast enough to prevent militarization, in which case the UN should consider disengagement rather than risk sending troops when it is too late.[50]

DDR efforts and donor support

As discussed above, DDR is increasingly being utilized as a technical solution to militarization. DDR efforts throughout Africa have been supported by the World Bank and UN agencies such as UNDP, UNICEF, UNIFEM, IOM and ILO, and other NGOs, but with mixed, if untested, results (Muggah 2005). UNHCR has also started to play a role in facilitating cross-border returns of demobilized 'foreign ex-combatants'. But challenges have emerged. A major obstacle is that the pre-conditions for DDR are seldom adequate. Other constraints relate to the usual challenges of mandate creep and turf battles. Another major challenge relates to inadequate resources for DDR, particularly with regard to the implementation of effective reintegration measures within sending states (Muggah 2006).

Despite these issues, DDR presents a possible entry point to ensuring sustained demilitarization of refugees and IDPs. Large-scale DDR operations are under way throughout the Great Lakes, including in Rwanda and Uganda. Given substantial funding made available to the MDRP and bilaterally, Rwanda and Uganda are currently heavily dependent on donor support and programming to implement effectively their demobilization and reintegration programmes (DRPs). Coupled with DDR, regional efforts at securing the border between DRC and Rwanda continue to be supported, though ongoing violence there has undermined the various peace efforts. MONUC continues to maintain an active presence in eastern DRC and intends to provide logistical support for the implementation of the border monitoring mechanism put in place in February 2005. Controversy about the mission's effectiveness continues, however, as recent attacks and reports of human rights violations committed by peacekeepers have accumulated in the past year.

DDR can also have unintended effects. According to Muggah, donors have called for a drastic reduction in military spending in Uganda to prevent the recurrence of civil war. The DDR programme implemented in 2002 is alleged to have contributed to the reduction of the armed forces by 40–50 per cent.[51] Perversely, however, planned and actual curtailment of military spending has inadvertently contributed to inward militarization, as the government has come to rely more heavily on the civilian auxiliaries, including IDPs, to protect settlements and camps. Thus, the government's response to diminished resources for military defence has resulted in the parallel growth of civilian militia groups, local defence units and 'home guards'.[52] The arming of a range of civilian militias has contributed to the proliferation of small arms and weapons in Uganda and has kept the price of weapons comparatively low.[53]

There have been some concerns about the potential negative externalities generated by DDR as well as sustained donor support. Rwanda is moving forward within the context of the MDRP amid some controversy for this reason.[54] In Guinea, limited donor interest in ongoing UNICEF efforts to demobilize child soldiers ('young volunteers') resulted in its premature termination in mid-2004. As a result, and against a backdrop of persistent armed violence, young volunteers remain armed and susceptible to military recruitment, particularly in the southern region of Guinea. The lack of sustained donor will to support DDR in Uganda and Guinea indicates the need for either more concerted lobbying or alternatives. Certainly, the time may be right to develop alternative strategies focusing on violence reduction and supported by NGOs and community-based organizations – as is currently under way in a limited fashion in northern Uganda. Described by Muggah as 'soft options', these might also include the introduction and strengthening of amnesty legislation, which includes the provision of certain types of immunities and freedom from criminal prosecution, as has been advanced in Uganda.[55] Other 'soft' options include promoting the protection of refugees and IDPs through demobilization efforts on the part of local civil society organizations and the establishment of child protection units to facilitate the integration of child soldiers into local communities.[56]

The UNHCR and its partners need to experiment with new ways and means to promote protection and to prevent both outward and inward demilitarization. Coercive or even voluntary disarmament, as advocated by proponents of DDR, may not always be the right answer. For example, in Tanzania the government's cantonment of refugees and severe restrictions on both their movement and access to income-generating activities appear to have at least partially contributed to the rise of criminal activity and the trafficking of illegal weapons in recent years. Ultimately, increased monitoring and community-based policing of refugees and host communities, as well as the provision of more appropriate economic and livelihood opportunities for refugees, particularly in protracted refugee situations, may alleviate the problem. The deployment of civilian police under a 'security package' (between UNHCR and the Ministry of Home Affairs) has been a positive development in this regard, but has done little more than scratch the surface. Indeed, overt government restrictions on the rights of refugees and their freedom to engage in political activities has contributed to increasing discontent among Burundians.[57] To address the problem of small-arms availability, trafficking and armed violence, the government could provide a more comprehensive and integrated strategy for sustained community policing and the monitoring of its borders, while giving greater freedom and opportunities for refugees to secure their own livelihoods.

Areas for further research and the development of institutional mechanisms

It appears that research on refugee and IDP militarization is rapidly growing as a distinct sub-field of forced migration and refugee studies. There is a myriad of policy-oriented assessments, guidelines and studies that highlight both the strengths and weaknesses of current approaches.[58] There is also a comparatively recent shift from reservedly qualitative and anthropological case-study assessments to empirical studies relying on large data-sets and quantitative assessments.[59] But these quantitative assessments are still nascent. Despite the tremendous advantages of comparative examinations of refugee militarization and conflict onset (or vice versa), the unreliability and limitations of existing longitudinal data-sets prevent rigorous hypothesis testing and statistical analysis. It appears that while expectations for quantitative research are high, the case-study approach is still preferred. Stedman and Tanner (2003: 10), for their part, have recently observed the impacts of refugee assistance on regional security: '[b]ecause research into refugee manipulation is so limited, we find it necessary to develop theory rather than test it and have chosen a case study approach for this purpose. Hence our findings about manipulation writ large are tentative and await further research, *especially work incorporating larger datasets and quantitative methods*' (added emphasis).

The opportunity for enhancing and developing policy-making in this area, particularly should larger cross-country quantitative studies be carried out, would be far-reaching. Much of the current literature on militarization is unable to test causal pathways, and often overlooks the way in which various actors, competing for political recognition, economic resources or the furthering of their own particular agendas, produce outcomes that are unintended and undesirable for all. As the previous chapters have made clear, even well-intentioned actors, such as humanitarian agencies, may contribute to the chronic insecurity of refugees and IDPs if their approaches are not grounded in robust local knowledge and diagnosis. Indeed, militarization may not result from a deficit of will, resources or even capacity on the part of humanitarian actors, donors or states, but rather its surfeit, combined with a weak grasp of the underlying political dynamics driving states and rebel groups to engage in armed violence.

The reliance on field-based data is both a strength and a weakness of the case studies presented in this volume. On the one hand, the data collected here are unique, and form a preliminary empirical basis for examination of the prevalence and distribution of both refugee militarization and arms availability in four African countries. Even so, it should be stressed that the statistical assessment presented in each case is necessarily limited, and requires further testing and verification. Though efforts were made to ensure comparability, the absence of legitimate and credible surveillance data, and the difficulties associated with access, obstructed a more nuanced assessment.

Taken as a whole, the chapters presented in this volume demonstrate the challenges of comparative case-study research. The Small Arms Survey (SAS 2005: ch. 9) has observed that public and privately available surveillance data, whether health- or policing-related, is extremely limited in Africa. Thus, fact claims must always be taken with an understanding of the limitations imposed by the quality of available data. Ultimately, the replication of these individual studies using similar indicators across country cases could improve their reliability and data consistency.[60] While the individual cases in this volume provide a good grounding for understanding the dynamics of militarization, future multi-country studies could provide a cross-cutting analysis and a further basis for theory-building on militarization.

Conclusion: UN reform and its implications for refugee security

There are new opportunities opening up for the rethinking and reform of protection and assistance for refugees. Owing in part to the transformations heralded by the vamped-up 'war on terror', principles of asylum and donor tolerance are under threat. International policy-makers and academics are reconsidering traditional concepts such as 'security' and 'development', even as they begin to explore the responsibilities attached to 'sovereignty' in a climate where security is trumping rights. This shifting environment is also characterized by a concerted effort by the UN and its member states to rethink the way it does its business, including its work with refugees and IDPs. Though this is ambitious, the agency and its partners are increasingly emphasizing the importance of 'human security' and the 'right of humanitarian intervention'. These concerns have been emphasized by the International Commission on Intervention and State Sovereignty, which released *The Responsibility to Protect* in 2001. Though controversial, the report articulated the 'right of humanitarian intervention' as 'the question of when, if ever, it is appropriate for states to take coercive – and in particular military – action, against another state for the purpose of protecting people at risk in that other state' (International Commission on Intervention and State Sovereignty 2001: foreword).[61]

The door of opportunity is likely to be opened farther still following the much-anticipated reform programme articulated by the UN's High Level Panel Report (UNGA 2004). The High Level Panel has also signalled a shift in how the UN and its membership interprets the nature of 'threats' and the sources of insecurity in a globalizing world.[62] Increasingly, states and international organizations have expanded their understanding of 'threats' to international peace and security to encompass lack of access to health and education, the prevalence of disease, economic deprivation and environmental degradation. Efforts to address the political and technical aspects of refugee militarization have thus evolved as the very concept of security is redefined and reformulated by international policy-makers. Moreover, the expansion in thinking on the security implications of protracted refugee crises has created new opportunities and challenges for host states, donors and humanitarian and development agencies to better coordinate their efforts. According to a recent study by Loescher and Milner (2005), 'the primary causes of protracted refugee situations are to be found in the failure of major powers, including the US and the EU, to engage in countries of origin and the failure to consolidate peace agreements'. They argue further that 'humanitarian programmes have to be underpinned by sustained political and security measures if they are to result in lasting solutions for refugees'. As the studies in this volume demonstrate, the issue of arms trafficking and the involvement of refugees in organized violence cannot be fully addressed without responsibility being taken by a variety of actors at the state and international levels to coordinate humanitarian and political responses to the refugee crises examined here.

The studies in this volume come at a critical time for the UN and the humanitarian sector as they continue to search for durable solutions to some of the world's most intractable and protracted refugee crises. The issue of refugee/IDP militarization and the concomitant challenges associated with small-arms control continue to present formidable challenges for refugee agencies, host and sending countries and donors alike. But as the concept of security has broadened in recent years, so too has the scope of responsibility for addressing refugee violence and arms trafficking. Future research should seek to incorporate evaluations of international and domestic efforts to confront these two related issue areas. This chapter concludes that the political management of conflict and the promotion of refugee and IDP rights are essential pre-conditions that must be satisfied as part of ongoing efforts to counter militarization and armed violence. Interventions should adopt a combination of 'hard' and 'soft' responses, depending on the particular circumstances. Ultimately, the effectiveness of any programme or policy response to refugee and IDP militarization will be greatly enhanced if the motivations driving key actors – refugees, states and rebels – to engage in violence and the trafficking of arms are taken into account. Evidence-based appraisals of the incentives and disincentives of the key actors who condition militarization would provide policy-makers and scholars with a broader range of policy options to address the problem of militarized refugees, ranging from disengagement to, in extreme cases, interventions under a UN peacekeeping mandate. Opportunities for future research are set forth here to encourage further debate on these and other aspects of refugee and IDP militarization; even as significant advances are noted and appraised.

Notes

1 See UNHCR (1991). For a compelling discussion of new challenges facing UNHCR with respect to refugee protection, see also Steiner at al. (2003).

2 For a stimulating review of the relationships between refugee assistance and the excacerbation of conflict, see Barber (1997).

3 For a thoughtful reflection of the shift in scholarly attention from international and inter-state wars to civil wars in the aftermath of the cold war, see David (1997). See also David (1998), Walter and Snyder (1999) and Brown et al. (1997).

4 Scholars concerned with the study of international security have thus turned their attention to non-state and transnational factors to explain how and why conflicts have occurred in recent years. See especially Gleditsch (2003).

5 Up to 937,000 people were killed during the 1994 Rwandan genocide, according to the government of Rwanda. For an overview of the Rwandan genocide with regard to the refugee security, see Mills and Norton (2002) and Goose and Smythe (1994).

6 While IDPs are not granted the same legal status as refugees, the Guiding Principles on Internal Displacement (UNOCHA 2000) were issued by the UN to recognize and uphold the protection and security of displaced populations. UNHCR often cares for IDPs and refugees in its operations, since the protection and humanitarian needs of both are similar in many states that have experienced both large refugee influxes and internal displacement, due to war, political persecution, etc. The Guiding Principles define internally displaced persons as 'persons or groups of persons, who have been forced or obliged to flee or to leave their homes or places of habitual residence, in particular as a result of or in order to avoid the effects of armed conflict, situations of generalized violence, violations of human rights or natural or human-made disasters, and who have not crossed an internationally recognized border'. See also Muggah (2003).

7 Yu (2002: 1) defines militarization as the 'non-civilian attributes of refugee populated areas, including inflows of weapons, military training and recruitment. It also includes actions of refugees and/or exiles who engage in non-civilian activity outside the refugee camp, yet who depend on assistance

from refugees or international organizations.' See also Lischer's definition (2005: 167).

8 Rather than focusing on militarization per se, some scholars have focused on the idea of 'refugee warriors'. Thus, conceptually, there may exist some ambiguity about whether militarization is an attribute of camps or an attribute of refugees. 'Refugee warriors' are the subject of Howard Adelman's (1998) essay. According to Adelman, the term was first coined by Zolberg et al. (1989).

9 Muggah and Mogire, this volume, pp. 7–8.

10 See Muggah, this volume, p. 91.

11 See Muggah, this volume, p. 91.

12 While neat conceptual categories, they are at times difficult to distinguish on the ground, since refugees and IDPs may simultaneously be both participants in a larger war and victims of external manipulation by those with war aims. The distinction is nevertheless employed by several authors to indicate how and in what contexts refugees and IDPs are militarized. Ostensibly political factors external to the refugee community or exogenous to the host state may affect the dynamics of one type of militarization without affecting the other.

13 For a good discussion of how militants manipulate refugee assistance to further their political aims, see Barber (1997). Aside from the cases in this volume, the struggle for resources and the manipulation of refugee aid have occurred among Afghani refugees in Pakistan in the aftermath of the Soviet invasion during the 1980s, Cambodian refugees in Thailand who fled the Vietnamese occupation in the 1980s, and Saharawi refugees in Algeria who were organized by POLISARIO to fight the Moroccan government from the 1970s.

14 See Milner with Christofferson-Deb, this volume, p. 59.

15 Their assessment that refugee camp militarization is 'no longer an issue in Guinea' is based primarily on interviews with fifty representatives from the government of Guinea, UN agencies, NGOs, health practitioners, civil society and refugees themselves during a field visit in September/October 2004. Respondents were asked: 'Do you feel that the presence of small arms or armed elements in the refugee camps in southern Guinea is a cause for concern today?' According to the two researchers, '[i]n all fifty interviews, the answer was "no"' (Milner with Christofferson-Deb, this volume, pp. 51–87).

16 Rwandan authorities had previously provided support for rebel activity by supporting the Banyarwanda Congolese and the Banyamulenge in a series of cross-border attacks into the DRC from 1996 to 1998. Rwanda also established a Tutsi–Banyarwandan political and military organization, the Rassemblement Congolais pour la Democratie (RCD), initiating a rebellion in eastern DRC in August 1998 that led to the outbreak of regional war between the governments of Uganda and Rwanda on one side and the governments of the DRC, Angola, Zimbabwe and Namibia on the other.

17 *Interahamwe* included former Rwandan Hutu army and militia members who massacred several hundred thousand Tutsi and moderate Hutus

in the 1994 genocide. Ex-FAR were troops of the Rwandan government at the time, who also participated in the genocide.

18 See Mthembu-Salter, this volume, p. 189.

19 The transitional government is currently consolidating its authority over the country and attempting to address the grievances of former dissident elements, including the Tutsi–Banyrwanda-based RCD. Establishing mutual trust between the transitional DRC government and the government of Rwanda is, however, complicated by the fact that the RDF is alleged to maintain a covert presence in eastern DRC, despite an October 2002 agreement calling for the full withdrawal of RDF forces from the region. The minority Banyamulenge continue to be subject to an ethnic cleansing campaign in the eastern Kivu provinces, contributing to lingering concerns that Congolese refugees in Rwanda may decide to organize themselves militarily to retaliate against government forces in the Kivu provinces, as occurred when the RCD joined forces with the RDF to capture eastern DRC in August 1998.

20 As Mthembu-Salter puts it: 'it is unlikely that the Rwandan government has sufficient trust for the Banyamulenge community and its political leadership that it would risk the strongly negative international reaction that would arise from its being caught assisting the external militarization of its Banymulenge refugees' (this volume, pp. 181–216).

21 In Tanzania, refugees were largely self-settled, until the past decade, when the government began to insist on repatriation and settlement in third countries. For a detailed discussion of the recent shift in Tanzanian policy towards Rwandan refugees, see Whitaker (2002).

22 See Muggah, this volume, pp. 89–134.

23 The UN has also recently approved an instrument on marking and tracing, as well as curtailing brokering and transfers of particular weapons types (UNGA 2004: 36).

24 For example, there is little evidence of firearms possession or weapons-related violence among Congolese refugees in Rwanda. Nyagatare transit centre, now since disbanded, was protected by RDF soldiers and administered by Rwanda's Ministry of Local Government, in partnership with UNHCR (MONUC 2005); at the time of the report, MONUC had no record of armed crimes and had no reports of weapons seizures. In the neighbouring town of Cyangugu, there was likewise no evidence of small-arms trafficking or illegal firearms possession between January and June 2004. Farther inland, Ntendezi and Coko camps, housing former Congolese combatants, contained soldiers who had been disarmed and were being monitored closely by the government. The researchers concluded that it was highly unlikely that trafficking of small arms was a concern for these areas.

25 In Tanzania, small arms and firearms mortality is reported to be a growing concern, as reports of weapons-related violence and crime have increased in recent years. The presence of firearms is also reported to be linked to the presence of refugees who gain access across porous borders, the militarization of refugees, economic hardship and criminal activity. Refugees crossing through unofficial entry points often sell their weapons within Tanzania for profit. Between 1994 and 1998, rebel groups in Tanzania

are also reported to have received arms shipments from manufacturers in eastern Europe and Africa to support cross-border raids, particularly among ex-FAR and *interahamwe* from Rwanda who were working to align themselves with rebel movements in Tanzania, Angola, Burundi, the DRC and Uganda. While there is no evidence that the government has supported the arming of these forces, nevertheless economic hardship experienced by refugees and lack of economic opportunities due to severe restrictions on their movement and activities may be creating incentives for them to obtain and sell weapons to support themselves. Poor conditions within camps and protracted refugee situations have made refugees more susceptible to involvement in the illegal trafficking of firearms: large, poorly policed camps have created an environment conducive to criminal activity, including illegal weapons trading.

26 At the time this volume was going to press, President Kagame indicated his willingness (and capability) to attack eastern DRC to counter the perceived threat of Hutu militia still residing there. Moreover, there is speculation among policy-makers, leaders and the media that Kagame continues to provide support to RCD rebels hostile to Kinshasa in part to mitigate the threat posed by the DRC and to maintain a strong grip on power in the region. In February 2005, Rwanda and the DRC implemented a joint verification mechanism to 'verify and clear all accusations between the two countries along their borders' (IRIN 2005a). Ongoing tensions and violent conflict in eastern DRC continue, however, to hamper long-term efforts to establish peace and security in the region.

27 Muggah, this volume, p. 113.

28 It should be recalled that refugee/IDP militarization has also been the unintended consequence of government policies that are put in place to defend or protect IDPs and refugees. In Uganda, for example, the posting of UPDF soldiers may have exacerbated the problem of militarization by making both IDP and refugee camps more susceptible to attack by the LRA. Similarly, the Tanzanian government's strict control of refugee movement to within 4 kilometres of a refugee settlement has contributed to discontent and grievances on the part of refugees, making them more susceptible to military recruitment.

29 Mthembu-Salter, this volume, pp. 181–216.

30 Mogire, this volume, p. 149 (referring to Durieux).

31 A promising development in this regard occurred in November 2004, when the heads of state of Rwanda and the DRC, along with nine heads of state of other countries in the region, signed the Dar es Salaam Declaration on Peace, Security, Democracy and Development in the Great Lakes Region in an effort to 'establish an effective regional security framework for the prevention, management, and peaceful settlement of conflicts and, to this end, evaluate regularly relevant sub-regional initiatives and mechanisms' (IRIN 2004b). The declaration prohibits the 'use of any territory by armed groups to carry out acts of aggression or subversion against other member states'. How effective these measures will be in stemming the violence between Rwanda and DRC and easing tensions between the two countries has yet to be seen, but the agreement indicates a willingness on the part of the Rwandan and DRC

governments to establish mechanisms for monitoring and promoting peace and security along their borders. It also highlights the willingness of the international community to provide active support for such measures.

32 For an excellent discussion of a shift towards a culture of 'voluntary repatriation' as a durable solution by UNHCR, see Barnett and Finnemore (2004: ch. 4). A striking example of the involuntary repatriation of refugees occurred in 2002, when the Tanzanian government, in conjunction with UNHCR, required that all Rwandan refugees return home by 31 December of that year; see Human Rights First (2003).

33 It is assumed that larger camps are more susceptible to military mobilization, recruitment, training, fund-raising and arms trafficking because of the lack of supervision. See Mogire, this volume, p. 142.

34 Muggah, this volume, p. 113.

35 See Mogire, this volume, p. 148.

36 See Mogire, this volume, pp. 137–78.

37 A joint mission by the Commission for Human Security and the Emergency and Security Section of UNHCR, Geneva, stated that 'the general safety and security of the refugees in the six camps is incomparable to their situation in late 2000/early 2001' (Mogire, this volume, pp. 54–5).

38 A UN Panel of Experts investigating regional compliance with the arms embargo against the DRC has accused the Rwandan government of failing to comply with the embargo by assisting and providing relief to Mutebutsi and his soldiers.

39 See Milner with Christofferson-Deb, this volume, p. 64.

40 See Milner with Christofferson-Deb, this volume, p. 74.

41 See Da Costa (2004).

42 See SPHERE Project (2004). The SPHERE Project was launched in 1997 by NGOs and the Red Cross and Red Crescent movement. As stated on its website: 'the Sphere Humanitarian Charter and Minimum Standards in Disaster Response sets out for the first time what people affected by disasters have a right to expect from humanitarian assistance. The aim of the Project is to improve the quality of assistance provided to people affected by disasters and to enhance the accountability of the humanitarian system in disaster response.' See also Inter-Agency Network for Education in Emergencies (INEE) at: <www.ineesite.org/>.

43 See Muggah (2005) and SAS (2005) for a discussion of the relationships between DDR and development.

44 For essays on the issue of the relief–development gap, see Macrae et al. (1997), Smillie (1998), and UNOCHA (1997). As stated in UNOCHA (1997): 'General Assembly resolution 46/182 gives an explicit directive that emergency assistance must be provided in ways that will support recovery and long-term development. The resolution clearly recognized the need to establish a strong link between relief and development activities within the assistance community and, in particular, within the United Nations system. It charges the Emergency Relief Coordinator (ERC) to help orient the interventions of the humanitarian relief community towards longer-term development objectives.'

45 See UN (1992), as well as the special edition on refugee livelihoods: Forced Migration Online (2004).

46 Currently, the Security Council is authorized only to send a multi-national or regional force under Chapter VI of the UN Charter.

47 See UNHCR (2000b). For information on UNHCR's 'ladder of options', see UNHCR (1999, 2000c).

48 Militarization may still be a problem, however, among Rwandan and Burundian refugees in Tanzania, as evidenced by reports of military training in Nduta in 1998, Muyovosi refugee camp in 1999 and Ngara in 2000, but such activities seem to be due mainly to government complicity.

49 Milner with Christoffersen-Deb, this volume, p. 165.

50 He also notes that the UNSC has learned that a humanitarian response to refugee militarization cannot be a substitute for a political response – even if the entity is paralysed and unable to intervene adequately. To the extent that a campaign of ethnic cleansing has occurred and is currently a problem in the region, however, he argues that the UNSC has gone far enough in terms of empowering MONUC to prevent the continuation of violence between ethnic Hemas and Lendus there. The recent killing of nine Bangladeshi peacekeepers in the Ituri district and the more recent killing of fifty militiamen in the same region highlights ongoing instability in eastern DRC, and the inability of MONUC to prevent ongoing violence within the region casts doubt on its ability effectively to prevent violence from spilling over its border with Rwanda.

51 See Muggah, this volume, pp. 100–1.

52 Among the civilian militia groups, the Arrow Boys, the Amuka and the Border Frontier Group have been trained and armed by the UPDF and have been given explicit government licence to protect their communities and households. See Muggah, this volume, pp. 95–6.

53 See Muggah, this volume, pp. 96–8.

54 In the case of Rwandan refugees in DRC, there have been frequent allegations that returned Rwandese had in fact been recycled into the RDF.

55 The chairman of the Amnesty Commission in Uganda has reported that 13,231 combatants from a variety of rebel groups were demobilized through the commission since the granting of the first amnesty in 1987 and another in 2000.

56 Muggah also described an innovative radio programme sponsored by the Ministry of Security and the Ugandan Internal Security Organization, initiated in 2004 to encourage LRA combatants to seek amnesty.

57 See Mogire, this volume, pp. 137–78 (citing Durieux).

58 See, for example, Da Costa (2004), *Refugees* magazine (UNHCR 2005) and UNHCR's New Issues in Refugee Research series at <www.unhcr.ch>. See also Terry (2002), Jacobsen (2000), Lischer (2005), and Stedman and Tanner (2004).

59 See Lischer (2000) and Gleditsch (2003).

60 Surveys conducted within particular countries of refugees and humanitarian workers which utilize similar questions would assist in generating

findings that apply to a broad range of cases. See, for example, Buchanan and Muggah (2005).

61 As stated in the report, 'the Responsibility to Protect' conveys 'the idea that sovereign states have a responsibility to protect their own citizens from avoidable catastrophe – from mass murder and rape, from starvation – but that when they are unwilling or unable to do so, that responsibility must be borne by the broader community of states' (International Commission on Intervention and State Sovereignty 2001: foreword).

62 The UN secretary-general has also recently released a report, *In Larger Freedom: Towards Security, Development and Human Rights for All*, further articulating the need to make progress 'towards peace, security, disarmament, human rights, democracy and good governance' through the promotion of a number of key Millennium Development Goals and reform of the UN system (UN 2005: introduction).

References

Adelman, H. (1998) 'Why refugee warriors are threats', *Journal of Conflict Studies*, 18(1): 49–69.

— (2003) 'The use and abuse of refugees in Zaire', in Stedman and Tanner (2003), pp. 95–134.

AFP (Agence France-Presse) (2001) 'Violence, militarism threaten refugee camps in Southern Guinea', 25 January, <www.unhcr.ch/cgi-bin/texis/vtx/home>.

Anderson, M. B. (1999) *Do No Harm: How Aid Can Support Peace or War*, Boulder, CO: Lynne Rienner.

Barber, B. (1997) 'Feeding refugees, or war? The dilemma of humanitarian aid', *Foreign Affairs*, 76(4): 8–14.

Barnett, M. and M. Finnemore (2004) *Rules for the World: International Organizations in Global Politics*, Ithaca, NY: Cornell University Press.

Bogna, P. (2005) 'Precarious security conditions continue to undermine relief efforts in key areas of the DRC', *MONUC News*, UN Mission in the Democratic Republic of Congo, 13 June, <www.monuc.org/news.aspx?newsID=7162>.

Brown, M. et al. (eds) (1997) *Nationalism and Ethnic Conflict*, Cambridge, MA: MIT Press.

Buchanan, C. and R. Muggah (2005.) *No Relief: Surveying the Effects of Gun Violence on Humanitarian Aid and Development Personnel*, Geneva: Centre for Humanitarian Dialogue and the Small Arms Survey, <www.smallarmsurvey.org.>

Da Costa, R. (2004) 'Maintaining the civilian and humanitarian character of asylum', UNHCR Legal and Policy Research Series, PPLA/2004/02, UNHCR Department of Protection.

Dar es Salaam Declaration on Peace, Security, Democracy and Development in the Great Lakes Region (2004) Dar es Salaam, Tanzania, 20 November, <http://www.reliefweb.int/rw/rwb.nsf/db900SID/MHII-672542?OpenDocument>.

David, S. (1997) 'Internal war: causes and cures', *World Politics*, 49(4): 552–76.

— (1998) 'The primacy of internal war', in S. Neuman (ed.), *International Relations Theory and the Third World*, New York: St Martin's Press, pp. 77–101.

Deng, F. (2004) 'Trapped within hostile borders: the plight of internally displaced persons', in K. Cahill (ed.), *Human Security for All: A Tribute to Sergio Vieira de Mello*, New York: Fordham University Press, pp. 28–51.

Durieux, J.-F. (2000) 'Preserving the civilian character of refugee camps: lessons from the Kigoma refugee programme in Tanzania', *Refugees, Conflict & Conflict Resolution*, 9(3), <www.ccrweb.ccr.uct.ac.za/two/9_3/p25_preserving_civilian.html>.

Florquin, N, and E. Berman (2005) *Armed and Aimless: Armed Groups, Guns, and Human Security in the ECOWAS Region*, Geneva: Small Arms Survey.

Forced Migration Online (2004) *Forced Migration Review: Livelihoods*, May.

Gleditsch, K. (2003) *Transnational Dimensions of War*, Manuscript, University of California and Centre for the Study of Civil War, International Peace Research Institute, Oslo, May, available at <www.dss.ucsd.edu/~kgledits/papers/transnational.pdf>.

Goose, S. and F. Smyth (1994) 'Arming genocide in Rwanda', *Human Rights Watch*, September/October.

Human Rights First (2003) 'Forced home? Focus on Rwandan refugees in Tanzania', *Africa Refugee Rights News*, 1(1), <www.humanrightsfirst.org/intl_refugees/intl_refugees_news/newsletter_01.htm>.

International Commission on Intervention and State Sovereignty (2001) *The Responsibility to Protect*, Ottawa: International Development Research Center, December.

IRIN (Integrated Regional Information Networks) (2003a) 'Guinea: situation in forest region remains complex says ACT', 2 July.

— (2003b) 'Refugees asked to move out of Conakry', 17 July.

— (2004a) 'DRC: special report on war and peace in the Kivus', 10 August.

— (2004b) 'Great Lakes: fresh threat challenges new regional declaration', 26 November.

— (2005a) 'DRC–RWANDA: joint verification mechanism now operational', 10 February.

— (2005b) 'Great Lakes: call for special fund for war-torn region', 21 February.

— (2005c) 'DRC: fighting between UN troops, militias leaves 50 dead', 2 March.

Jacobsen, K. (2000) 'A framework for exploring the political and security context of refugee populated areas', *Refugee Studies Quarterly*, 19.

— (2002) *African States and the Politics of Refugees: Refugee Assistance as Political Resources*, Feinstein International Famine Center Working Paper no. 6, January.

Lischer, S. (2000) *Refugee Involvement in Political Violence: Quantitative Evidence from 1987–1988*, UNHCR Working Paper no. 26, July.

— (2001) *Refugee-related Violence: When? Where? How Much?*, MIT Working Paper no. 10, Center for Migration, December.

— (2003) 'Collateral damage: humanitarian assistance as a cause of conflict', *International Security*, 28(1): 79–109.

— (2005) *Dangerous Sanctuaries: Refugee Camps, Civil War and the Dilemmas of Humanitarian Aid*, Ithaca, NY: Cornell University Press.

Loescher, G. (2001) 'Protection and humanitarian action in the post-cold war era', in A. Zolberg and P. Benda (eds), *Global Migrants and Global Refugees: Problems and Solutions*, New York: Berghahn Books, pp. 171–205.

Loescher, G. and J. Milner (2005) 'Protracted refugee situations: domestic and international security implications', *Adelphi Paper*, no. 375, London: IISS.

Macrae, J. et al. (1997) 'Conflict, the continuum and chronic emergencies: a critical analysis for linking relief, rehabilitation and development planning in Sudan', *Disasters*, 21(3): 223–43.

Mills, K. and R. Norton (2002) 'Refugees and security in the Great Lakes Region of Africa', *Civil Wars*, 5(1): 1–26.

MONUC (UN Mission in Congo) (2005) 'Thousands of Congolese Banyamulenge refugees leave UNHCR transit center', Press release, 13 June, <www.monuc.org/news.aspx?newsID=7162>.

Muggah, R. (2003) 'Two solitudes: comparing conflict and development-induced displacement and resettlement', *Journal of International Migration* 41(5).

— (2005) 'No magic bullet: a critical perspective on DDR and weapons reduction in post-conflict contexts', *International Journal of Commonwealth Studies. The Round Table*, 94(379): 239–52.

— (2006) 'Rethinking disarmament, demobilization and reintegration in Sudan', *Humanitarian Practice Network Exchange*, winter.

Nairobi Protocol for the Prevention, Control, and Reduction of Small Arms and Light Weapons in the Great Lakes Region and the Horn of Africa ('Nairobi Protocol') (2004) Nairobi, Kenya, 21 April.

Newman, E. and J. van Selm (eds) (2003) *Refugees and Forced Displacement: International Security, Human Vulnerability, and the State*, Tokyo: UN University Press.

Ogata, S. (2004) 'Human security as framework for post-conflict nation-building: lessons from Iraq to Afghanistan', in K. Cahill (ed.), *Human Security for All: A Tribute to Sergio Vieira de Mello*, New York: Fordham University Press, pp. 3–14.

Rieff, D. (2003) *A Bed for the Night: Humanitarianism in Crisis*, New York: Simon and Schuster.

SAS (Small Arms Survey) (2005) *Weapons at War*, Oxford: Oxford University Press.

Sengupta, S. (2003) 'No Escape from west Africa's wars: both rebels and governments recruit in refugee camps', *International Herald Tribune*, 20 May.

Slim, H. (1997) *Doing the Right Thing: Relief Agencies, Moral Dilemmas and Moral Responsibility in Political Emergencies and War*, Nordic Africa Institute Report no. 6, Uppsala.

Smillie, I. (1998) *Relief and Development: The Struggle for Synergy*, Humanitarianism and War Project Occasional Paper no. 33, Providence, RI: Watson Institute.

Smock, D. (2000) 'Humanitarian assistance and conflict in Africa', *Journal of Humanitarian Assistance*, 3 June, <www.jha.ac/articles/a014.htm>.

SPHERE Project (2004) *SPHERE Project Handbook*, <www.sphereproject. org/index.htm>.

Stedman, S. and F. Tanner (eds) (2003) *Refugee Manipulation: War, Politics, and the Abuse of Human Suffering*, Washington, DC: Brookings Institution Press.

Steiner, N. et al. (eds) (2003) *Problems of Protection: The UNHCR, Refugees, and Human Rights*, New York: Routledge.

Terry, F. (2002) *Condemned to Repeat? The Paradox of Humanitarian Action*, Ithaca, NY and London: Cornell University Press.

UN (United Nations) (1992) *An Agenda for Peace: Preventive Diplomacy, Peace-making and Peace-keeping*, A/47/277, S/24111, 17 June, <www.un.org/Docs/ SG/agpeace.html>.

— (2005) *In Larger Freedom: Towards Development, Security and Human Rights for All*, January, <www.un.org/largerfreedom/>.

UNGA (United Nations General Assembly) (2004) *A More Secure World: Our Shared Responsibility. Report of the Secretary-General's High Level Panel on Threats, Challenges and Change*, A/59/565, 2 December.

UNHCR (United Nations High Commissioner for Refugees) (1991) *Report of the Working Group on Solutions and Protection to the Forty-second Session of the Executive Committee of the High Commissioner's Programme*, EC/SCP/64, 12 August.

— (1997) *Refugee Camp Security in the Great Lakes Region*, Inspection and Evaluation Service, EVAL/01/97, April.

— (1999) *The Security and Civilian and Humanitarian Character of Refugee Camps and Settlements*, Executive Committee of the High Commissioner's Programme, Standing Committee, 14th Meeting, EC/49/SC/INF.2, 14 January.

— (2000a) *The State of the World's Refugees: Fifty Years of Humanitarian Action*, Oxford: Oxford University Press.

— (2000b) *Handbook for Emergencies*, 2nd edn, <www.unhcr.ch/cgi-bin/texis/ vtx/publ/opendoc.pdf?tbl=PUBL&id=3bb2fa26b>.

— (2000c) *The Security, Civilian and Humanitarian Character of Refugee Camps and Settlements: Operationalizing the 'Ladder of Options'*, EC/50/SC/INF.4, 27 June.

— (2005) *Refugees Magazine: How Secure Do You Feel?* Issue 139, <www.unhcr. org/cgi-bin/texis/vtx/publ/opendoc.pdf?tbl=PUBL&id=42d65e9c2>.

UNOCHA (UN Office for the Coordination of Humanitarian Affairs) (1997) *Humanitarian Report 1997: The Link Between Relief and Development*, <http://www.reliefweb.int/ocha_ol/pub/humrep97/link.html>.

— (2000) *The Guiding Principles on Internal Displacement*, New York: UNOCHA.

Walter, B. and J. Snyder (eds) (1999) *Civil Wars, Insecurity and Intervention*, New York: Columbia University Press.

Whitaker, B. (2002) *Changing Priorities in Refugee Protection: The Rwandan Repatriation from Tanzania*, UNHCR Working Paper no. 53, Evaluation and Policy Analysis Unit, February.

Yu, L. (2002) *Separating Ex-combatants and Refugees in Zongo, DRC: Peacekeepers and UNHCR's 'Ladder of Options'*, UNHCR Working Paper no. 60, August.

Zolberg, A., A. Surke and S. Aguayo (1989) *Escape from Violence: Conflict and Refugee Crisis in the Developing World*, New York and Oxford: Oxford University Press.

About the contributors

Astrid Christoffersen-Deb is completing her doctorate at St Antony's College, University of Oxford, while pursuing her medical training in obstetrics and gynaecology at Harvard University. As a Rhodes scholar, she carried out research on the medicalization of female genital practices in Kenya as well as on cross-cultural notions of human personhood. Research carried out for the Small Arms Survey was inspired by her interests in the public health of developing countries. Her current research examines changing notions of personhood at the beginnings of life in the context of reproductive technologies and stem cell research in North America and the United Kingdom. In 2004, she was named a Trudeau Scholar.

James Milner is a doctoral student at St Antony's College, Oxford. He has worked as a consultant for UNHCR in India, Cameroon, Guinea and at UNHCR headquarters, and has served as an adviser to the UK Home Office and the European Council on Refugees and Exiles (ECRE). He is currently co-director of the 'PRS Project: Towards Solutions for Protracted Refugee Situations' at the Centre for International Studies, University of Oxford. Through the project, he has recently co-authored a number of works with Gil Loescher, including 'Protracted refugee situations: domestic and international security implications' (Adelphi Paper no. 375, 2005), and articles in *International Affairs*, *Survival* and the *Journal of Conflict, Development and Security*. His current research focuses on the relationship between protracted refugee situations and the politics of asylum in Africa. In 2003, he was named an inaugural Trudeau Scholar by the Pierre Elliot Trudeau Foundation.

Edward Mogire completed his PhD on 'Refugees and Security' at Bradford University's Department of Peace Studies in 2003. The same year he was Ford Foundation Research Fellow at the Bonn International Center for Conversion. Since October 2003, he has been a researcher at the European Research Centre at Kingston, University of London. His research interests focus on refugees, security and terrorism.

Gregory Mthembu-Salter is a freelance writer and researcher on African political economy, living in South Africa. For more than a decade he has written Economist Intelligence Unit reports on Africa, with particular emphasis on the Great Lakes Region. He is a long-time contributor to *Africa South of the Sahara, Africa Contemporary Record, Africa Confidential* and a range of South African newspapers. Recent other publications include a chapter on Rwanda in *Lion Cubs? Lessons from Africa's Success Stories* (Policy Exchange, London, 2004) and chapters in *Hide and Seek: Taking Account of Small Arms in South Africa* (Institute for Security Studies, Johannesburg, 2004). Mthembu-Salter received an MA in economics from the University of Cape Town in 2003 for research into unrecorded trade between Rwanda and Burundi. This was also the subject of a consultancy for the World Bank. Mthembu-Salter has conducted research for organizations including Action Aid, Cape Town's Centre for Conflict Resolution, the Johannesburg-based South African Institute for International Affairs and Institute for Security Studies, and Geneva's Small Arms Survey, about topics including the role of mediation in resolving civil conflict in Rwanda and Burundi, the effectiveness of the Sierra Leone human rights commission, firearms proliferation in South Africa, money laundering in South Africa, and the diamond business and organized crime in the Democratic Republic of Congo.

Robert Muggah is based at the Small Arms Survey at the Graduate Institute of International Studies in Geneva, Switzerland, where he oversees the design, implementation and management of large-scale research projects in over thirty countries. He is also a professional fellow of the US-based Social Science Research Council and a doctoral candidate at the University of Oxford. Trained in political economy and development at the Institute for Development Studies (Sussex) and the University of Oxford, he specializes in post-conflict recovery and reconstruction. His present focus is on the design, implementation and evaluation of disarmament, demobilization, and reintegration (DDR) as well as 'resettlement schemes' for displaced populations. He has worked and undertaken research in several countries affected by acute violence or emerging from conflict, including Brazil, Burundi, Colombia, Republic of Congo, the Democratic Republic of the Congo, Haiti, Kenya, Indonesia, Nepal, Papua New Guinea, the Philippines, the Solomon Islands, Sri Lanka, Sudan, Togo, and Uganda, in partnership with the World Bank, the European Commission, UNDP, UNHCR, WHO, IOM and various bilateral donors. He is published widely in mainstream newspapers as well as policy and peer-reviewed journals.

Sue J. Nahm received her BA *magna cum laude* from Yale University in 1997, and her MA (2000) and MPhil (2004) at Columbia University. She is currently a PhD candidate in political science and Andrew Wellington Cordier Fellow at Columbia University. Her dissertation focuses on the links between refugee militarization, UNHCR policy and international security; her research interests encompass international relations theory, the security implications of refugee flows, human rights and the United Nations system. She has taught international relations theory courses and served as a teaching fellow in human rights at Hunter College and Barnard and Columbia colleges. She has also researched and worked in various capacities on humanitarian and security issues for the International Rescue Committee, the Consortium on Security and Humanitarian Action (Ralph Bunche Institute, CUNY), the International League for Human Rights, and the Office of Coordination of Humanitarian Affairs (OCHA).

Index

driver hijacked, 159; Emergency and Security Section, 17, 64, 231; Executive Committee (ExCom), 16, 19, 165, 232; field security officers, 17; Guékédou (Guinea) office attacked, 62; *Handbook on Emergencies*, 234; Humanitarian Security Officers, 17; 'ladder of options', 16–17, 164, 206, 209, 210, 211, 229, 233, 234; Macenta (Guinea) office head killed, 51, 62, 63; policy of depoliticization, 161; position on refugee/IDP militarization, 232–5; programme in Guinea, 54; recognition of soldiers as refugees, 25; Refugee Security Liaison Officer, 17; relations with national liberation movements, 163–4; response to militarization, 7, 10, 21, 36, 220; screening procedures of, 115; 'security package', 167, 224; source material from, 8; statutory obligations of, 90; verification exercise in Guinea, 71–2

US Committee for Refugees (USCR), 54, 59, 60, 62–3, 158, 231

war by proxy, 12
war on terror, 6, 238
West Nile Bank Front (Gorogoro) (Uganda), 94
World Bank, 207, 235; Multi-country Demobilization and Reintegration Programme (MDRP), 117, 232
World Food Programme (WFP), 156, 187

Young Volunteers (Guinea), 52, 61–2, 71, 75, 76–7, 79, 221–2; demobilizing of, 67–8; disarmament of, 55, 80
youth gangs, 68

Zaire, 12, 14, 19, 167
Zambia, 2
Zimbabwe African National Union (ZANU), 139
Zimbabwe African People's Union (ZAPU), 139

BICC

The Bonn International Center for Conversion (BICC) is an independent non-profit organization dedicated to promoting the transfer of former military resources and assets to alternative civilian purposes. Established in 1994 in Bonn, Germany, BICC provides specialized research and consultancy services in the fields of demobilization, disarmament and reintegration, as well as security sector reform to international governmental and non-governmental organizations.

Bonn International Center for Conversion
An der Elisabethkirche 25, 53113 Bonn, Germany

Phone: + 49 228 911960   Fax: +49 228 241215
E-mail: bicc@bicc.de
Website: www.bicc.de

Small Arms Survey

The Small Arms Survey is an independent research project located at the Graduate Institute of International Studies in Geneva, Switzerland. It serves as the principal international source of public information on all aspects of small arms, and as a resource centre for governments, policy-makers, researchers and activists. Established in 1999, the project is supported by the Swiss Federal Department of Foreign Affairs, and by sustained contributions from the governments of Canada, Finland, France, the Netherlands, Norway, Sweden and the United Kingdom. The Survey is also grateful for past and current project support received from Australia, Belgium, Denmark and New Zealand. The Small Arms Survey collaborates with research institutes and non-governmental organizations in many countries, including Brazil, Canada, Georgia, Germany, India, Israel, Jordan, Norway, the Russian Federation, South Africa, Sri Lanka, Sweden, Thailand, the United Kingdom and the United States.

Small Arms Survey
Graduate Institute of International Studies
47 Avenue Blanc, 1202 Geneva, Switzerland

Phone: +41 22 908 5777   Fax: +41 22 732 2738
E-mail: smallarm@hei.unige.ch
Website: www.smallarmssurvey.org